KISS ME
AGAIN, PARIS

BLICK VOM EIFFELTURM AUF PARIS

DM 70.- ÷50% v. 140.- „Neue J

Aufnahme Atlantic·Neumann·Leipzig

m 30.5.37 171

KISS ME
AGAIN, PARIS

a memoir

RENATE STENDHAL

IF
SF
publishing

Copyright © 2017 by Renate Stendhal
All rights reserved.
Published by IF SF Publishing.
San Francisco, California
www.ifsfpublishing.com

Printed in the United States

ISBN 978-0-9859773-8-2

Cover and interior design:
Ingalls Design, San Francisco

Author photo on cover:
Louise Kollenbaum

First printing

To Kim Chernin, true love and life companion

*Some names in this memoir have been changed to preserve privacy.
Most of the women depicted in the photographs are not identified by name,
but all belonged to my intimate Paris circle of lovers and friends.*

*Some unconventional style choices have been made in the production of
this book. This is mainly to reflect its cinematic nature.*

SEX AND OTHER SACRED GAMES (with Kim Chernin, 1989)

"Using the insights of both Anglo-American and French feminism, the writers explore the possibilities of an authentic sexual identity within patriarchy; of reclaiming a lost history of female power; and of more fluid constructions of gender."

— *Library Journal*

GERTRUDE STEIN: IN WORDS AND PICTURES (1994)

"The amateur . . . could hardly wish for a better introduction than Ms. Stendhal's ingenious marrying of newly discovered and well-known photographs with familiar and unfamiliar texts."

— *The New York Times*

"After an astonishing, playful essay, the book opens into a revelatory combination of quotes, quips and 360 photos of Stein and her wildly brilliant circle."

— *Elle*

Gertrude Stein was the recipient of a
Lambda Literary Award in 1995.

CECILIA BARTOLI: THE PASSION OF SONG (with Kim Chernin, 1997)

"This book . . . chronicles the twin careers of Cecilia Bartoli—a still-young world star possessed of real vocal endowment and an estimable degree of innate musicianship, who wields in performance a restless, unleashed charm—and of her mother, Silvana Bazzoni, a lyric soprano ex-chorister of the Rome Opera."

— *The New York Times Book Review*

THE GRASSHOPPER'S SECRET: A MAGICAL TALE (2002)

"Renate Stendhal has definitely found the magic wand that transforms stories into mysteries."

— *Compulsive Reader*

TRUE SECRETS OF LESBIAN DESIRE: KEEPING SEX ALIVE IN LONG-TERM RELATIONSHIPS (2003)

"What a compassionate and useful little book, so full of heart and good sense. Renate Stendhal brings to her work deep understanding about intimacy that will benefit any couple ready to take the next step in love and passion."

— Carol Queen, Ph.D., author of *Exhibitionism for the Shy*

"Tracking all these mutual quests for honest relationships, Stendhal's small and beautiful volume almost made me wish to be in one myself. I'll keep it handy, should the occasion arise."

— Alix Dobkin, singer/songwriter

LESBIAN MARRIAGE: A LOVE & SEX FOREVER KIT (with Kim Chernin, 2014)

"Every lesbian couple—perhaps every couple, period—should have this straight-shooting guide on their shelf."

— Brooke Warner, She Writes Press

"The book's bottom line is also its very first: "You care about your marriage; you want to keep your love alive and passionate." With warmth, wit and a wealth of wisdom, this refreshingly realistic look at relationships is perfect for any marriage: gay or straight, legal or not."

— *San Francisco Examiner*

KISS ME AGAIN, PARIS (2017)

"I've now read Renate Stendhal's fascinating manuscript. Her writing is terrific and I felt as though I were there with her in the Paris she describes so well—it's the 1970s and Renate's world is filled with artists and bohemians and exiles, of beauty and sexuality that doesn't recognize boundaries. This book illuminates a perspective that we don't often get—the erotic pull of women attracted to women. I'm not convinced we are the right publisher for *Kiss Me Again, Paris* [because] in some ways we are too conventional."

— Reader's Report, Algonquin Books

An excerpt from the book earned a pre-publication award from the Women's National Book Association, juried by Deirdre Bair (*Simone de Beauvoir: A Biography*).

CONTENTS

THE STRANGER

4

THE LEATHER JACKET

5

RUE DU DESIRE

6

MO AND LULÚ

7

1

PARIS BY NIGHT

THE WOMAN IN RED

It was the last night of Mozart's *Così fan tutte* at the Paris Opera, and I was without a ticket. My press pass had already served for opening night. No problem. In the crowd coming up the stairs, I picked out an animated group of Parisians in tuxedos and evening gowns. The oldest among them, a monsieur with a white silk scarf, was holding the fan of tickets for all of them in his hand. They had to be box subscribers, patrons who tend to leave seats available for friends and random guests.

With my aviator scarf over my leather jacket I fit the group to a T. I followed my lively troop unnoticed, past the marble giants on their thrones in the vestibule—Rameau, Lulli, Gluck, Handel—and up the majestic sweep of stairs to the first balcony. *Voilà*, it was just as I had imagined. I took a seat at the back of the box with ease, grateful that you don't have to belong to the rich in order to enjoy their privileges. The more expensive the seat, the less interference from all sides. At least in the City of Light.

During my early days in Paris I had developed my "bohemian" technique—a necessity, given the empty pockets I brought with me from Germany. When an exceptional film opened and people were already lined up around the block, I would mix in up front, making myself invisible. Not that I was usually overlooked. It had to do with energy, catching the right moment to make the move, then sending out the message, "I belong in this spot, you just didn't notice until now." If for once I didn't get away with it I would hold up a piece of baguette or a croissant I had at the ready in a paper

bag. In Paris, every cinema has a bakery next door, and Parisians understand stepping out of line for the urgency of a croissant. At the Opéra or the
Théâtre des Champs Elysées, where patrons tend to be more hawk-eyed, I
usually found a person who welcomed a chat with a stranger and invited me
into the line. Sometimes I simply waited on the sidelines until the crowd got
into motion. In the first excitement of the doors being opened, I joined the
rush and slipped through the line.

     In Germany, such a thing would have been unthinkable. Every
German ticket controller was a moral authority, a "stiff-back" watching over
rules and regulations as if patriotism depended on it. I was light-years away
from of my childhood home, I was among the French who guard the temples
and palaces of art with the relaxed assurance of serving a *grande culture*.
Wasn't that what I was doing, too—serving culture, seeing an opera
a second time?

     As far as I was concerned, culture in Germany was dead. What could
possibly be left after the massacre of intellectuals, poets, artists, gays, Jews?
My parents, teachers, all of them good Germans, had been busy forgetting

what never happened—so how could they possibly have known? The war was over—what war? That new Germany, country of Herr und Frau Sauber-mann, Mr. and Mrs. Spic-and-Span. Iron-clad respectability. Sex unclean, not to be mentioned. Homosexuality a crime. No craving for family and motherhood: perverse.

My Hamburg school friends and I found it hard to breathe in the scrubbed air. We lived in the haunted places of the past—the Vienna of Mahler and Wittgenstein, Kafka's Prague, Gertrude Stein's Paris, the Berlin of the twenties, when typewriters stood at the ready on café tables. I dreamed up different identities for myself—literary, gay, Jewish, while I played the good girl to my mother's face and rebelled behind her back. Coming of age in Germany was living with bated breath, waiting for some kind of exit, release, an explosion of truth. Just break the silence, break the primal taboo. Everything else will follow.

Goodbye then, forsaken *Vaterland*. I made it to Paris with two metal suitcases, one with clothes, the other with books and diaries. Paris would wash Germany out of my hair. Perhaps even suck the German marrow out of my bones. I was young then, and dramatic. I was twenty-three. I was ready.

Did it matter that I didn't have a penny? I paid for my classes with jobs paid under the table. My attic rooms in different *quartiers* looked out over the city, up six or seven floors on narrow back stairs with automatic lights that clicked off between floors, so you had to grope along grimy walls for the next switch. There was a primitive WC at the end of a hallway, but I always had a friend or lover with a big tub in a white-tiled bathroom. A lover to squeeze through the Metro stile together on a single ticket. The vendors at my neighborhood street market let me negotiate for parched greens and bruised fruit. Making do without meat didn't matter as long as I could hang out in cafés and write about my love affairs. I was proud of my free-dom, proud even of my deprivation. Every now and then I had a feast: fatty, over-sugared sweets I loved to pine for in the window displays of mid-Eastern bakeries—thick, roasted almonds in beds of golden-green jelly squares.

Wasn't this the life everyone wanted? The bohemian romance of unheated garrets, beautiful women, and broken hearts that turn artists into Artists?

Now in my thirties, I got paid to write about culture. Culture? Paid?

I used to be a know-nothing next to my older Hamburg friends who were already intellectuals and artists. I was the Good Girl trying to go bad by secretly reading Sartre, Jean Genet, even de Sade in the classroom, hiding the books on my lap, and what did it teach me? There had to be another life waiting for me.

When my friends and I went to art exhibitions, concerts, or the opera, I couldn't put words to my feelings. How was it possible that they had opinions about everything? What was an opinion? How did one make one? My longing for the world of literature, art, sophistication burned me up. I would grit my teeth, determined to read a text, any text, twice, three, four times—until I could formulate its argument to myself. If I managed to repeat a thought aloud in my circle of friends, wasn't that an opinion? Whatever it was, I felt I had tamed a piece of the alluring, alien beast that one day I would master.

I had finally made friends with the beast. As a "cultural correspondent" for the German radio and press, I was cheered by the irony that the *Vaterland* was paying for my Parisian life. Unless it was a devil's bargain? That voice always in my head. Asking me to prove that Paris, my Paris, wasn't a myth or make-believe—that I had really got away.

Sneaking into the opera tonight, I had once again proved it to myself. I looked around the circle of boxes, that abundance of plush, red velvet, and gold that seemed only a breath away from a luxury bordello. My unknown companions were bent over their programs, anticipating a production that had been called sensational in the press. An occasional curious look brushed over me. I almost expected them to invite me into the conversation: what did I think about modernizing Mozart? I was prepared to tell them that this provocative *Così fan tutte* (I had already reviewed it) would be as scandalous in Spic-and-Span-Land today as it had already been in Mozart's day and age. Paris applauded the two well-bred sisters, Fiordiligi and Dorabella, for their sexual daring, their way of outwitting their deceitful fiancés. The two were tricksters, sisters of mine.

What would my box companions say if they knew I was here for an encore without a ticket? They didn't know I had to stay in practice. I couldn't afford to lose my touch.

Not too long ago, I had taken my lover Claude to the opera to show off my bohemian skills. Like any ambitious, attractive actress, Claude couldn't help drawing attention to herself. We got caught. It was one of those errors one makes when one is blind with desire. Being found out and stopped like a schoolgirl brought me right back to Germany. Suddenly I was with my mother, whose fury over any lapse in good behavior could push her over the edge, especially if there was the shadow of anything sexual: "*Du Schlampe!* (Slut!) What shall the neighbors think?! You should be ashamed of yourself!"

Claude had laughed off the gaffe, finding the whole thing amusing. "I'll dance Carmen for you right here, if you like..." She had flung her arms into a Flamenco pose in the middle of the foyer, throwing me glances. When I told her about my mother, my shame of being German, she looked me up and down, "Leave it to me, *chérie*, I can think of a few more rules for you to break..."

But why spoil my opera night thinking of Claude the Treacherous? I'd much rather look forward to Mozart's two rebel sisters, sung not by the usual walruses of the opera stage but by pretty singers with small waists, dressed up in corsets.

I always brought a pair of opera glasses to the theater. They served to entertain me during tedious old ballet "hams" I had to review because Nureyev had resurrected them or was dancing in them. But even when I was watching *Swan Lake* or *Giselle*, I liked to train my binos on the Corps de Ballet and follow the poisonous, longing, adoring glances the lesser dancers cast at the prima ballerina. Oh, the boredom of being frozen in one endless graceful pose—until the next pas de deux of the soloists is finally over and a new pose can be taken! I knew it all from my own romance with ballet, taking classes as a girl, then suddenly getting serious and spending a year in a professional ballet company. My first-hand knowledge gave me an advantage as a critic. Sometimes my opera glasses led me to a new star in the making—a corps girl who filled her poses with such abandon that every bend of her swan's neck seemed artistic inspiration or perhaps spiritual ardor. Such a discovery could easily make me forget the cold acrobatics of the soloists and open up a field of dreams.

From the back of my box I scanned the oval of the balcony and was rewarded by sophisticated hair-twists and milk-white *décolletés*.

Hold on...

A flash of red caught my eye. This was the woman with the asymmetrical haircut I'd passed as I followed my animated group to their box. She'd come running up the sweep of stairs from the opposite side. Something about the way she leapt past me like a tall gazelle—all aflash in red—had stayed with me. Her henna-red hair flying off the side of her face like a single wing.

Now she was sitting in a box almost across from me, accompanied by a man. I confirmed the elegance of her appearance before the lights went halfway down for the overture. From my position I saw the haircut from the longer side, following her jaw line and ending in a slightly extended tip near the corner of her mouth. With a movement of her head her long, narrow-cut eyes came into view. Her mouth appeared small and full like a bud. I could not read her expression, but I studied her neck. The neck, if you ask me, is one of the most interesting parts of a woman's body. This neck was longer and less boyish than Claude's, but still. There was something musical and sensuous in this neck, her head inclined as if she were soaking up Mozart in a summer breeze. As I had already seen the opera I could afford to divert part of my attention. Once the curtain went up, her low-cut white blouse shimmered in the light reflected from the stage, framed by the chili red of her jacket. Her companion had a dark ponytail and was wearing a white turtleneck under his dinner jacket. He bent toward her, made remarks into her ear and passed her his opera glasses. His hands looked surprisingly small and delicate. Was it a woman?

The moment the applause welled up at the end of Act One, I went to the spot where the half-round of boxes led to the vestibule. The doors had hardly opened and the first rush of spectators spilled out toward the bar and buffet stations in the foyer, when the couple appeared. They quickly passed me on the way to the stairs. I followed them, admiring the red *tailleur* she was wearing. How could anybody fly up a staircase in a tight, barely slit skirt? The clash of the chili red with the henna of her hair was refreshing, bold. Her red shoes had jeweled heels, and she was carrying a jeweled handbag that could not fit much more than a lipstick. He, by contrast (I had decided it was a he when I noticed the size of his shoes) carried an elegant shoulder bag. What a couple! His gait had a dancer's swing, whereas hers was understated. No mincing, no showing off. I had seen her run like a winged gazelle, and now she walked as if she were wearing sandals. But perhaps she was simply floating on a cloud.

I followed them back down the grand staircase, past the naked-breasted statues with candlesticks on their heads, until they both turned into a hallway that ended at the stage door. I quickly took in as many details as possible—the way her hair with its oblique line brushed her neck; the way her companion talked to her, touching her elbow. People were crowding around the stage door. All of a sudden, she turned and looked over her shoulder. Had she felt my stare in her back? My breath caught. Her gaze stopped on me for the briefest interval. I was shocked by her piercing eyes. Her face expressed neither surprise nor interest enough to match the intensity of this gaze. I went to the nearest bar and got myself a glass of Champagne to calm my nerves.

Afterwards I was restless. I wandered around, baffled by the short skirts worn by women with bulky legs. As I didn't want to be on the constant lookout for the stranger in red, I mosied over to the exhibition wing. Ballet paintings from the nineteenth century: *le galant* in his high hat standing ready in the wings or waiting in the classroom near the girl who raises her leg together with her tulle skirts. Not much has changed in the world of ballet.

The intermission seemed interminable until I noticed the dark-skinned *ouvreuse* standing at the entrance of my box with a stack of programs, eyeing me. I looked back with curiosity as she undauntedly held my gaze. I raised my glass to her; she smiled. I waited. She approached.

"Don't we know each other?" she asked.

"You seem familiar," I said. "Remind me?"

"The Women's Film Festival last fall?"

"Right," I said, searching my memory. "Great party."

Her afro framed a round face with a big, sensuous mouth and lively eyes that seemed ready to laugh or tease. Compared to the aureole of her head, her body in the tight *ouvreuse* uniform looked small and trim. There had been many attractive women in the party crowd. Could I have overlooked her? Distracted by Claude, perhaps?

"Do you like the performance?" she asked. "Even a second time?"

"How do you know?"

"I worked downstairs in the orchestra on opening night. Right center section." The area where the press was seated.

I bowed slightly to acknowledge her compliment. "Do you remember every spectator at opening night?"

"That very much depends."

"I see. And at daytime, you are a private detective?"

"You might say so." She laughed impishly and looked at my mouth. "I study music and remember certain notes."

"I can see *Così* again and again," I said. "I like the production. For once the women are players, too."

"Dorabella and Fiordiligi know what they want." She gave me a telling look.

"And what do they want?" I flirted back.

"Variety," she said with emphasis.

"Who wouldn't want that?"

"I would!"

"Well, aren't we a match." It was my turn to look at her mouth. "Which instrument are you studying?"

"Piano and voice."

"Mezzo?" Her talking voice had a pleasant timbre and her full lips were appetizing. "Which is—or would be—your favorite role?"

"Cherubino. Perhaps Oktavian, but Mozart is easier…"

"Trouser roles, I see. Unfortunately there aren't that many." I tried to imagine her chocolate skin in the silver suit and powdered wig of Octavian in Strauss's *Rosenkavalier*, one of the sexiest roles in the operatic repertoire.

"Unfortunately, in real life there aren't many either!" She let her eyes wander over my theater jeans.

"But that very much depends," I quoted her, enjoying the warmth rising in my body.

"On what?"

"Who you turn to. During intermission, for example."

She laughed at me from the corner of her eyes as if that were too good to be true. The intermission bell rang.

"Next intermission?" I proposed. I saw a certain shimmer in her eyes.

"Agreed."

Back at my seat, I tried to place my new date at the party where she had seen me. Had I flirted with her? Had she flirted with me? Had we kissed? There was an ease between us as if no effort had to be made to be more than strangers. What a promising night. I might be doubly rewarded for sneaking into *Così* a second time.

I kept an eye on the box across from me. In the last moment before the doors were closed, the woman in red reappeared with her companion. This time she let her opera glasses slowly wander around the auditorium. Could it be that she had noticed me when she turned around for that one-second look? As the opera went on, I observed that she didn't fuss over him to get his attention. Her hands made no movement toward him. The two put their heads together and exchanged remarks while Mozart's deceitful young men, disguised as "Albanians," made their move on the sisters. He pulled something out of his jacket pocket—a pen—and she scribbled something. She was taking notes.

I was back at my post in the vestibule just as the curtain went down. This second intermission, unusual in a two-act opera, gave me another chance to find out about her. Why, in fact, did that seem so important? I couldn't explain it to myself. With Claude and our shared taste for adventures, I had enough passion in my life. Why then was I troubled by the stranger as if her unreadable gaze held an answer? I had no time for further reflection. In the next moment, the couple (but were they a couple?) rushed past me again on their way downstairs. Apparently they knew someone in the cast or in the orchestra and had to use every minute to pay their respects. This time, however, she was looking around as if searching for someone. Not me by any chance?

I followed them at a polite distance, hoping they would stop for a drink. I had to make a connection before the evening was over. I wanted to make her look at me for more than a second. What was I going to say? "Don't we know each other?" Any banality would do, as it had with my *ouvreuse*. But again the couple hurried to the stage door and disappeared. I swallowed my disappointment. I had a rendezvous after all.

In front of one of the gilded mirrors of the foyer I contemplated my image. I was *d' accord avec moi-meme*, as the French would put it—okay with myself. My slicked-back hair and the white aviator scarf over my leather jacket made me look like...who was it? David Bowie's brother-sister? I felt I cast a proper figure in Little Versailles, among the gold candelabras and lascivious statues, the medallions and frescos with naked nymphs swooning over Apollo. The mirror was guarded by the statue of a muse with a mighty leg. The contrast between her and me seemed to incite women to crane their necks. Or was it some other contrast? In certain moods I looked too young and soft-boned, my eyes unguarded, my mouth too full for a boy. And boys usually don't glow the way I did this night. My reflection showed that I had done more than listen to glorious music for the past two hours. And the night wasn't over yet.

"What do you do between intermissions?" I asked the music student-*ouvreuse* who was leaning in a niche of the vestibule, one silky brown leg crossed over the other. "Are you allowed each time to see the entire opera?"

She nodded. "If it's really packed, I go down to standing room."

"I envy you. When I first got to Paris, I had an usher job in a cinema. I watched Catherine Deneuve in *Belle de Jour* at least thirty-five times. I learned a lot."

"I'd say," she said slyly. "Tonight there are enough empty seats, in any case. The first loge is completely empty..." She made a movement with her head toward the stage, inviting me to follow her. She opened a nearby door with her key. In the semicircle of boxes and loges she indicated the loge directly to the right of the curtain. She looked at me expectantly.

"*Coté court*, stage left," she said pointedly. "Right across, you have the loge of the Phantôme de l'Opéra. I'd rather not suggest that one..."

I stared at the loge on the right. What was she suggesting, exactly? The loge with its scarlet velvet canopy was flanked by two colossal half-naked caryatides. The first one had a strikingly shiny belly as if—like the feet of certain saints—it had been fondled for centuries by caring patrons. I remembered having been in one of these loges next to the stage. There was a small, dark entryway. One had to turn a corner before getting to the chairs. It occurred to me now that this meant nobody could directly barge in on the occupants. The architect must have had something in mind with this arrangement.

"Are you sure?" I searched her face. Could she be that bold?

"It's almost always unoccupied. You can't see much of the stage but—"

"Drop a rose into the diva's *décolleté*?" I made a movement of throwing, landing my fingertips lightly on the open neck of her uniform.

"I'm going to listen in the loge." Her tongue moistened her lips. "The garden scene and the rest…"

The garden scene meant the seduction of Dorabella by Guglielmo, her sister's fiancé, although in this production it wasn't clear who seduces whom. It was the sexiest scene. My companion was watching me, waiting. I knew her, I thought, even if I didn't recall the details. In Paris, every woman knew every other woman.

"I'm free after this intermission," she said with urgency.

"Free—for Guglielmo?" I assured myself with a long look into her eyes.

The way she looked back was my answer. We nodded at each other. As I turned to leave, I saw her expectantly chewing on her lower lip.

THE GOOD GIRL

My "Dorabella" had barely disappeared from the loge when I remembered the box on the other side. I was stung by the impression of red disappearing through the door. There was no doubt. For a second, the silhouette of the man with the dark ponytail was visible in the doorframe.

I should have been there at the end of the last scene, should have stopped them on the way out, said something, anything, to get her to talk to me. For one wild moment, I cursed my mistake. But how could the charming *Mozartiade* in the loge be a mistake? I had never so literally experienced Mozart's phrasing, his rhythms and repetitions, his painful *douceur* and piquant gallops. I was still out of breath, butterflies all over my skin.

"Wanting to dance at two weddings at the same time? You'd better wake up!" My mother's voice. Wanting was dangerous. Wanting too much pleasure was greedy and would be punished.

Did I want too much pleasure? Was I greedy?

This was the Good Girl, *das brave Mädchen*, popping up like a weed that needs to be plucked the moment it raises its ugly head.

Of course I am greedy. Greedy, and grateful. Enthusiastically grateful to all women, especially the Parisians. Because they are alive, because it's so easy for them to find the way, the most natural of all ways, into the arms of another woman. Because the City of Light attracts them like a thousand merry little fishes...every day a new swarm, a new school! The mere thought of this glittering rush caused my mood to somersault as if spring had broken and I was strolling through a May night instead of a cold and wet night in March.

I walked down the Avenue de l'Opéra on a high: all women were beautiful, bedecked in red *tailleurs* and tight uniforms, smelling of cinnamon, carnations, and all kinds of imponderables. In a mood like this night, every single one of them had to be loved, embraced, enchanted, had to melt like butter in the sun, like snow on the tongue.

Was this Mozart's effect on me? "We could try this again," she had whispered during the final sextet of *Così*.

"Which opera is next?"

"*Arabella*."

"The last performance again, like tonight?"

She had buttoned up her uniform with a conspirator's smile, calmly tucking her blouse back into her skirt. "Just like tonight."

There was a fleeting scent of spring in the air. The cast-iron grates around the trees on the boulevard glittered. The globe-shaped lights of the Café de la Paix shone like lemonade moons in the puddles of the sidewalk. Ivy boxes in front of the glassed-in terrace sported pink alpine violets in defiance of the winter spleen. Yes, I was in love with them all—Claude with her dark almond eyes; my *ouvreuse* and her promise of a da capo opera night; the stranger in red with her intense, unreadable gaze, whom I would find again, even if I had to search for her all over Paris, wander every street, go to the opera every single night.

Arriving at the Palais Royal I stopped to look at the programs announced under the awning of the Comédie Française. The showcases were unlit; the Comédie didn't need to advertise. A little group of tourists in winter coats was huddled at a display window featuring Molière's *L'école des femmes*, trying to decipher a review. I had seen the play and knew the review. My colleague from *Le Monde* had provided the sycophantic applause that was expected at the most ancient, venerable, and most conventional theater of France.

"But our German paper said it wasn't worth it," a young man with a little hunter's hat remarked, speaking German. Had he read the critical review I had published a week ago? "If *Le Monde* liked it, we must go," the others decided, and the little group marched off with confidence.

My mother had tried to steer me toward journalism from the moment I mentioned writing, at age fifteen. But in my friends' eyes, a journalist wasn't a serious writer. My mother had no idea what a writer was. Anything touching upon "Vissi d'arte," Puccini's famous aria about a "life for art," was deeply suspicious to her. She would not have invited Tosca, the diva living openly in sin, to her little soirées where she served self-baked pizza—a first in my parents' circle, my mother's own avant-garde.

Throughout my school years, she had kept a keen eye on the men courting me. Where was the professor, diplomat, publisher whom she would push on me and marry alongside me? It was all she knew. It enraged me. It broke my heart to see her limitations. Could a woman ever be free? Free to be herself? In my darkest hours, when my mother tried to console me, she always came back to her panacea: "All you have to do is wait. You are so young, *mein Schatz*. Do journalism and wait for the right husband. It will all fall into place."

I strode down Rue de Rivoli, along the backside of the Louvre. From this side, the museum loomed like a fortress, a dark, repetitive reminder that the laws of culture, the rules of the game, excluded women. The stone-framed windows stared back at me in blind, monotonous indifference, until the first narrow passage—just wide enough for a horse carriage, barely accommodating a city bus—allowed me to slip through and enter the court-yard. Had I "slipped through" by becoming a journalist?

Chairs were scattered everywhere on the paths, taking on the personality of human beings, refusing to get in line with the geometry of French park design. As if set up for a theater piece, they were waiting for the curtain of the night to lift and magically set them in motion.

The smell of rain and earthworms, and I was back on the wet, dreary streets of Hamburg when I was a teenager, coming out of a theater with my parents; the forced conversations about the play we had just seen. It never was about the play, never about a mad passion for theater or art—just the self-congratulatory pride of belonging to the educated classes, like the other families of my parents' circle. The only pretense of life in these night streets was the polite blabber of the young man who had been invited as my "cavalier," for whom I wore mascara and heels and a dress with a belt so tight I came home feeling strangled.

No wonder the first man I moved in with after school was an intellectual, a writer with unwashed hair. Franz, or rather Frantisek (in honor of Kafka and all things Prague) spoke with the slowness of a poet searching with a lantern for a word, while his full mouth held a self-ironic smile. His thin, slightly stooped frame was crushed by the coat he insisted on wearing: his grandfather's war coat, a stiff, brown affair with a huge collar, once probably meant to stave off Russia's winters, now making him suspicious in Hamburg's bookstores. He studied medicine because it would be "exotic" to be a writer and country doctor like certain modernist poets he admired.

We also thought it "exotic" to sign marriage papers to get me a cheap "newlyweds" flat when I dropped out of Hamburg University for the Munich Academy of Dance. A marriage license was meaningless; it surely wouldn't impact bohemians like us. I hoped all this would teach my mother a lesson, but it taught me that you get punished for fooling around with bourgeois mores, giving up your name and hanging up your freedom at the coat-nail of Mrs. Newlywed.

I strode past the Carrousel with its klutzy Arc de Triomphe that replaced the palace where Marie Antoinette had failed to escape in time from her executioners. Sometimes I still had Frantisek's voice in my head: "Once you start doing journalism, you'll never write."

What did he know about it? I had once shown him one of my poems and heard him talk to the others about his "little poetess." Probably back then, I had to give up language for a while to find my own words. Get out of my head, into my body. Diving headlong into the beauty and strict discipline of ballet had been an act of rebellion against him and everyone else.

Leaving the Louvre, I bounced down the steps to the Seine to check out what the lovebirds were doing in the shade of the quays. Nobody there, of course, given the weather. I had been part of these couples often enough myself, smooching to the background music of the barges creaking against the quay. One of my early lovers, Jules, a set painter, had lived on a barge but never invited me to put my foot on it. He was proud of knowing every spot on the banks, under the arched passageways, where it was worth the risk. It was his favorite way of doing it, and I could see his point, doing it fast, in a hurry, like the river that had to rush to the Atlantic that very night.

I'd made my way to Paris with the same rush. Frantisek and the Hamburg friends had picked me up in Munich on their semester break, on their way to the south of France. I was ready to train all summer. As a late-comer to ballet I couldn't afford to take a break.

I had my driver's license, but my controlling husband wouldn't let me touch the wheel of his battered VW. Friend Käferstein (a name taken in honor of all things Jewish) gallantly opened the driver's door of his Opel for me. He watched with a self-satisfied smile as I stepped on the gas and sped ahead of Frantisek and the other friends. Not a word when the needle went up above 120 km/hour. We stopped at the last gas station of the *autoroute*, at the gates of Paris, gazing at the shimmering, gray mass of the city I could almost touch with my hand. When Frantisek and his VW reappeared a good half hour later, his face filled with anguish and reproach, I didn't know yet that I had got to Paris for good—and that getting there first, I'd left him behind.

Sometimes a meaning takes a while to catch on.

NIGHT WANDERER

The Seine was lapping up high, swollen and excited from the rain storms of the past days. The illuminated Gare d'Orsay across the river threw a lick of polish on the cobblestones of the quay. My marriage to Frantisek seemed like a story lived by someone else. My imagination had been stirred by women as far back as I could remember. A little girl with a dark page cut mesmerized me at age five because she was half French and her parents had a marble statue in their garden in Berlin, where I grew up. I remembered a children's ballet from that time, the little girls dolled up in brocade as in a painting by Velázquez. I was permitted to touch one girl's crinoline dress, entering a magical realm I never completely left.

The fairy tale of femininity...

What made it so fascinating was that I was never entirely part of it. I was and I wasn't. I was in love with the tale but I didn't fit the bill, no matter how hard my mother tried. There wasn't a day in my childhood and youth that wasn't touched by the dream my mother, my older sister, and I were supposed to share—graceful manners, beauty, charm, all difficult to define and difficult to escape. My parents didn't have money after the war, but my mother, cook and baker par excellence, was ambitious and endlessly creative. Throughout the fifties, she tailored entire wardrobes, ball gowns, and coats, making us look like members of a social class she was determined to join. We sometimes joked that she would also make our shoes if only she had time. My knack for being a trickster must have originated with my mother. While she baked and bustled and hosted, my sister and I smiled, curtsied, and pirouetted in apparent unison. Our planet of womanly virtues was graced by admiring visits from "outer space": my father circled around us at a distance, but always brought his favorite toy, a camera. His big, leather-bound photo albums filled a prominent space in the bookshelves and fed my mother's hunger for family stardom.

What a charade, my family. A painted merry-go-round with one tune, made in Germany, made for my mother. Her devotion to home and hearth exacted a price. If we didn't perform properly, she erupted in cutting criticism. If we betrayed her standards of decency—by complaining to friends about the family, for example—she fell into a pained silence that could last for days. In my teenage years, the threat of her disappointment taught me that love was an effort and compliance an inescapable deception.

Looking back now, how early was I aware that my mother controlled everything, even my father? As a child already? My father—the discreet royal consort, my sister and I, her doll princesses. She was wearing the pants, demanding, commandeering, while her "better half," my father, catered to her, indulged her, and shut up. I watched his discrete victories, like calling me Luise, the name he wanted me to have against my mother's will. He liked to trace his family line back to the Prussian Queen Luise, a claim my mother resented and refused to believe. But he kept calling me by his pet name (picked up by Frantisek and the friends, who called me Lou). I knew it was his secret male privilege to get a part of his daughter away from my mother, to fantasize having me all to himself.

Masculine, feminine. How arbitrary those points of view were. It was all make-believe, a mere fantasy, shifty as a mood. In my coming of age I had taken femininity to an edge, pretending, protecting my mother from myself, and then stepped out, leaving my ballet slippers and everything else behind.

I leapt at the branch of a sycamore bent low over the riverbank, letting the raindrops splash over my face and hair. Feminine, not feminine. The same kind of fantasy declares "Paris is a woman," makes me the lover and her the beloved. Paris, a woman in perpetual performance, brilliant, showing me—as she did everyone—exactly what I longed to see. Like Claude the Treacherous, in her uncanny ability to guess my desires. But there were other similarities, too. Like a curtain coming down between acts, Paris could

make you a stranger, an outcast, from one moment to another, with a shift of mood or weather, you never knew what. An indifference shutting you out cold while everything exciting was still there at arm's length, if only you could grasp it.

Claude had disappeared from view. It wasn't the first time we had been cooling our affair. No explanation. No warning. How many weeks? Five, six? We had never gone longer than a fortnight. What was she waiting for?

A Bateau Mouche was chugging up the Seine toward the Pont des Arts, ferrying along the warm-wet glow of a private party, now disappearing under the bridge on its way upstream to the Quai des Grands Augustins, Quai des Orfèvres, melting into the haze.

I flipped the butt of my cigarette into the river and continued along the quay toward Notre Dame. Passion was a roller coaster: you just had to hang in there.

I was whistling Ferrando and Dorabella's love duet when someone whistled back at me like a mockingbird. It was a good-looking guy sitting on a bench with provocatively spread legs, presenting his packet. I grinned at him.

"Hey," he said, "in the mood for a *tête à tête*?" Of course, he didn't say *tête à tête*, he said an obscenity that sounded just like it.

"Perhaps, if you were Mozart."

I said it in my normal woman's voice. At night, with my long legs and the long stride I have adopted, I am rarely taken for a woman. The world of the night is an unfair world. Men are everywhere on the go, hanging out around the *pissoirs* and bushes, on the benches in squares and along the quays, ready for some adventure. How many women are just as awake at this moment, barely past midnight, and in the mood for a little excitement—if only there was something out there catering to them. But what? Little tea huts around the Tuileries with a sofa and a candle? A row of tents along the banks of the Seine, adorned with colored flags to signal sexual preferences?

A clicking-rolling sound approached from below the Pont des Arts. Out of the shadows, a narrow figure rushed up with rowing movements—a girl on roller skates, sporting a phosphor-yellow cockscomb. She stopped sharp in front of me and stared at me with smeared mascara eyes.

"Got a cigarette?" she said with a brazen voice.

"Sure do." I pulled my cigarette case from my leather jacket. I usually prepare a few "active" cigarettes for a theater night in order to avoid having to roll them at intermission. The young woman blinked when I opened the case and held it out to her. She suspiciously peered at my face, the silver case, my hands—then she got it.

"Can I have two?" she said with eager, childlike trust.

"Go ahead." When she had fished out two of the last four cleanly rolled cigarettes from the case, I asked, "Anything else you need?"

"Got fire myself," she grinned. With a brief military salute at her cockscomb, she added, "Have a good day, pal," and rolled off clicking along the cobblestones. A moment later someone whistled. A young guy with a similar hairdo rolled out of the shadows and followed her. I heard them laughing as if they had just cracked a big joke.

I was strangely touched by her salute. What had she seen in me that would link us as "pals"? She had no idea that I'd been a rookie like her once, pretending to be invincible when I strolled through the city by day and by night, convinced that Paris belonged to me.

At first I, too, had a companion. Blue was a musician from Guadeloupe who lived in a collective with friends of mine. He used to play a mournful saxophone in the metro and at night, on a fresh high, set out to wander. I accompanied him and listened to his stories from the Caribbean Islands. Childhood stories about his grandmother who took him with her to the graveyards to talk with the dead. He told me he understood the cooing of the pigeons on the roofs. I told him about Gertrude Stein's *pigeons on the grass alas*, and he assured me Gertrude was a great Shaman who understood them, too. He kept a privileged dialogue with God. When I smoked some dope and read a few pages of Castaneda I had no trouble keeping up with him. I'd been smitten with Paris even before I got there; I couldn't wait to make it mine. Without a second thought I slipped into the nomadic lifestyle of Blue. I cut my hair and adopted his garbs—jeans with a short jeans jacket, T-shirt, tennis shoes. He sometimes introduced me to friends and clochards, and from the moment one of them took me for a guy, he used my father's pet name, presenting us as "Brothers Lou and Blue." We got a kick out of it.

The last traces of youthful fat disappeared from my face. It happened that the women at the bakeries and cheese shops in my quartier greeted me, "*Bonjour, Monsieur.*" I was twenty-eight when I became invisible to the ordinary world of men. No more catcalls or marriage proposals coming at me. The eager looks up and down my body now came from gay guys in the metro or in the streets, and I quickly learned to enter the fantasy game their eyes invited. When I exchanged a few words with them on occasion, I dropped without effort into the deeper voice I used in my conversations with Blue. I kept the tempo of his walk and the length of his steps long after losing sight of him.

A good year ago, my friends told me that Blue was back in Paris. Some young theater company had engaged him for a play. We went to see the performance at the Biennale des Jeunes Artistes, a festival for young theater folk, where the play got attention, and there I met Claude and the rest of her troupe. Shortly after the end of the run Blue disappeared again—I figured he had taken a boat back to Guadeloupe. But sometimes during my night wanderings I continued to be "Brother Lou" and felt his smooth gait next to mine as if he'd been one of Jean Genet's dark angels, forever chosen to protect me.

If my mother could see me now, I used to think. It was as if the city took me in and peeled my old skins away. Still, there was always another remnant of the Good Girl to be shed—an obliging smile, a readiness to turn my eyes away. Don't look! The classical motto of so-called innocence as soon as there is anything interesting to see. Anything sexual, *louche*, forbidden. How is a girl supposed to take her place in the world if she isn't allowed to see the world? I found out soon enough that a woman who can't look also can't desire. She can only entice in order to be desired. Women's eyes are passive eyes; they wait for something to enter them and blow their minds.

I continued walking, feeling the ease of my stride. Had I wanted to, I could have stepped right into the gaze of that stranger in red and made her look at me, stop her in her tracks and take her by the arm: *Let's get out of here!* I was free. My life was anything I wanted it to be. An adventure. A *coup de théâtre*. A loge with bordello-red chairs and velvet trimmings.

What if someone started an opera revolution that dedicated the first loge on the right in every opera house to women's own purposes? Women are not eager, after all, to slouch on park benches, hang around pissoirs or crouch in the bushes at night, in the cold. I imagined what it would be like to plunge some more hesitant lovers into the fantastic tumult of the orchestra.

What the battle cries of Wagner's Valkyries might trigger in
some of them...

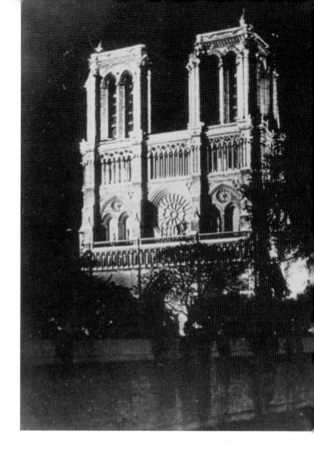

I was approaching Notre
Dame. The cathedral looked like
a dramatic stage set gleaming
in the haze.

We would need to divvy
up the acts for the use of the
first loge on the right: the
romantic-morbid lovers would
clamor for the last act in which
the heroine dies of consump-
tion, kills herself, is killed or
buried alive. Nothing could be
more enticing when la petite
mort was at stake, the "little
death" of orgasm, as the French
call it. My newly discovered
Dorabella, in fact, was quite a revolutionary. No hurry, no sticky sentiment,
not even names. Simply waiting until the right opera is on the program and
the last performance comes to an end...

I started up Blvd St. Michel. Shakespeare & Co was illuminated,
probably after a reading. At the corner store of the boulevard, Gibert Jeune,
with its thousands of secondhand books and paperbacks outside under
the yellow awning, students were still browsing. A few young women were
hanging out with them, visibly less interested in the books, their umbrellas
tucked under their arms.

A limo stopped at a nightclub; I watched a gaggle of girls in sleeveless
taffeta dresses peel out and run up to the line of cars that were looking for
parking. They didn't have the least trouble running and skipping in their
flimsy footwear, as if they'd worn stilettos since first grade. They were clacking excitedly across the wet pavement, sweeping up the taffeta skirts around
their legs as they ran.

LA COUPOLE, MIDNIGHT

On Blvd Montparnasse the night was in full swing. Cars were parked right down the middle of the wide boulevard, between the Dôme, Le Select, La Rotonde, and La Coupole. There was a merry chaos of valets and people, some in evening attire, flagging down cabs, stepping in and out of honking cars and limousines, shouting, laughing. I felt drawn to my night hangout like a sugar addict to her favorite bakery. I scanned the crowd inside La Coupole, groups of revelers piled in between the frescoed columns; tables loaded with bottles, Champagne coolers, glasses, plates. Waiters in long aprons zipped in and out of the kitchen swing door, large pewter trays hoisted on one shoulder, stacked with oyster pyramids on ice. It was the post-midnight speed, driven by alcohol and big tips. The rest of the day the waiters would be loitering at the tables for a chat. They knew their clientele. Legs crossed, leaning confidentially onto the tables, one thumb hooked into an apron string, they would be as oblivious to impatient patrons as to the couples huddled too closely in the corners of the leather banquettes.

There were tables not set for dinner at the side of the bar where the view over the vast hall was limited. I ordered a glass of Champagne in honor of *Così* and the soon-to-follow last act of *Arabella*. I drank to the old adage that sex is best when there are no names attached. Well, sometimes. Anything is true sometimes.

Alone at my table with my glass of Champagne, in my leather jacket and silk scarf, I was expected to be out for no good. A blond girl-woman between two men at the bar made efforts to catch my eye. She was too young to be so willfully flirting, in a slinky dress that showed her bony shoulders, her mouth over-painted. I kept an eye on the trio, wondering what they were up to. Was she looking for a foursome? Or for a way to escape her two cavaliers?

Where would the woman in red have gone after the opera? Brasserie Bofinger? Maxim's? Was she here? Why had she suddenly turned around as if she knew damn well I was following her? I still felt the shock of being discovered, caught *in flagranti*, my breath stopped in some wild expectation, mixed with fear. Why fear?

I'd barely asked when I spotted a redhead at the opposite side of the large hall. I strained my eyes but too many people covered my view. A long neck, an elegant naked shoulder visible at a table. I couldn't tell if her companion with the ponytail was with her. "Haven't I just seen you at the opera?" It would be the easiest thing in the world, something I'd done a million times. Chatting up a stranger was as easy as doing a pirouette. I readied myself to leave my table when the red-haired woman got up. The illusion fell with the sight of a petite person in a mini dress. There was nothing asymmetric about her. Nothing of a gazelle.

What was it about the woman in red? Her *nonchalence*, the flying ease of her movements? The way she leaned into the music? The invitation of her rosebud mouth against the piercing coldness of her eyes? Was it the instant rush to want to break through that barrier of indifference and reach her, reveal the mystery of her body, her person?

How would I ever find her again?

Paris est tout petit pour ceux qui s'aiment d'un aussi grand amour... "Paris is a small nothing for those who share so big a love," Garance teases her gallant suitor in *Les enfants du paradis, Children of Paradise*, when he fakes a surprise meeting with her. She plays along with a knowing smile. The kind of smile Claude the Treacherous smiled.

I ordered another glass, then another. The extravagance was my celebration, my toast to adventure. What would be next? Who would be next?

A group of night birds pushed through the central entrance doors, a ring of excited men around a woman; the flash of a camera. The flock made its way down the main passageway. People craned their necks; waiters stopped and stared. The center of attention—a dark head with a page cut, proud, bobbing with pleasure from the flattery—could it be Claude? Claude returning to Paris for a new theater project, with a throng of admirers already sidling up to her?

I suddenly felt tipsy and out of control with the desire to run up to her and elbow my way into her circle, see her throw her head back with exaggerated surprise and delight. Was I hallucinating? Claude's *carrière* wouldn't yet produce such an *entrée* even if she had been ready for it from the moment she set her foot onstage. But with her, nothing was ever predictable. What did I know about what she had been plotting during her absence? She had been gone long enough to prepare some outlandish return.

Two *messieurs* in tuxedos jumped up at the back with raised glasses, shouting, "Mireille, Mireille!" and the throng settled around their table. Mireille, indeed. She could have been Claude's sister with a more tailored haircut, less boyish, but the same seductive almond eyes. It took a while before the excited twitters in the birdcage ebbed back to the normal din and everybody returned to their oysters and Champagne.

It took me a while longer to cool down. The air had changed. There was a readiness to take off into a higher pulse; it was the time of the night when *vedettes*, famous people, showed up. I noticed the restlessness of heads turning more frequently to the entry doors. The young woman with her two cavaliers at the bar kept checking whether I, too, was looking at the doors or perhaps in the opposite direction, at her. I did. I smiled at her, touched by her childlike shoulder blades. She smiled back, whispered to the two men, and then they all looked at me.

At this moment, a dark, rough-edged voice nearby caught my attention. Something in the cadence sounded like a diatribe. It had to be Stéphane. My first Paris lover. I looked around. Impossible. What was wrong with me tonight, seeing phantoms wherever I turned? She was the last person I wanted to encounter. I hadn't seen her in years, although since meeting Claude, Stéphane had been on my mind again. Perhaps because both of them were theater women. Perhaps because they had more in common than theater. Hanging out with Claude backstage and at her rehearsal space had made me wonder when I would run into Stéphane. I had tried to imagine what it would be like, but I still wasn't ready for it. I was tempted to move out of sight. How was it possible that I was once so young—a good ten years younger, enthralled by a woman who was my incompatible opposite?

But there she was, in a quartet of women whose eyes were eating her up. She was holding forth with the particular animation that would grip her when she talked about her political ideas, her chin raised, projecting her words with a little bite or snap. The same feathery brown hair barely covering her ears, the tight, ambitious mouth, the eyes with the childish expression of self-delight.

I had fallen in with Stéphane at the first Paris appearance of the Living Theater, a New York underground group. I went because the group was a sensation, and it was true—their performance was like nothing I'd ever seen on a stage. The all-out violence of war and oppression; the chaos of naked bodies; loud, barking voices seemed to come right out of my German nightmares—the scenes of persecution, torture, and death that filled my dreams as I grew up. At the climax, the group was standing in a bleakly lit circle, and in a daisy chain of mayhem, each member got shot down by the person standing next to them.

When everyone had left, I was unable to get out of my seat. Near the exit of the circus tent space, two or three audience members were talking to the director. I went over and hung back with the little group. One of them was Stéphane. With her unadorned looks, short-cropped hair and dark, edgy voice, she was the first person who ever made me wonder: boy or girl? I couldn't get my eyes off her while she was conspiring to organize a free performance by the revolutionary troupe. I introduced myself and asked if she would call to let me know the date and place? There was the question of a big enough stadium and getting around the police department. She was cocky. She would set up the event as a happening, without a permit. But a week later I got her call at my au pair job: the police had stepped in. There was no question of an illicit, free performance. The company had moved on. Speaking French on the telephone still was a major challenge for me, but I managed to express regrets over her failed coup and suggest a coffee.

It was the end of my first year in Paris. While Stéphane was doing *théâtre d'action*, political street theater, I took classes at Place Clichy, a building with several dance studios, creaking stairs, huge, unwashed windows, tiny, sweat-soaked dressing rooms. Day after day I walked through the political unrest of the student revolts, literally walked through half of Paris, as there were no metros or busses running. After a few weeks, the streets up to Clichy were lined with mountains of garbage so high you couldn't any longer see the third-floor windows of the houses. Everyone supported the general strike and most cars took up pedestrians wherever they could be seen walking. I used to wear a long, belted military-style coat and a self-made streetboy's cap. Drivers would lean out of their car windows and shout, "*Hé, gavroche*, want a ride?" Being called "street urchin" in French was a *tendresse*, a compliment, and I usually followed the invitations, even though there wasn't a single time that I didn't have to go into laborious battles to fight off the men's seduction. It forced me to speak with a certain speed and panache. I took it as a sport, a contrast to my mostly nonverbal days of ballet training, getting special lessons in French flirting.

On my coffee dates with Stéphane, I didn't flirt, and neither did she. We talked about politics and art, nothing personal. It was the way Frantisek and the friends talked, the way two boys talked. I was sure Stéphane was gay in every cell of her body, although she never let on. I never uttered a word about being married. Sometimes I felt we were observing each other across our café table with the curiosity and reserve of aliens, one French, one German. I was painfully aware that being German was a personal as well as collective shame nothing could wash away. The humiliation of the German occupation of France was an unavoidable legacy. Stronger than my attraction to Stéphane, history and my hobbled language skills kept me at one remove, an outsider who feared to intrude or commit a faux pas.

Now that I saw her again, a few tables away from me, I was reminded that there had been other elements in the picture as well. I hadn't wanted to reveal myself to her because of her unwillingness to take me in unless it was on her terms. How could I break into her urgent political discourse to tell her about a husband, a troubled relationship, a private tug of war over who I was spending time with?

Was I just imagining it? Stéphane was turning around, scanning the bar side of the café. She was looking at me. Her gaze stopped short, turned blank. She looked away and went on talking as if I didn't exist.

I stared at her profile, watching her talk, her hands gripping the air.

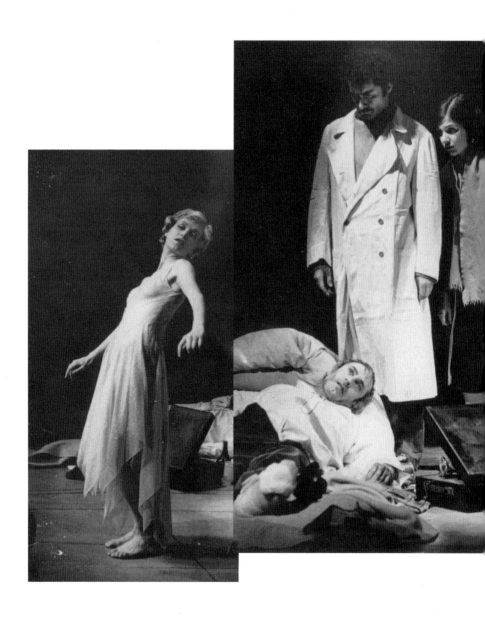

She was laying it on. I could tell how pleased she was with herself in front of her audience, myself included—the guest of honor. The three women nodded, laughed, applauded. And I had to give it to her—as always, she was fascinating. I remembered her street theater improvisations, watching her small-boned body burst into the energy of an attack bird, her hair spiked like wet feathers. She radiated the pleasure of being herself without making any effort. You had to be born a boy to own her greedy, childlike entitlement, or maybe you just had to be French.

I was fed up seeing her and not being seen. I went over to her table.

"*Salut*, Stéphane," I said, "is it you?"

"It's me," she said, the tiniest pleased smile on her mouth.

"I thought you didn't recognize me." I waited a beat. "When you turned a moment ago and looked straight at me."

"I didn't," she said, poker-faced. "No idea you were here."

I had to grin, knowing her all too well. "It's been a while," I explained to the three women who eagerly looked on. "I'm an old pal of Stéphane's from the barricades." They laughed.

"Are you still doing it?" I asked her. I felt like saying, are you still doing your old tricks?

"I'm doing video now," she said with an understatement that couldn't fool me, "and teaching activism. At Narbonne." She hit a pause. "You? Still *onstage*?"

The old competition between us was playing out. She had never forgiven me for finding her political theater repetitive, for not getting fired up by French politics. Descending into the streets for combat or heading out to some factory in the suburbs to do agitprop was not my idea of theater avant-garde. When I was looking for something more "artistic" Stéphane considered me spoiled, bourgeois, an amateur. I didn't have what it takes.

"I write about it now," I said. "I'm a cultural correspondent for the German press." I knew I wouldn't impress her. Why did I try?

She lit a cigarette, inhaled deeply, lowering her chin in a sort of nod. I noticed how good she was at not taking me in. She looked either right through me or at something else, the room, her cigarette smoke, the bowl of pommes frites between their four espresso cups. Was it possible that our old story was still that much alive for both of us?

"You know," she turned to her clique, "this comrade of mine once rejected working with one of the best directors we've got. He wasn't good enough for her." She checked the open-jawed faces around her.

I felt for a moment like a cyclist pedaling after the chain has slipped off. Her distortion of the story was so broad I didn't know where to start.

"Yeah," I said. "I was satisfied. I already had a big role, you know. Broadway dancer turns into Angel of Death." I paused. "Could it get any better?" I asked the astonished trio.

Stéphane huffed.

The play, a world premiere on the experimental fringe, got noticed and had a long run. The dance sequences soothed my frustrated ballerina dreams and taught me what it was like to be in the spotlight. For a while I continued to ride the wave with bit parts on TV, film, advertising. Then I met Ruth Henry, a cultural journalist for the German press who one day asked me to cover ballet for her when she had too much on her plate. I said yes; I saw writing ahead of me. It turned out there was enough demand in Germany to want another voice reporting from the Paris front. At the same time, a young, fashionable theater director offered to be my Pygmalion, but I declined. Stéphane couldn't believe it. I didn't want to be someone's starlet or *Schatz*, tied once again like a puppet to someone else's power. I wanted my own.

I took my leave with a noncommittal bow, savoring the hush that fell as I went back to my table. The quartet soon left, which I booked as a territorial victory, but a shadow remained. A painful part of my early Paris days had intruded into my night. I lit the last cigarette from my silver case, chewing on the smoke.

Had I made a mistake walking off the stage?

The trio at the bar was getting ready to leave. The girl-woman passed me on the way to the bathrooms, shooting me a wounded, curious look, perhaps wondering how I could have forgotten her. I watched her strut down the passage next to the bar with her bony shoulders, her little shoulder bag bumping against the side of her butt. I could see her effort. She was too young to be sexual in her own right. Her walk gave her away.

At a table farther back, I detected a well-known actor, all by himself, not looking around, not looking at anybody. It was one of those things that make French cafés what they are, the fact that nobody blinks an eye about people hanging out with themselves any time, day or night. Women too. Unthinkable in a German pub or restaurant. Pubs in Germany were gross, drunken cruising grounds, obvious ships of fools. In France, sex is all-pervasive in a subtle way because sex is part of culture and therefore art. In Parisian cafés and *bistrots*, where waiters in uniform maintain agreeable formalities (and there's always enough light to read), you are invited to feel private in public, as comfortable as at home, only more so as you don't have to feel lonely.

I stared at my empty glass of Champagne. The din of voices and dishes suddenly tapped on my nerves. All it took was running into Stéphane and my celebration had turned into a wet mop.

Why did it still matter what she thought?

Something about Stéphane's capacity for indifference, for shutting me out, stuck in my bones and made me wonder if my dismay over Claude's absence played against my first Paris heartache. There was something about Stéphane. Now there was something about Claude. Something haunting, unsettling, like a déjà vu.

The last time I had partied at La Coupole, I was with Claude. Claude, a talent on the rise who outshone Stéphane and captivated everyone with her smoldering promise of sex. I remembered our talk that night, how we disagreed in the way we typically disagreed about anything unimportant because of the deeper sexual tension between us, the always unsettled tug of seduction and surrender, top and bottom, boy and girl. We had argued over the heydays of bohemian life before the war, when Kiki de Montparnasse reigned over the *quartier*. Was it a myth that the café night life was wilder in the Roaring Twenties and the thirties than today? Was it true that a notorious young surrealist woman artist had peed one night into a gentleman's top hat here, at La Coupole? It was a story that had gone around forever; I'd heard it from my journalist colleague Ruth Henry, who knew the artist, who didn't elaborate. Claude claimed to know it was true. It was nothing compared to what she'd seen with her own eyes just yesterday. She was adamant about it. The way she provocatively cocked her head on her stubborn neck told me she would insist on being right no matter what I said. She dared me to contradict her and I obliged. I couldn't resist. I loved to watch her more dangerous moods, the glint of anger and pleasure in her almond eyes. I

never knew to what extent she was doing this stuff herself. I sensed the innuendo in the positions she took, but she kept her secrets, and so did I.

I didn't tell her that I knew who that surrealist artist was. I had met Meret Oppenheim in my theater days when Ruth Henry took her to see me as "Broadway dancer turned into Angel of Death." Ruth used to host afternoon salons at her Art Nouveau apartment on Blvd Edgar Quinet—a small "art museum," stuffed with books and photographs, paintings and collages. Meret was just then having a comeback after a long disappearance into depression and silence.

She was still as striking in her sixties as she'd been in her twenties, in Paris, when Man Ray took a spectacular series of nudes of her. Picasso admired the fur-lined bracelet Meret had made for herself. That led to her "Fur-lined Teacup," which was snatched up in 1936 by the New York Museum of Modern Art, making the young German-Jewish artist a sensation over night.

"Too much, too soon," she explained, sitting across from me on Ruth's bulky sofa. How could she tell, back then, if she really was an artist? Was it talent or just looks? Artist-subject or beautiful object of desire for men like Max Ernst or Giacometti (and certain women)? Not knowing the answer, she said, was her undoing. Ruth showed me pictures of the furry cup, saucer and spoon, an object considered the surrealist *objet* par excellence. I grasped its absurdity, its feline elegance and sexual aura, and I got the joke of Meret's calling it "Le déjeuner en fourrure" (Luncheon in Fur) as an allusion to Manet's provocative painting "Le déjeuner sur l'herbe" (Luncheon on the Grass).

That afternoon, Ruth, in her role as *salonnière*, hostess, and caretaker, pressed upon Meret that she would need an assistant now that she was getting famous again and the Paris gallerists wanted her work and all the art magazines and the American feminists wanted to interview her. "My German *protégée* here needs a job," Ruth said. "Lou will help you write your checks and all that."

Meret looked me over with a self-mocking smile and anxious eyes. "But what are we going to do with you?" I imagined she wasn't sure how to share her studio space with another person. I wasn't sure how to handle her beauty and artistic power.

"We could of course dress you up as a Moor-boy," she said, peering at me like an apprehensive, but curious bird, "and send you to the door with a silver tray to receive the *cartes de visite...*"

Another surreal idea, given the primitive, monkish atelier she occupied in a dilapidated back alley on Avenue Jean Moulin. The idea pleased everyone, and we started working together every morning for a number of years. The little she paid me (reluctantly, always anxious about money) was a blessing while I was on my way to becoming an independent journalist.

I followed Meret from the simple atelier in the 14ème to a luxurious studio apartment in the Marais, the Jewish *quartier*, and while the price of her paintings and objects shot up, she kept wearing her jeans and maintained the monkish lifestyle of her past, thin as a rail, with short-cropped salt-and-pepper hair. Every day, after our work hours, we sat down for a midday meal of an apple and two modest wedges of cheese, one of Camembert, the other of Gruyère.

I wasn't ready to let anyone in on what my years with Meret Oppenheim had been like. They were a time of self-provocation, learning about the advantages and disadvantages of being young, having to face my lack of experience and courage next to her intrepid creativity and brilliance.

No, this intimate apprenticeship and the closeness I had to her, and yet never had, I did not share with Claude.

O U T   O F   T H E   B L U E

The following night, I listlessly polished up a book review and went to sleep early.

The phone was ringing. Ringing in my dream? I blindly scrambled to my desk. *The woman in red is calling!* I found the light switch.

I stared at my clock.

"*C'est moi...*"

"Good God, Claude!" I was shaken. "You're still alive?" The silly question brought me to my senses. It was just like her to call out of the blue, after weeks of stubborn silence. In the middle of the night.

"Oh yes, very much alive." Honeyed hues of a string instrument in her voice.

"Where on earth are you? Why'd you disappear? Have I done something? Are you mad at me?"

"Lou, I haven't been alone here..."

"What? What do you mean?"

"I didn't know how to tell you."

It took me a moment. "That there is someone else?"

"*Pardonne-moi*, Lou. I should have let you know...a while ago."

I was stunned. "How long has this been going on?"

"Is that important?"

"Of course it's important! What are you thinking? At the very least, tell me the truth!"

"Okay then. It's new."

"Someone else has turned your head overnight? While I wasn't looking?"

"If you like."

"Who is it? Do I know her?"

"No."

"Oh, come on. Out with it. I'm sure I know her. I know every artist, actress, dancer, painter, poet, journalist, multimedia nut in our circles."

"No, there's no connection—if that satisfies you. But I can't say more right now."

"Why? You want to simply let me starve here forever? With no message? No nothing?"

"I know. I'm sorry, Lou. It was all a bit...too much." The sudden deep vibrato in her voice alarmed me. "But you understand, don't you? That one wants some privacy? And if the other doesn't want to—"

"Are you telling me you are forbidden to talk?"

Silence.

"You let her stop you from coming clean with me?"

Her laughter was a bit too relaxed for my comfort. "We weren't that dirty, were we? Lou, you know how it is when everybody starts getting wind of..."

"Am I everybody? Are you out of your mind?"

"I guess I am..." The sigh with which she said this finished me off. I noticed my disheveled reflection, looking like a ghost swimming in the black window above my desk lamp.

"Is she also putting you into a chastity belt? For everyone else?"

"Don't be mad at me. I'll call again when I'm back in Paris, okay?"

Click, went the connection.

With shaky hands I lit a cigarette. Why now? After all this time?

She had gone to the south of France, I'd finally heard from Aicha in her theater group when I got unsettled enough to inquire. No return date known.

Was she alone? Or was she...?

Aicha's clown face had produced wide eyes in protest. With both hands she had fanned away the horrid thought. Aicha was always convincingly dramatic when she lied. Claude's family lived in the south and her mother was in poor health. I had believed it.

Fool!

It couldn't possibly be over. Part of me wanted to laugh and dismiss the whole thing as an act of theater, a typical Claude act, designed to fire me up, knowing exactly how to get to me. Another part of me was flustered. *We weren't that dirty, were we?* What the hell did that mean? It had hurt like a needle bursting my balloon. Was there something I didn't know about her? Something sexual I had missed? Impossible.

Don't be mad at me, Lou! She had to be kidding. The sound of her voice, so near as if her hands were on my body. In a series of snapshots I saw the scenes I had imagined of our reunion, the new beginning. Excited phone calls, hot confessions, a sudden knock at my door, maybe even a tear. I dropped my head on my desk. Why hadn't I managed to keep her on the phone? Too stunned to ask the right questions, too hurt to invite her to talk. I had provoked her with anger instead of—what?

Cool down, I told myself. Are you forgetting that you've missed her before—and then not missed her at all? The last time we had a lull in our affair I also thought we were done, and I was dead wrong.

I had most likely mistaken her call. Hung over from La Coupole, torn from sleep, I had got it all wrong. How could I have missed the deeper vibration in her voice, the ease of laughter, the intimacy of her calling me in the middle of the night, "*C'est moi...*" Her playful refusal to unbutton her secret—it was all a tease. "If you like..." She was playing with me, playing coy in order to prepare me for aa surprise.

A few months ago, on a nasty November day, I had been coming back from a dance performance in the northern suburb, St. Denis. There were only ballet fans and working folk on the train. I was thumbing through the program notes when I felt that I was being watched. At the other end of the car, someone was peeping at me over a newspaper. Between a beret and the unfolded *Libération* I made out a pair of dark, narrowed eyes. I was intrigued. The look kept coming at me, stinging, hot.

The confusion lasted only a heartbeat. Claude must have been at the show without my noticing her. I had never seen her wear a beret pulled down over her ears. She dropped her paper barricade, lowered her chin and trained her eyes on me from under her lashes. The beret framing her face made her look like a *lycéenne*, a schoolgirl, the precocious kind.

Her white, ungloved hand went up to her coat collar. A button was loosened, then another. She paused. Another button. Beneath her dark duffle coat a peach-colored cardigan appeared, a color that from the distance could be mistaken for skin. She started over with her cardigan, one button at a time. I was suddenly aware that a couple of stations had passed and only a few more people had come in or gone out. Nobody was blocking my view and nobody seemed to be aware of what was going on. But Claude had noticed my nervous glance and the corners of her mouth gave away her satisfaction. Was this the Good Girl, unnerved by Claude? I couldn't stop my eyes from darting around. The Good Girl didn't know how to play this game. Claude was in her element, slightly torqueing her body right and left to make sure I noticed her progress. She had planned this like a performance, aware of the weak Metro lighting, the late hour, the numbness of people riding home. She had chosen the colors with care, peach tone over skin tone, to keep her revelation for my eyes only.

The Good Girl scanned the compartment again. The cardigan had scores of little buttons. How far would she go? Would there be time? Part of me wanted to speed her up and get there—where? Another part was ready to move over and finish the unbuttoning myself. One button, one kiss, one button, one kiss.

The train rattled into the Pigalle station. A throng of people pressed in. I jumped up to look for her above the crowd, but she had slipped away.

That very night, as I was prowling around the telephone in my flat, she had knocked at my door to follow up on her suggestion.

To let us begin again.

She might be back in Paris already, might even be on her way this very moment, just checking in to make sure I was home. I changed into a pair of bottle-green sweatpants with a matching top, a gift from her. I quickly made order in my flat, remade my bed, even fluffed up the pillows. I longed for a strong drink, but my stomach refused. Instead, I picked a branch from the pot of mint from my kitchen, brewed it and settled in my chair by the window, my Thinking Chair, the tea at my feet next to the ashtray. Claude would come. She loved to come to my place. My rooms were bigger than her tiny boudoir in her collective. I had rooms with a view.

I propped my feet up on the low ledge of the window and watched the smoke of my cigarette float over the night-gray roofs of Paris. I had lucked out with this garret a few blocks north of Montparnasse, made of three *chambres de bonnes*, maids' rooms, glued together into one eccentric apartment. The kitchen was towel-size and the bathroom primitive but at least my own. The windows, however, were not much different from those on the classy lower floors. They reached almost from floor to ceiling, shaped in the proportions of a human body. I had my theories about the steep cultural divide between the long, elegant French windows and the squat, stunted German kind. But culture was not on my mind at this moment, as I stared at the tired flicker of the Eiffel Tower in the distance. I listened for the hum of the elevator in the sleepy building, the clanking of the glass-and-metal doors. The rapid steps on the last flight of stairs to the top floor, approaching my door.

2

CLAUDE

AMOUR FOU

Claude, Claude, Claude. A name she had chosen because you can't tell which gender it refers to. When Claude first came to Paris, everybody went by a new name, and the lesbians were nothing more than a big commune living without clothes in a suburban villa. ("Villa Nude," as my pal Charlie liked to remind people, each time with a dirty grin on her moon face.) It's a funny thing about Paris women. They all seem to descend from somewhere else and quickly become Parisians, without shedding the tang of their local accents. There's no need. All it takes is an address in one of the *quartiers* and Paris takes care of the rest—until August when they all disappear again to where they came from.

Parisians born and made, together with expatriates of all sorts and colors, used to drive out to the suburb on weekend pilgrimages to have a look at the lesbian house and perhaps, with luck, spot one of the inhabitants. It was a house in an unkempt garden with a few trees and lilac bushes. A slate roof covered two stories of beige stucco walls—a color the French favor on the walls of their houses. (I call it baguette-beige.) The windows were framed by faded bricks and wood shutters painted sky-gray. In short, it was an ordinary house with an extraordinary aura.

Claude used to live there, together with the circle of the acclaimed writer Monique Wittig, who was at the center of everything to do with women's erotic awakening. The most beautiful, most sexy Parisians were her admirers, followers, worshipers. Wittig went by the Grecian name Théo,

short for Théophane, as everyone, especially lovers, now preferred short, boyish names.

I had met her and fallen under her spell some time later, and it used to vex me that Claude didn't want to tell me anything about the beginnings. Was it jealousy, wanting to keep me away from Théo, even in my thoughts? She would listen to my questions and pull up the curtain of a Mona Lisa smile. *It's so long ago, all that*, she would say. *But now I am here, with you.* She would mark the last seven words with a physical innuendo, coming closer without making a move. I would forget to insist on answers; I either had to puzzle over this sudden intimacy or instantly take her up on the promise it implied. Each time her hard, almost edgy face with its high cheek bones softened. She pursed her lips with expectation. The veiled fire in her dark eyes drew me in and wouldn't let go. I could look away as much as I liked, but at some point I had to face her again. She kept a stubborn silence and waited for me to break it—and there was the pull again in her gaze telling me, *Now I am here, with you...*

Claude never told me her real name. How could she possibly be a Josette or Evelyne or Marie-Jo! Just as she never knew my real name. Nobody in my circles knew much about my past, but that was because we all had new lives, new names, and the past didn't matter. What mattered was now, and what mattered right now was sex.

Claude and I had started like strategists, carefully plotting the moment which my friend Christiane Rochefort loved to analyze in her writing: the *Augenblick*, the moment of "the gaze." The moment when you look out of a train window and meet the eyes of a stranger. Compelled by a mysterious power, you leave your train, cross the platform, enter the stranger's compartment. The train sets off. *Amour fou.* That's how it was with Claude—almost.

I had gone to the Biennale des Jeunes Artistes, the experimental theater festival, to see Blue onstage. I was eager to hear his saxophone again, his exotic stories, his ramblings about God speaking through the pigeons on the roofs. The piece was called *Acharnelles*, a word creation by Claude, as I would learn. *Acharné* means insistent, obsessed, and *charnelle* is the female form of *charnel*—carnal, of the flesh.

Five actresses were tied to posts with long red cords around their waists. Five archetypes: housewife, whore, nun, secretary, and young girl. They drowned each other out in fugue-like layers and chaotic rants. I recognized snippets from Virginia Woolf ("Women alone stir my imagination") and Simone de Beauvoir ("One is not born, but rather becomes, a woman"). Every now and then they broke into chansons with ironically altered lines. Instead of "*Je ne regrette rien,*" they sang "*Je ne répète rien*" (I don't repeat anything) to repetitive, synchronized steps as if they were showgirls or

The Supremes. They were accompanied by Blue's saxophone, a percussionist, and a bass. At irregular intervals they all started running to escape their fetters, got aggressive, threatened and sabotaged each other to the point of exhaustion. According to the typed, one-sheet program, their motto was, "Any oppression creates a state of war." Each of the characters took a turn, slipped into military fatigues, donned a soldier's cap, and reestablished order with the help of a short whip. The wildest and most furious rebellion came from the young girl. She used her fists and kicks like a boy and finally managed to tear off the red cord. Streaming with sweat, the short, thin dress glued to her body, her face in the final tableau painfully and triumphantly raised to the light—this was Claude.

The play was schematic but well choreographed. The style was part variety show, part Theater of Cruelty. All five of them threw themselves into their roles with physical recklessness. I liked the fact that the women were agents, not just passive victims. I shared this observation afterwards with Claude in her dressing room, once I had sufficiently hugged and admired Blue.

"Just victims of men?" Claude asked

and slightly drew back her chin. "That would be too simple, no?"

"Just what I meant." I was surprised how much softer she looked up close. "Letting the musicians improvise onstage adds an interesting commentary to your piece." I heard my slightly pompous formulation, saw her smile, and thought: do I already like her to the point of talking pretty to her? Indeed. She had been the focus of my attention during the entire play. In her fatigues, she had reminded me of a young samurai. In profile, she sometimes looked like an American Indian boy, camouflaged in a girl's flimsy summer dress. But close up, her edgy features receded and one only saw her eyes, dark, almond-slanted eyes burning with a secret promise. When I told her I was a journalist, she looked at me with interest.

"The musicians provide the cultural background," she informed me.

"That says it, in very few words," I complimented her. "You are taking some risks with your social critique. But do you only give girls, I mean, very young women, a chance?"

She fixed me for a moment, either because she was wondering what I meant or because she had heard the *double entendre* in my question.

"Personally..." she took her time, "I give everybody a chance." It seemed to amuse her to include me. "It's up to the next generation, however, not just—" We were interrupted by friends and admirers who were pushing into the dressing room. In the hallway, I spotted Liane, a Vietnamese theater photographer who worked with Ruth Henry and other journalists and had once been a flirt of mine. She was wearing her usual Mao suit in washed-out workers' blue. Her shoulder-length black hair looked ironed into a feline shine.

"Are you taking photos of *Acharnelles*?" I asked her. "Could I get a few? I want to review it. What do you think of it?"

"Fabulous," she said in her husky voice that always seemed to emerge from a tunnel beneath her throat. She dragged me back with her into Claude's dressing room. "Brava, Claude! Fantastic!" They hugged. "You've made quite a step since your last play—what was the name again? And your jazz musicians—superb! Where on earth did you dig them up? This piece will show real well in the photographs. By the way, this is my friend Lou..."

They discussed a photo shoot. Claude called Aicha (who had played the housewife), and they went over the rehearsal and performance schedule. I stood by and watched, admiring Claude's beautiful, strong neck and the forms of her body beneath the damp girl's dress. I registered that her gaze also wandered over to me. Should I perhaps join Liane's photo shoot under some pretext? Following a sudden intuition, I asked if I could interview her for my article.

"Any time," she said with that look of many meanings the French call *un certain regard.*

The interview idea was a strategic coup, but I was certain that she herself (although she never admitted that much) was already in the game.

We met at the Clauserie des Lilas because it was only a few Metro stops away from her training room at the Cité International, the student campus south of Paris. During our interview she teased me by slyly quoting the formulations I had used in her dressing room. All kinds of things "added an interesting aspect"—for example, setting up a work rendezvous at the Clauserie des Lilas, a café known for its *dragueurs*, its cruisers. She stressed the word "chance" and made a point of thanking me for "being given the chance" of seeing her name in a foreign newspaper.

She explained the genesis of her play and her philosophy of a theater that everyone could understand—political, but not Brechtian, please! She didn't think much of Brecht's "distanciation." She was into emotion, and she believed in poetic imagery like her European and American avant-garde colleagues whose names she ticked off for me—Robert Wilson, Peter Brook, Richard Foreman. Hats off, I thought, she is placing herself right up front with the best. But it would take more than cockiness and much more than talent to get there. As if reading my mind, she launched into a tirade about the "old boys club" of the stage. She was touching in her fierceness, but after a while I found myself sagging; she seemed to be addressing an audience of equal-minded obsessives, not me.

I brought her back by asking her opinion about last season's theater productions. We compared notes and from the way she observed me, I recognized a certain rivalry and smoldering envy because I knew as much as she did. I had been more often at the important theater festivals than she. (I used the occasion to inquire if she had ever run into Stéphane? She said she didn't remember.) I had the better arguments, I thought, and she insisted more stubbornly on hers when we disagreed. But she did so with such heat that I was charmed and asked myself more than once: how would she be in bed? I told her about my pal Blue and our night wanderings; she told me she used to be part of the circles of women gathering at the Café Flore. She mentioned the "chance" of having met Théo, the poet, early on and having traveled to Lesbos with her. What an initiation. It was my turn to feel a stab of envy—or was it jealousy?

"Now I think I've said a lot, in very few words," she concluded, slyly quoting me again.

"Not enough," I contradicted and held her gaze longer than I should. "We could say more, in very few words..."

I waited and felt the well-known pulsing in my body.

She had propped her chin into her hand. Her index finger seemed to hide her mouth on purpose, and now she closed her eyes as if she had to think for a moment—or as if she already envisioned the scene. A rather pleasant scene, according to her facial expression. It was easy, then, for me to add,

"Should we give each other a chance?"

She laughed. The look she gave me seemed to admit that the idea was quite agreeable to her, but that she wouldn't pronounce herself. I wondered how she managed to send two contradictory messages in one gaze and appear completely relaxed about it.

This was not the look I wanted. It wasn't *the gaze* à la Christiane that would have forced me right out of my chair to trail after her, no matter where. Not yet. But she invited me to watch the rehearsals on the last day of the Biennale. She allowed me to become a groupie.

B L U E   T A N G O

Playing groupie gave me permission to look at Claude without restraint for a whole day of exercises, followed by a rehearsal for the final performance of *Acharnelles*.

Before the last show, I was taken along for shopping at a student supermarket. The group, together with two understudies, had planned a quick meal at Matou's in the late afternoon. Matou, who worked at the Crazy Horse Saloon, was also a groupie (Aicha's, to be exact). I was stunned when I saw the treasures, the fine patés, triple-cream cheeses, peanuts, prosciutto, tea cake, and two bottles of quality wine that appeared on the table in Matou's simple student room. Only a fraction of it had been actually bought at the store.

"The state won't support actors so we need to support ourselves," Claude said in a nonchalant voice.

Later I learned that a master thief belonged to the group. Rachel, who played the nun, provided the five not only with food but with an entire wardrobe. When she went "shopping," she managed to pick the right size and model of pants and jackets for each member of the group. In the supermarket, all I'd seen was Rachel swinging her large blue cape through the aisles quickly and apparently in the best of spirits.

The final performance confirmed my impression that Claude acted without any thoughts about her effect or appearance. She was drop-dead gorgeous one moment and brutal, ugly the next. I believe that only women who aren't classical beauties can achieve this shift between extremes that makes the sudden appearance of beauty breathtaking. The most striking example for me had always been Maria Callas, both in her voice and her looks. Now I saw it alive onstage, in Claude. Her radical disregard of feminine niceties gave her violent Girl a baffling innocence. All the contradictions of a girl who knows nothing and yet already knows too much, touched a chord in me.

There was a moment when the Girl's defiance crumbles. She looks around, sees that the others have turned their back and disappeared. She is alone. The disbelief drives the air out of her. Her arms hang from her body; all muscle tone gone. She is just a child, after all. She turns to the audience, looks at them with an urgent appeal. The trust in her eyes, the painful naïveté of this appeal brought me to tears.

The other actresses were good, too, but there was a reason why Claude was the leader of the troupe. Offstage, at the rehearsals, I had no doubt she was flirting with me. But then, they all were. All seven of them seemed to be acting permanently on some imaginary stage, making a show of themselves and demanding attention. The extroverted Mediterranean element. But when I had a moment alone with Claude, she seemed to hold back. It was enticing not to know what to make of her. Perhaps she simply refused to be distracted when she was working. In that case, I would wait. I had put my cards on the table at the Clauserie. It was her turn.

After the last curtain call, wine and cheese were served behind the stage. Friends and fans gathered; Blue and his pals started playing oldies. Claude appeared in a pinstriped pantsuit with a stiff white men's shirt and tie. I did a double take, not recognizing her in this outfit, hair slicked back, dark shadows around her eyes. I stayed at a distance. I wasn't sure this man-costume—if it was indeed a costume and not her usual outfit—was a turn-on. Her ambiguity was switched off into a one-sided and therefore less interesting stance.

The manager of the theater space brought out Champagne and toasted the Théâtrales as the sensation of the festival. The group performed their doo-wop number "*Je ne répète rien*" for our entertainment. For me it didn't have the same charm as it had onstage when Claude danced between the others in her thin summer dress.

Claude commanded, "Tango communale!" emptying her glass. By

now everyone was quite tipsy. The group formed a circle around her. She snapped her fingers at Blue and the band played a jazzed-up version of "Blue Tango." I recognized the old classic on the spot. My father, who had been a prize-winning tango dancer in his Berlin youth, had taught me the dance at the same time he got interested in taking photographs of my sister and me. During my early teens, I had obsessively practiced the steps and danced his favorite "Blue Tango" with him.

With her smooth, languid cross steps and *ruedas*, rotations around her partners, Claude led each member of the group across the dance floor. I felt my resistance melting. Her butch outfit and hair, combined with her panther-smooth footwork, took on a sexy cachet. Every one of the actresses danced so well that I could tell they had rehearsed this "communal tango" as ardently as their entire theater performance. Liane and other guests clicked and flashed their cameras and everyone hollered applause.

The last "promenade," danced by Claude and Aicha, landed them in front of my feet. Aicha freed herself with a deep curtsy worthy of a court jester: "Your turn!" Handing me the dance, handing me to Claude. Her smile was knowing and sly, as if this, too, had been choreographed. How would an outsider fare who only just got permission to be a groupie? I tried in vain to read Claude's face. Her raised chin, her lowered eyes ordering my hand into her leading hand revealed nothing but the pride of the master bestowing an honor.

Was it an honor? Was it flirtation? Was it a setup?

I hadn't mentioned in our interview chat that I used to be a ballet dancer. I knew that theater people looked down on classical ballet as a performance art that could only inhibit and stiffen you. Now we would be dancing. Everyone was watching.

"Blue Tango"—even with Blue's jazz and bossa nova slides—awoke the memory cells of my body like a song from childhood. I noticed the hush around us and Claude's puzzled, sideways glances. She tested my mettle, plunging into fiery, quick-footed maneuvers she probably didn't expect me to pull off. Now and then a frown flew across her brow, warning me that she might try to trick me. The others clapped and shouted Olé!

I didn't reveal what a turn-on this was to me, dancing with someone who was my equal on the tango floor—a dancer made to order, made to be my lover. Same height, same strength, so it seemed, same mastery. This was a game of challenge and I wasn't going to lose my head. As if she sensed my state of mind, my determination, Claude made a mistake in a *pasada*. Instead of crossing over, she almost stepped into my leg. She slightly stumbled and immediately let go of me. With a flourish addressed more to our audience than to me, she bowed out. "A bit stoned…" she muttered while everyone hooted. I could see in Aicha's face that this wasn't usual for Claude.

Afterwards she seemed to avoid me. She disappeared for a while. When I went to look for her, she was hanging out in her loge with Liane, who had brought her contact sheets of the performance. I joined them and marked a group photo for my article. Unfortunately, none of the shots rendered what I had seen in Claude. The photos were altogether lacking in energy. But Claude heaped one compliment after another onto Liane. I kept my mouth shut. Could she possibly be seductive with Liane, in my presence? I trailed off again, leaving the two of them alone with their magnifying glass.

The band was playing African rhythms and Claude joined the dancers.

She looked tipsy or stoned or both. She danced by herself, wearing her men's shirt, sleeves rolled up, her eyes closed as if nothing and nobody else existed in her universe. I didn't let on that I was paying attention to her and felt she was playing the same game. She was dancing provocatively, showing off for me, I felt. I danced with Liane and shuffled along with Blue, listening to his tales of a spectacular theater career.

Just as I was ready to leave, Claude veered toward me as if drawn by a magnet. How had she managed that, with her closed eyes?

"Lou," she said, placing her hand on my arm, "I didn't get a chance to talk to you tonight..." She looked confused. "You still have some questions for me, no?"

I had to laugh. "I sure do."

She came closer.

"Questions with few words," I specified, staring at her unabashedly.

Her drug-veiled eyes seemed to open. I read a sudden hunger in them. Now she was so close to me, I thought she was going to kiss me.

"But not to worry, I'm in no hurry," I said, backing away.

"Leaving already?"

We pseudo-embraced in the French fashion. *Comme par hasard*, as if by chance, my lips managed to brush her ear.

"Wait," she said. "I'm free tomorrow afternoon..."

CROCE DELICIA

The door to her apartment was open. I announced myself by shouting hello and heard, "Come in!" I followed the sound of her voice through a communal living room with a patch-up of furniture, then through another open door. Her boudoir was a tiny room plastered with photos, notes, sketches, theater posters, and framed newspaper clippings. A large reproduction of "The Lady and the Unicorn" hung over the sofa. The door was decorated with an antique kimono, a chair covered with Indian shawls. Next to the tiny desk at a window a little ficus tree was potted in front of shelves with books, masks, and tchotchkes. Claude was sitting on the floor, one nimble leg folded beneath her, brushing her cat.

"Don't mind the clutter. There's still some space left." She pointed to the sofa. "I'm almost done with Minou." She gave me the briefest probing look as if to make sure I was what she desired to see.

"You've got the whole history of theater on your walls," I said. I randomly inspected this and that picture instead of sitting down. But I was incapable of taking anything in—apart from the lady with the unicorn whose way of holding her mirror made me think of the gifted narcissism of Claude's troupe.

"Minou has been much neglected these last days," she said. "She resents it."

I was tense with a mixture of impatience and intentional reserve. It was her invitation; the ball was in her court—that was all I could think of. I sat down on the sofa. After staring a while at her prune-blue velvet pants and the shimmering orange, gold, and turquoise colors of the kimono behind her, I noticed that we had fallen silent. There was only the fine, stroking sound of the brush and Minou's purring. Had she forgotten me?

"Turn around!" she ordered and the cat rolled to its other side. Claude praised Minou who went into a long stretch before pressing her delicate black head back against the brush. Every now and then Minou whacked the brush or grabbed hold of it as if pouncing on a prey.

"No," Claude said, "we're not playing. Roll over!"

She knew exactly what she wanted and how to apply the brush in order to get the cat to do her bidding. At moments a little laughter escaped her throat and she murmured tender words like *Minou Minou mon p'tit choux...* I watched, spellbound, the way she dug her fingers into the silky fur of Minou's neck. Her teeth bit down on her lip. I could hardly stand it. She looked up at me right then. It was a shock to discover and confess our desire in the same moment. Impossible to look away; impossible to let go of her.

There it was—*the gaze*. How long did it last? The time it took to die a thousand little deaths. Until Minou leapt up, electrified by the first involuntary movement we made toward each other, and raced off, the hairs on her neck standing on edge. Without turning her eyes away, Claude stretched out her prune-blue leg and kicked the door shut.

Slowly, inch by inch, we approached each other until our faces were so close that I could feel her breath. I saw desire and pain in her face. Carefully, sensing her way, she moved her mouth around the outline of my lips without touching me. I felt the warmth emanating from her skin and lips. Her eyes were fastened on mine but at the same time they seemed to be listening, concentrated on the energy swelling and ebbing between our faces. I noticed the movement of her nostrils, the small temptations to move in. She quietly backed away, took a breath. The ball was still in her court. Behind her closed lips her tongue was working, just like mine, imagining touch, taste. Her hesitation when I got too close. Holding our desire instead of leaping at each other. She clenched her teeth. The effort created a slight opening of her lips and she drew in her breath through her teeth. I heard my own sigh, saw her close her eyes for a second. Then she looked into my eyes again—probing? demanding consent?—and the tip of her tongue appeared between her lips. I was aware that my shoulders fell. My head bent backwards.

"Today we'll just kiss," she murmured when we sank onto her rug.

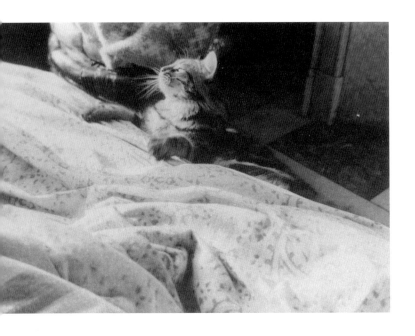

She stopped my hands from meandering over her body. Her face, the dark strands of hair over her temples and cheek bones, the tempting hollow of her neck below her jaw where I felt her rapid pulse, were all I was allowed to touch, her mouth the only place she let me enter. I complied, reluctantly, at moments furiously. I wanted to fight her, break down her resistance. There were moments when my fingers in her mouth sent a shiver through her. Her breath stopped, and her muscles seemed to relax all at once as if she had given herself over. But she didn't give in. She kept the lead, kept me aware that it was her turf, her decision. Almost in spite of myself, I stayed a step behind her, burning to know what exactly she had in mind.

At some point she got up and pulled a rose from a vase by her window. A dozen silver-pink roses with a big ribbon—an admirer's bouquet.

"Bring it back when it's... you know," she said, waiting to see if I would catch on to the operatic story—the flower given as an invitation for the lover to return.

"*Croce delicia*," I quoted from *La Traviata*. Torment and delight.

I turned the rose over. "Two days," I said.

At the second rendezvous, Claude shoved Minou out of the room and closed the door. She looked at me searchingly before she pulled me onto the chair at her tiny desk.

"Don't turn around until I tell you to," she ordered. "I've got a surprise for you."

I heard the slipping of clothes, fabric brushing over skin, being shed, something silken, rustling, the sound of the sofa. Silence.

"Now," she said.

She was half stretched out on the sofa, one arm behind her head, leaning against a pillow like a figure by Klimt. She wore the kimono which I had admired at her door the first time. It was draped around her in a way that left the central strip of her body uncovered. My gaze fell as if following a waterfall down her smooth, gold-toned skin to her navel and below. I was speechless. My eyes wandered back upward and met her probing, burning gaze.

"Today you must only look," she declared.

If I can stand it, I thought. I nodded. She watched as I turned around on my chair, crossing my arms on top of its back to create a barrier, a cover for myself. She closed her eyes and surrendered to my look as if taking a sunbath. I stared at the work of art with its two dark poles—the black meshes of her hair around her face and the precisely drawn black triangle where the folds of cloth disappeared between her legs. Her face with her closed eyes looked edgy and bold, her lips pale. Her body with its hidden curves could have been the body of a young warrior, wrapped in the gold, orange, and turquoise hues of a far-away morning land.

The freedom she gave me, the freedom to look, shocked me. I was afraid she would open her eyes again too soon. But she held still and at some point my eyes felt raw; the image began to quiver. A paralysis came over me, an almost desperate yearning. I felt weightless, drawn into her radiance. I know, something inside me said, I know...as if any separation between us had dissolved.

Impossible! I started. I was losing myself...to what? To her? Within a second, I saw her image sharply again and studied it with alarm. What had been going on? What had she done?

She opened her eyes. The devil knows what she read in my face. She managed a smile. I had no idea how to respond. Gone was the perfect image from a moment ago. With her almond eyes and her pointed smile, she was suddenly feminine. Almost imperceptibly, she pulled her kimono to one side so that the small, compact round of her breast appeared.

My forced passivity was suddenly unbearable. With one leap, I left my chair and threw myself onto her. I noticed surprise and a flash of triumph in her eyes. Had she been waiting for this? In the next moment, she turned the situation around and, with feline speed and agility, was on top of me. She locked my arms above my head on the sofa edge and her kimono flew open; a naked samurai woman pinning me down. Her strength and power stunned me. I registered the weight of her hips and thighs on mine, and we were both breathing heavily, staring at each other.

"Not today!" Her voice was husky.

She held her grip on my wrists. I struggled against her. I refused to be tamed.

"One kiss," I pleaded, "just one!"

She hesitated. Slowly, deliberately, I bent my head back, opened my lips and offered her, as she had done, the tip of my tongue. The spark, when

I felt her tongue on mine, ran like a hot wire through my body.

She stopped. Gave me a surprised look. Then satisfaction spread across her face. She was inspecting me.

"Just one kiss, ha?" She laughed. "I've got to get to my training."

With a quick move she freed me, got up, and closed her kimono. I watched her gather up her clothes.

"You were unruly today." She cut me a look. "You need some further initiation, don't you agree?"

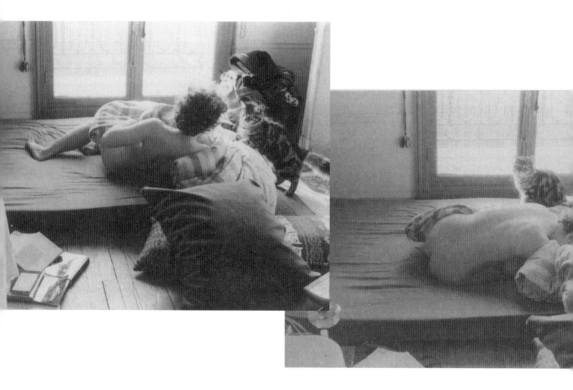

OBSESSION

Footsteps. Someone following me. Who? Coming closer, haunting. I can't see, but I know this is Germany. Darkness. No, the steps are ahead of me. Someone trying to escape....

I woke up with a sense of dread. That dream again. The same dream had pursued me for I don't know how long. Always the sense of being followed and in danger. Then it's suddenly me following someone. As if in the beam of a flashlight, I sometimes see white socks and shoes walking ahead of me. Walking fast. I feel an alarm, an urgency. Who is it? I walk faster, faster, but the distance remains the same.

A waft of stale tobacco. I remembered. I had spent the night in my Thinking Chair by the window. Half dreaming, half remembering, not bothering to get into bed. Not bothering to clean out the ashtray. Half sleeping, half waking. Waiting for Claude.

I tore the window open to a dull, gray sky and trotted down the stairs to the bakery a block away. I felt a Claude crisis coming on. I had to fortify myself.

"*Messieurs Dames,*" I greeted the line of people inside the well-lit, well-polished bakery.

"*Bonjour, Monsieur,*" a distracted chorus answered me. There were one or two uncertain "*Bonjour, Mademoiselle.*" Short hair, jeans, no lipstick—it was as simple as that. As usual, I could tell from the dense atmosphere that everyone was politely holding back a desperate impatience to get to their

baguette in the morning rush. Woe to the customer who would be called upon and had failed to make up his or her mind. I had often enough been knifed by looks from both sides of the counter. Did I want a croissant? Or rather a *pain au chocolat*? Did the baguette look more promising than the slim *flute* this morning? Or did the larger *pain de campagne* have the right look of a crusty coat with a dense, doughy interior? It takes years of living in France, scrutinizing bread on bakery shelves day after day, to successfully pierce the deceptively innocent look of a loaf and detect the powdery, air-holed dryness that can hide inside. Like detecting inhibition under the dressed-up, sexy surface of a woman, but with women I didn't have the problems I had with baguettes. Even taking too long counting out one's francs pieces could create a terrifying shuffle of feet at one's back.

I had already wolfed down a good chunk of my (acceptable) baguette in the street when I thought of an egg for breakfast. I stopped at my corner café and picked a dull white egg from its plastic pyramid stand on the counter. I sprinted back up the seven floors. I had a pronounced dislike for the glass cage elevator with its cumbersome swing doors, its clanking iron gate, and slow rattle. Every stop necessitated a polite interaction, holding the tight doors open and helping neighbors squeeze in or out. I wasn't in the mood to help anyone in or out, especially this morning with Claude on my mind.

Here I was eating a lonely, boring, cold egg and a piece of plain baguette, thinking of the little hotel above Nice that Claude had found for us. Each morning we had a breakfast of toasted baguette, butter and lavender honey, served with steaming bowls of *café au lait* on a little terrace overlooking the perfectly blue sweep of the Baie des Anges. The Bay of Angels.

What if Claude was breakfasting right now with her new flame on that same sunny terrace? How I had misread her phone call! She hadn't returned, hadn't knocked at my door. I was starving in cold, rainy Paris, where spring never seemed to arrive, and didn't even know when she would be back.

If I weren't so rattled I could at least have had a "Luncheon à la Meret Oppenheim," a fine piece of cheese or two and an apple, to comfort myself. Had Claude really not given any hint? Every time I got to the moment when she sighed, I felt a small knife turning deep in my back.

A change of wallpaper was needed. I jumped on my Vespa (driven straight up from Italy one summer) and zipped over to my café. I had picked Le Rostand with its big windows because it was situated right across from the Luxembourg Gardens and almost had the air of a garden café. It was also near the Sorbonne, in a spot where everyone hung out: students and professors, writers and gamblers, tourists, cruisers, and the little old ladies, *les dames du quartier*, who came in from the park for a chat and a *verveine*, the indispensable lemon-verbena potion of the French. I liked the cozy-stuffy fifties style of the café—upholstered banquettes, peach-and-apricot table lamps, portraits of the poet Edmond Rostand (creator of the long-nosed *Cyrano de Bergerac*) in pompous frames. Waiters strutted through the aisles in crisp uniforms, supervised by a bulldog *patronne* who had her throne at the cash register by the bar. The coffee was first class and the tables were squares of polished mahogany, big enough for cups and plates, books and papers.

I was surprised to find my friend Christiane wrapped in a cloud of smoke at one of the back tables. I hadn't seen her in several weeks. Her head of gray wisps was half hidden behind a pile of manuscripts. The St. Germain publisher of her books was practically around the corner.

"Has someone died?" she asked.

I threw my leather jacket onto the banquette across from her and let myself drop into the sagging pad.

"Set up my memorial stone."

Christiane pushed her glasses a bit further down her nose and looked at me with curiosity. "Oh dear." She shoved her manuscripts to the side. "Lovesick?"

I made a face as if tasting mustard in my hot cacao. Christiane was of an age where sex was no longer all that important, which sometimes made me question my own escapades in her presence.

I held up my thumb and index finger to Pierre, the waiter. Pierre was small and unsightly. With his sullen moustache he controlled the café and the other waiters. He had a weakness for me. The right amount of tips and chats had tamed him. A thumb signaled, "An espresso." Thumb and index finger, "With cognac. Urgent." Pierre winked at me, causing one corner of his mustache to twitch.

"Claude has eloped," I filled her in. "She finally called but won't tell me anything. No idea who it is."

"Ah, Claude," she said with raised eyebrows. Of course she knew Claude. Everyone knew Claude.

"How could I get hooked like that? I feel like a novice—jealous and sick of it."

She took a thoughtful puff of her cigarette. "Logically this is a shock," she said, and I was comforted by the fact that everything had a logic. Finding the simple rationale behind things was a habit with Christiane. "Is there perhaps some retaliation in the cards? You had some hot-cold periods with her before, if I remember correctly?"

"If you don't cool things off every now and then, how can you start the fireworks again?"

Pierre swung his small oval tray with my espresso and cognac onto our table. Christiane raised her eyebrows again. I wasn't sure if it was the cognac or what I had said.

"I can't let go of her." I lit one of Christiane's Gauloises and sank deeper into my banquette. "It's an obsession."

"Your kind of passion-obsession?" She gave me a sly look. I looked back at her cat eyes, the color of water with a few drops of blue ink.

I didn't catch her meaning, but an image clicked off in my mind. That night with Claude. The night in the red room. The night I truly possessed her for the first time. Claude had a way of resisting surrender, like a boy who first had to be vanquished, thrown to the ground, before he was willing to change into a girl.

"Yes, the sex was really..."

I heard the replay in this conversation. Years ago I had filled Christiane's ears with my heartache over Stéphane. I was spending a hasish-fogged night at a party that Christiane also attended. It was one of those parties where everyone was stoned and argued about politics, the politics of sex. I noticed the small person with gray wisps of hair sitting on the floor all night, her back against a wall, intimately talking with one woman after another. I wasn't talking. I was in pain. Maybe I was crying. At some point, she turned to me and asked what was the matter. There was such open curiosity in her cat-eyes that I felt compelled to tell her something more or less coherent about my troubles with Stéphane. "I've smoked too much," I added miserably.

"Does it help?"

I shook my head. "Just self-pity. I hate it."

"Well, that's at least one person who has empathy with you."

I must have stared at her, bleary-eyed. A clearance opened in my hashish brain, and I saw the possibility of an older self feeling compassion for a younger one.

That's how Christiane became my friend and soon afterwards, my savior when I had to move out in a rush. Christiane let me crash at her house until I got back on my feet. As we picked apart my relationship with Stéphane, I found out that Christiane Rochefort was an intellectual who was passionate about putting her mind to work. Thinking was a creative endeavor, she told me. I had never thought of it that way. Did my past efforts of seizing thoughts and trying to hold on to them for dear life qualify? I had no problem anymore forming opinions. I was a critic. But creative thinking? I loved to imagine Christiane winding up and down the hallways of her mind with little light bulbs sparking as she passed.

I washed down my cognac with coffee and a tinge of doubt. It wasn't my style to comfort myself with cognac in the middle of the day. But surely Claude's phone call gave me license.

"I like obsessing," I said in order to say something.

"Precisely. Could you imagine feeling passionate without it?"

"It would be of no interest if the butterfly couldn't escape any moment."

"Claude, a butterfly? I would have thought a bit of a scorpion rather, no?"

"It's always both with her. Everything about her is so ambiguous. *La Sylphide*, you know? There's this moment in the ballet when the hero dances with his betrothed and the sylph gets in between. She's invisible, of course, or is she? He dutifully executes his bridal pas de deux, but he's already lost to the enchantment—the obsession. It's haunting, and hot."

"The elusive object of desire."

"Elusive and embodied. The erotic paradox. That's what I always thought about Meret Oppenheim's work, like her teacup lined with fur…"

"Elusive indeed."

"Things don't go together, even clash, and yet it's perfect because it's so erotic. That's what got me into ballet, in fact. Working excessively with the body in order to transcend the body. Weightless grace—and ecstasy."

"Feminine mystique and masochism?" She looked at me as if I were an interesting specimen. "I can't quite imagine how you'd fit into this ultra-feminine ideal."

"Well, I didn't really fit the mold. I was always better with the things the boys did. But I knew what dancing was about. Just pouring myself out, completely. And what a turn-on, all these perfectly molded bodies in the same room with me."

Christiane eyed me and exhaled her smoke to the side. "*La fillette aux muscles d'or,*" she said, quoting a French writer. Indeed, the "girl with golden muscles" was what I was missing right now.

"Damn Claude," I grumbled. "Why can't I get what I want?"

"In fact, you got exactly what you want, if I'm not mistaken. A certain distance, a challenge, a rival. In short, back to the hunt you adore."

I was sure there was a time when Christiane, too, adored the hunt. I rolled myself a cigarette. Christiane's filterless Gauloises were scratching my throat.

"It keeps you busy, distracts you from what it's really about. I mean, remind me: have you ever loved someone? Really loved?"

"She just called me, so I'm on her mind."

"Do you sometimes wonder if you're chasing after the wrong thing?"

"How can I know it's wrong if I don't have it?"

"You sure know how to avoid my question."

"Are you saying *you* know what love is?"

"No, but I know what power games are. And how passionately they avoid love. When have you tried it last?"

"Tried to love? If you love, why would you have to try? If you have to try, why call it love? But hey," I looked at my watch, "we've got work to do. I know I'm a pest." I looked around for Pierre and felt her silence.

"While you're waiting for news, you could go to the Bretagne with me for a week, if you like. I am going down again this weekend." Christiane's literary success had afforded her a country house so she could escape the winter drizzle any time. This was the reason she had not been *au courant* about my loss of Claude. I remembered the first trip I took with her, her eccentric way of driving fifteen miles an hour on the smallest roads in order

to avoid endangering any furry or feathery critter with her Mini. I was never again able afterwards to speed through the countryside the way I used to.

At nightfall, we stopped to relieve ourselves in a *bosquet*, a little patch of forest, and found we had dropped right into a chorus of nightingales. It was in the thick of their mating season. They seemed to own not just their territory but the entire night. A web of luminous trills was stretched across the sky and we were caught in their net. Christiane, in her small waxed rain jacket and rubber boots, was standing under a tall tree like a child in a fairy tale, motionless, her hand stretched out, willing a nightingale to swoop down to her.

There was something in the way she looked at me now as she invited me again. A few more drops of ink had come to darken the water. Child's eyes. Pleading. I remembered her need to talk through the nights, to be consoled for her incapacity to go to sleep, night after night.

"Too bad. I can't leave. I've got to review this new play at the Champs-Elysées, and the Ramses exhibition. And then the Belgian ballet avant-garde comes to town…" I squirmed in my seat. "But thank you—I could really use a trip right now." Another half truth. A trip to Nice perhaps, on the trail of Claude.

"She'll reappear," Christiane assured me. "You know how long new enthusiasms usually last." She was already back to being the sly cat. I felt a rush of optimism and pressed her hand.

"I'll miss you." I meant it. "If only I knew who my rival is. Who on earth could be such a new thrill for Claude? Any hunch?"

"Aftershocks," she said through a cloud of smoke. She said it in English, pronouncing it *uffteur shocks*. "Expect a few more when she gets back. But right now, as nothing is known yet, the hunter has license, no? Knowing you, I bet you can successfully distract yourself."

Right she was, even if a certain sarcasm in her advice wasn't lost on me.

DISTRACTION

I drove the few blocks to Jussieu, to Club Cinq where initiation for lesbian novices was offered in the afternoons. I knew the club had been one of Claude's favorite playgrounds, and perhaps still was. I had never gone with her as I wasn't convinced that novices were my cup of tea. Now I wondered if she had found this new, unknown flame at Club Cinq.

About thirty women were sitting in a circle on the worn carpeting, some on their coats, leaning against the billiard tables or the walls. A few were perched on bar stools they had dragged in. Umbrellas were stacked in a corner near the door. A big, handwritten poster announced an evening with Théo at the Beaux Arts. The discussion circled around men and fidelity. I listened to the usual French stories about *maîtresses* and *putes* (mistresses and prostitutes), keeping an eye on the door in case somebody of interest showed up.

But as Claude wasn't going to show up, the only stranger who could seriously interest me was the woman in red. She had never appeared in my circles, and I couldn't possibly sneak into the opera every night. Where should I go looking for her? There were the cafés where prominent lesbians could be spotted at any time, day or night, but I didn't like to hang out at the obvious cafés. Could she possibly prefer the company of men? I knew a bunch of women holding a monthly salon, "Cocolette," in honor of Colette and Coco Chanel. They could have added Gertrude Stein ("Logic and fashion are the reason why French people are exciting and peaceful. Logic and fashion…"), making it "Salon Cocolettrude." A poetry circle gathered (predictably) right next to the Montparnasse cemetery, and rumor had it that they were bringing back the fashion of drinking absinthe. Another inspired flock was investigating "Vagina and its Discontents" on Sundays. An expatriate writing club met twice a month near the Louvre, at Café Rumpelmayer, where members fed each other Schwarzwälder Kirschtorte from little porcelain plates. Should I make the rounds again? Perhaps my best chance would be Toutparista—the sightseeing tours to the historic lesbian bars of Paris. (Who had come up with that idea?)

There was no possible distraction in the room. Unless.

I noticed that the woman next to me let her eyes wander over me more than once. Auburn-red hair. Shoulder-length curls, a pale complexion and freckles. Sitting with a rounded back like a scared rabbit. She met my gaze and gave me a questioning, two-second smile. Long enough.

"Why so tense?" I asked close to her ear. My smile assured her there was no reason to be alarmed. I put my hand on her neck for a little squeeze. To my surprise, she cast her mascara eyelashes up for a second, then down to close her eyes, accompanied by the slightest bending of her head. How little it takes to signal consent. I eagerly studied her face as if I could read on the spot how far the consent might go. The black lashes on her pale skin looked charming and she had a delicate mouth.

"Your first time here?"

"Hmm…" She nodded with closed eyes. "Feels good."

"Are you interested in this chatter?"

She stretched away from under my hand and yawned. Then she looked at me, pressed her lips together and slowly shook her head. No. I saw little sparks in her eyes: *do you have a better idea*?

"How about a glass of wine? I can give you a personal introduction, if you like."

Her smile was half embarrassed and half sly. She got up instantly.

"Where?" she asked. Picking up her coat she let her breasts brush against me. Talk about shy little rabbit! She had been sitting there huddled up not because she was scared but because she was bored. She wouldn't try to turn butch on me, would she? Did she notice that I had made the first move?

We strolled up Blvd St. Michel toward the Rostand. She was curious

about my accent. I let her guess and when she opted for Scandinavian I was pleased and, as usual, relieved. I had my old investment in remaining incognito. I had picked up in no time that even a good three decades later, the German occupation and French collaboration were sensitive topics for the French who preferred not to be reminded. True, the "German beast" elicited a certain fascination. But more, far more, resentment. A resentment that compelled me to speak the best French I could muster. I didn't want to be ignored in the detached, polite fashion most exiles were in Paris—especially if they came marching in with a thick Teutonic accent. I wanted to belong, which meant being invited home by Parisian women.

The red-curly newcomer wasn't interested in where I came from. She told me she was from Lyon and had only recently started working here. She had a job in a media office. Her name was Valérie. I told her I was a journalist.

"Then we've already something in common!" She seized my sleeve with an enthusiasm that gave me a start. "Great leather jacket..."

"So old it's falling apart," I said. "Careful." I gently freed my arm from her grip. "I need to find a new one. Very soon." What I meant to say was, *Careful to remain the little rabbit I thought you were...*

"How did you find out about Club Cinq?" I asked.

"Doesn't everybody know?" (Surely everybody who knows Claude, I thought.)

We had arrived at the Rostand. The place was almost as crowded as it had been in the afternoon. People were eating their *steak frites* and *carottes rapées*, which the menu translated as "raspered carrots." I checked with Valérie and ordered two glasses of red wine on the way to a niche table in the back. Pierre eyed my companion and sniffed his nose, his mustache twitching along. Twice the same day and each time a different date? I shrugged. *C'est la vie.* Pierre had no idea how simple it was to make a rendezvous with a stranger at a club, café, bus stop, anywhere. A rendezvous—and soon enough a honeymoon trip to the south of France...

Valérie shook her locks and inspected me from under her lashes while she studied the menu. Did she want to order something to eat? She didn't.

"Okay, I promised to tell you what's what," I said. What kind of personal introduction would Claude have given in my place?

Valérie lowered the menu and expectantly propped her chin in her hands, looking like an *écolière*, an obedient student. I felt inspired to introduce the charming absurdities of the Paris scene like a school lesson, while we sipped our *rouge*.

Let's see. A number of women had started getting together at the Café Flore on Friday nights, and almost immediately another gathering started at the Deux Magots next door, across the little street that cuts into Boulevard St. Germain. As was to be expected, those who went to the Flore refused to step into the Deux Magots, and vice versa. This followed a long tradition, one café always trying to out-fashion the other. A generation ago, the Flore had been the proud bastion of right-wingers and pro-Nazis, driving the leftist intellectual crowd over to the Deux Magots. Then the mood shifted. The Sartre-Beauvoir clique, getting tired of tourists standing in line to ogle them, went into hiding...at the Flore.

I was warming up to my mock lesson.

The café rivalry, carried with the French passion for argument, escalated into a veritable culture crisis. Veterans of each faction would post themselves at the doors with flyers, promoting their café with some celebrity historically linked to it. As Sartre and Beauvoir were out, having been switchers, the Deux Magots faction picked Joyce as their patron saint. James Joyce had favored their café. The Flore crowd opted for the chansonnière Juliette Greco, a bohemian who had started out in the French Resistance. At the height of the battle, sentinels were set up to linger near the Metro station St. Germain, ready to lunge at any promising-looking woman and dissuade her from getting near the wrong café.

The unruly Friday night occupants of the upstairs room at the Flore called themselves PATs, short for...

I stopped. I had the impression Valerie wasn't listening. Was she bored? Every now and then she shot me a glance like a dart. Wondering perhaps whether I was making it all up? I was wondering, too.

"Do you know what PATs stands for?"

My *écolière* produced a little frown.

"*Plaisirs d'Amour Toujours*, or Pleasure at All Times. And can you guess what their mottos is? 'Anything goes...to bed'." Claude's motto par excellence.

A flush chased her cheeks. "You are pulling my leg, aren't you?"

"But their opponents across the street," I went on with relish, "the other faction, they set themselves up as clean-shaven moralists."

Valérie pressed her pretty lips together to hold back a giggle.

"They called themselves OVA—*Ordre et Vérité de L'Amour*. Another way of saying monogamy. But the PATs started calling them OWLs, short for 'Order Without Lust.' That stuck."

"In English?"

"The OWLs are snobs. Picking Joyce! Just to remind everyone that a man can be a genius, too?"

"But OWLs sounds better than PATs." She looked pleased with herself.

"Sure—to a media expert's ear. But wait until you're on the analytic couch of the OWL boss, where everyone else has already been, to confess your sins..."

"I would have no objections to a couch right now." She fixed me, little sparks in her eyes.

"That's charmingly put."

She quickly averted her eyes, cheeks flushed again. Her moments of shyness or embarrassment suited her well, making her look young and undiscovered.

"*Disarmingly* put," she corrected me, locking me into her stare again as if I were the rabbit and she the big snake.

What was I thinking? That one redhead could replace another just because I said so? That a visit at Club Cinq would get me instant gratification? Well, maybe, but Christiane's "distraction" had better fit my fantasies. Anything to stop me thinking of Claude.

"This introduction you offered—did you mean anything practical?" I felt her shoe at my pants leg. "Or just theoretical?"

"The practical part is all about being docile," I teased her, as if there were still a chance that she would get the message.

She looked down at the table as if she had just booked a victory. Then her gaze leapt forward again. "Well?"

"Not tonight, I'm afraid." I felt a tinge of regret when her face clapped shut. "I still have work to do. A radio show, tomorrow morning. But you'll let me treat you, yes?"

At the door, I waved at Pierre, who would think all the wrong things about our exit.

Valérie went over to the Metro station Luxembourg. I watched her walk around the curve of the closed park, walk into the dusk in her proper, dark blue coat, hair fanned across her shoulders in orderly curls. There was something childlike and forlorn in her walk that gave my stomach a lurch. I wanted to run after her. This is who she is, I suddenly saw, that brashness is just a silly pretense. Her bravado tries to hide her inexperience. Why didn't I see through it?

Run after her? Like in the dream that had come back to haunt me this morning? White socks and tennis shoes walking ahead of me, away from me. An urgency, alarm.

I slowly moved down Blvd St. Michel in the evening rush to pick up my Vespa, feeling bereft and like a fool, not liking myself very much.

STARS ALL OVER THE SKIN

Late at my window, in my Thinking Chair, I pulled Valérie's business card out of my pants pocket and turned it between my fingers. Why had I been troubled seeing her walk away?

I thought of the little sparks in her eyes. *Disarmingly put*! Her foot at my jeans leg! How could she get so many things wrong so fast? Not long ago, however, before Claude's call, I wouldn't have minded. I would have been curious, perhaps charmed. I would have played along with her naïve advances to see where the forthright front would lead and where it would break.

My eye fell on the big mirror from my ballet times, broken off at two corners from too many transports up and down Parisian stairways. It had acquired an odd, harp-like shape. Cornering the window, it seemed to double the size of the room. I had taped the picture of a young Balinese dancer over one split-off edge. Claude had placed herself in front of the mirror one day, in the pose of the dancer. Hips to one side, arms to the other, head following her hips without turning, hands and fingers extended in upward curves.

It was one of those moments when she forgot I was there. She disappeared into her purpose, her pose which was more than a pose. She had moved my chair out of the way so the ficus tree at the back created a scene, a mood for her. She began the tentative motions of a dance in dialogue with herself, and I held my breath watching her and her double from my quilt-covered mattress on the floor—a shy Asian temple girl and a coy young prince from *1001 Nights*.

My trouble, I realized, wasn't Valérie, it was Claude. Claude walking away from me. I went over her phone call again, refusing to believe it was over. She was simply doing what I was doing—trying to distract herself.

I picked up the phone on the first ring. "You again?"

"Waiting to hear from me, Lou, weren't you?" Her way of speaking was slow, caressing.

I automatically joined in. "Waiting? When I knew you'd call?"

She laughed with surprise. "You knew—of course you knew I'd call! And what, tell me—what would I say?"

I soaked up her voice, trembling a little. Should I hold back? Should I move in?

"Are you tired of her?"

"Her..." She seemed to be tasting the word.

"You told me you weren't alone. Remember?"

"Remember, remember, the month of September..."

The ready laughter, the slowed speech, the singsong. She was stoned. But not too stoned to slip me a message. September had been our time in the south of France. Was this the message I wished to hear, or were we on treacherous ground?

"Are you calling because you're alone again?"

"Alone, not alone, what does it matter? I needed to hear you, talk to you. I knew you'd forgive. That call the other day. You must have been mad at me..."

"I thought you were mad at *me*. You had eclipsed—and not a word in ages. What did I do to you?" There it was, I'd confessed my trouble.

"See? I shouldn't have called. I knew it would upset you and I never want to upset you, Lou, you know that, don't you?"

I couldn't help laughing, but it wasn't a happy laugh. She laughed, too, in a stoned way.

"Am I upset or is this a setup?" I tried to provoke her.

"Oh Lou, if we could laugh together and not be upset! It's gorgeous down here. A little night breeze...I'm not even wearing a jacket, hardly anything. You should see how tanned I am..." Her velvety voice unnerved me. "That beach behind Julien's, remember?"

"I'm not sure I remember. It's been a long time."
Was I going to ruin this talk?

"Way, way too long! How did that happen? What happened, Lou? Why aren't you here?"

"Perhaps I'd tell you, if you weren't so stoned…"

"You are so right! Don't listen to my nonsense. But I am serious, I'm asking. Why can't we enjoy ourselves again? It's such a marvelous night. You love this kind of night. You once said, a night with stars all over our skin…"

I'm not sure I remember, I wanted to say again, but I remembered only too well.

"Just tell me what you are doing with her, whoever she is. If she is."

"Oh Lou, she is! She is… How can I ever—?"

"Then tell me about her."

"You don't want to talk about us?" She sounded taken aback.

"Can't you tell me the truth?"

"But I want to! I want to be honest. I hate myself when I—" Her voice suddenly cracked. "Lou, tell me what I am doing, why I am doing this…"

"I wish I knew, Claudine."

"I ask myself all the time, why? Why?"

"Yes, why?" I asked gently.

"I only know…I feel lost without you." Her voice was thick with tears. "I wish I could see you."

"Why don't you, then? Why don't you come back to Paris?"

"Couldn't you interview me again? Like, starting over? I'm absurd!" She half laughed and half cried. "Lou, help me—I am drowning… Help me!"

"I'd do anything," I murmured. *If only you'd let me.*

"Yes, yes, you would." She blew her nose. "Listen to me," she whispered. "*Should we give each other a chance*? That's what you said to me, remember?"

I was struck that she hadn't forgotten.

"Like in the beginning. The way we danced…our tango! I still see their faces…" She laughed, then sighed. "We haven't danced in so long! Couldn't we imagine just for a moment? I take your hand, there's the music.... You hear it, don't you, Lou?"

I heard her voice of dark honey and longing. I felt weak-kneed and torn.

"My hand on your back, we look at each other, we take a breath, we—" There was a sudden pause. "Wait. Hold on—" Her clipped, director's voice. I heard a muffled sound. Another voice, low, but a woman's, I thought. She must be cupping the receiver with her hand. I made out a distant, "I'm coming!...Shh!"

Then her high, girlish, angry voice, "Oh, why do I have to go!"

The phone went dead.

I slowly paced back and forth through my rooms. The confessions she made when she was stoned often revealed the truth. *I want to be honest... Help me.* She had been hedging in her first call, holding me off. Preparing me. *Starting over...* I knew she meant it. But she wasn't free. Not yet. *Couldn't you interview me again?* The charm of her wishful thinking, believing her magic could sweep all obstacles out of the way. Her fierce impatience with impediments. It was all I needed...for now.

I leaned out of the window and closed my eyes, trying to feel the night breeze of the south of France.

LE KATMANDOU

A few nights later I was still convinced. Such a call doesn't come out of a vacuum. It is made because change is in the air. She was thinking of me. She was on her way or had already arrived. I suddenly couldn't stand my passivity.

There was a time when the Katmandou was everyone's hangout, when Claude and I went there to dance the nights away. It was still the favorite spot for old-timers, and if you were new in town, you would always end up at the Katmandou. Claude liked to joke that the club would be her retirement home, so she insisted we "keep it alive long enough." Le Kat would be her first place of landing after her long escape.

A lonely dyke was sitting at the bar with a beer, looking me over. Two couples were hanging listlessly in their club chairs near the tiny dance floor. A chanson by Barbara was thundering through the speakers. In an attempt to lift the mood, Carmen had set the disco ball turning.

"Hey, Lou!" Her trumpet voice out-shouted Barbara. "*Vot's new*?"

I shrugged and swung myself onto the stool at the end of the bar. "Too much to do," I shouted back. "The newcomers!" I added.

Carmen grinned knowingly. "Looking for someone? Haven't seen you in a while."

Carmen knew her flock. A while, for her, meant two weeks, fourteen nights, each one smelling of treason. She refused to take in that the private women's parties were hotter than Le Kat. Carmen was from Argentina, had chocolate-brown skin and slight buckteeth. She had kissed me with these somewhat wolfish teeth with vehemence; I didn't remember much else from our bustle behind the bar.

"Yeah. Checking on *you*."

She fussed with her bottles, looking flattered. "Courvoisier?"

Carmen had a knack for remembering every client's taste and favorite drink. In this case, however, Courvoisier was Claude's preferred "nightcap." Was it a hint? The way Carmen eyed me, she either knew something or was waiting for me to spill the beans about why Claude wasn't at my side. I couldn't let on what I knew or didn't know and get into Carmen's rumor mill. When she served me the Courvoisier I wouldn't have ordered and was close enough to communicate without shouting, I told her my latest "novice" had been playing footsy with me under a café table.

"They learn fast nowadays," she grinned the same knowing grin.

"A propos: has anyone brought in a pretty music student, chocolate skin and afro?" Distract her from what I really wanted to know.

"Nope."

"Or a red-haired goddess?" I described the stranger.

"Goddesses, nothing but goddesses!" Carmen said with comically crossed eyes.

She trumpeted the latest gossip for my edification. Yvette Marteau, a somewhat dubious advocate, had dragged in two men. There had been a brawl because the men didn't behave: they asked the lesbians at the neighboring tables to dance. Moira, an Irish woman, had slapped her girlfriend who had insisted on taking the whisky bottle away from her. Her very own bottle, after all! Carmen's fleshy upper arms and shoulders were bulging out of her white undershirt. She propped her arms on her hips and, with owner pride, let her gaze wander across the shelves where her clients' private bottles were lined up, ready to go.

A draft from the vestibule announced new arrivals. Could it be Claude? Claude in a huge white mohair shawl with snowflakes glittering on her dark head, her face blushed from the cold, eyes shining with mischief—the way she had once arrived at the club, after making me wait an ungodly hour? A whole cluster of women spilled in, some sporting mechanics overalls and short haircuts, others wearing long hair and long skirts. I watched the "boys" helping the "girls" out of their coats. The full-moon face of Charlie, one of my pals, appeared in the tussle. Charlie belonged to the cavaliers who are always on call for the female sex.

"We just had a meeting for May First," Charlie beamed and hauled herself onto the stool next to me, "and guess what? We refuse to march behind the OWLs this year!"

I usually enjoyed the day in the street when the Parisians turned out in high color for the union parades to applaud the wildly costumed lesbian and mostly naked gay contingents. This time I wasn't in the mood. Even the wild partying afterwards didn't catch my imagination. Was I getting old?

"There were plenty of newbies again." Charlie winked in the direction of the women who were dragging the club chairs into a circle.

"Are they planning to do group terror here?" Carmen scowled. She preferred couples who made out and drank a lot. But she ended up helping the women pull another chair or two into the circle to get them seated and ready to place their order.

Charlie was waving to some latecomers. In the next moment, I was kissed all over by Skylark, accompanied by a repeated, resonant "Wow!" Her brass-colored Rasta curls shook with misgivings over our encounter here, in the "hunting lodge." Her ample body was dressed in a tight Indian suede vest with tassels, two layers of skirts, and moccasin boots. Her presence displaced enough air in the room that the dyke at the bar turned around.

"You have *manquéed* a *fabuleux assemblage* again," she declared in an attempt to speak French. She looked around reprovingly as if I had wasted my whole life here at the bar. "We are *décidées* to go to the parade *très beaucoup en costume!*"

"She plans to go dressed in a fig leaf to shock the OWLs," Charlie said under her breath, lighting a joint.

Meanwhile Skylark announced with fanfare: "I make *pour moi* a cape with zodiac signs and nothing *autre!*"

Skylark, as she had named herself, was a "city-nomad." She travelled around with backpack and guitar, performing Carol King and Joni Mitchell songs wherever she came to roost. I had met her at a music festival in England, where she tried to drum up interest in "Pocahontas Meets Emily

Dickinson," an opera she planned to write and star in. She had followed me to Paris and to every place where interesting women were hanging out. That was how, after a night of smoking dope, I paid for my mistake of getting too close in a London bathtub.

In the shine of a tea light on the edge of the tub, Skylark with her wet Rasta curls had looked like a magnificent brass lion—the kind you find as a wall relief at the entry to villas in the Mediterranean. The mouth of the lioness spewed arcane poetry (maybe she was reciting her opera) and I hardly caught a word, although I considered myself pretty fluent in English. My hashish brain finally realized she was putting on a show for me, and I kissed her, partly to shut her up. By the next day it was clear to me that there was no vibe between us. But she had already made up her mind to take her nomad life to Paris—in my footsteps, for God's sake.

By now "Parlez-moi d'amour" was resounding through the bar. There was no night at the Katmandou without "Parlez-moi d'amour." Everybody sang along and two women from the circle of chairs started waltzing. The couples next to the dance floor got up as well. Skylark harmonized for our entertainment. Not long ago, Claude and I had danced this waltz together at Le Kat, my one hand in the back pocket of her jeans, taking it easy. I always enjoyed the way she led, strong and supple like a cat. I'd taken a few puffs on Charlie's joint. Cat? Why was I drinking another Courvoisier?

Claude's Minou was a jealous cat who made mischief every time I spent the night. Once, when we were in the middle of a stormy embrace, the cat toppled Claude's favorite lamp with a bang. We had to sweep up the glass splinters before we could return to our topic. When we locked Minou into another room, she went on a rampage there. Once she went straight up the wall, which I took as a compliment. A few times we jumped on my Vespa and fled to Aicha's Hotel Violet, when the red room was free.

I was suddenly fed up with the flickers

of the disco ball. I was missing Claude with every bone in my body. There was no trace of the stranger who could have done more than distract me. Luckily, the dyke at the bar offered Skylark a drink: two compatriots had found one another. It didn't take long before they were pushing onto the dance floor. Skylark made sure I didn't miss the fact. Edith Piaf was blaring "Milord" and Skylark was blaring in unison. Charlie, who had moved over to the May First circle, was hanging onto the chair of a long-haired elf.

The place was suddenly packed. I saw Carmen hand a customer a drink with a paper umbrella stuck on the ice, her wolfish teeth beckoning with laughter. The women at the bar were all hanging on to her like parched desert foxes, ready to bite. My brass-lion-headed friend was howling to the moon and the stomping, head-bobbing women around her looked like they were going to join her in some delirious bacchanal. My eye fell upon a woman with a visor cap on her white-blond boy cut, Catherine Dubois. I hadn't noticed her arrival. Katman Cat, as she was called among the *habituées*, spent every night at the bar, spreading good vibrations. She was so tanned and leather-skinned that she looked one, if not two, generations older than everyone else. Wearing a cravat with her shirt and vest, she was swinging her large bootie while she steered her girl on the dance floor with tight elbows and minimal footwork, like a sea captain proud not to waste an inch of space. The pleased grin never left her face, no matter how much she drank. Every night another girl. I watched the girl shriek as Katman Cat whirled her off the floor in between the tables. Hell, I thought. Could I possibly end up like this myself, a decade or two from now, with nothing better going night after night than whirling some new girl around like a carousel horse?

I stuck a tip into Carmen's pickling glass with the good-weather frog on the counter.

"No redheaded goddess tonight," I said when she came out from behind the bar.

"Giving you sleepless nights?" Carmen's narrow eyes seemed to move even closer together.

"Not me," I said punching her shiny upper arm. "An old flame of mine who is in a bad mood right now."

Carmen grinned with one corner of her mouth. "Come by again."

HOTEL VIOLET

It was a relief to be out in the air. A slight, refreshing drizzle came at me as I drove home. But instead of continuing toward Montparnasse I found myself turning back toward St. Germain and the Seine. In a few minutes I had crossed the river and was at the Porte St. Martin, the *quartier* where Aicha's Hotel Violet was located, at the heart of the garment district. I was making a left turn off Rue du Faubourg St. Martin when I was almost hit by a car. Had I overlooked the red light in my Courvoisier and hash haze? I was sharply awakened by screeching brakes, then the car, a gray Citroën, glided past me. I saw a shocked face staring at me, pale, with black slanted eyes, and for a moment I thought I had seen Claude.

What was I doing here?

The area was dead at night; most of the little wholesale fashion boutiques with Algerian, Jewish, Moroccan names were shut down without any lights in their window displays. Most were locked behind chain curtains and rough metal shutters. The usual piles of empty fabric rolls and discarded clippings were stuck in boxes and garbage cans on the sidewalks. I parked in a side street and walked over to the hotel. Apart from the frosted Art Nouveau windows with dim light shining through from the lobby, the hotel seemed lifeless. It was even hard to read the name at night, written in flowery filigrees above the entrance door.

Hotel Violet was one of the oldest, dustiest Art Nouveau hotels in Paris. It was owned and managed by Aicha's father, a *pied noir*, an Algerian

Frenchman. Aicha occupied a maid's room and makeshift kitchen at the end of a hallway on the top floor, directly adjacent to a big bathroom with two doors. One door opened to a hotel room that was laid out entirely in red; the other, usually locked, led to Aicha's hallway. Film crews liked to use the hotel for scenes from the Belle Epoque, but when the rooms weren't sold out, Aicha's friends had the privilege of spending luxurious nights at the Hotel Violet. And as Aicha was a genius in organizing, she usually managed to keep the bathroom—and with it, the red room—available.

I stopped in the entrance, peeking in at the sleepy lobby with its leather club chairs and dimly lit reception counter. The night concierge was probably already asleep or watching soccer in his backroom. Just as I was debating whether to walk in, a taxi arrived, and a group of men piled out. They looked like Middle Eastern business men, in fine, tailored coats and cashmere scarves. They entered the hotel in a jovial mood and I watched them chat with the night clerk who disappeared and reappeared with a stack of brochures, which all of them discussed at length. I could probably have walked in unnoticed, quietly climbed the stairs and walked down the carpeted floor of the hallway to the door with the number 72…

Clearly I was not in my right mind. It occurred to me that at any moment Aicha could show up, wandering in or out. Aicha and the other members of the theater group loved to pile up in Aicha's tiny abode, smoke dope, and climb out of her kitchen window to a primitive roof terrace from where one could count chimney pots around an almost full circle. At any moment, another cab could arrive and bring Claude along to spend the night with her new lover.

I withdrew to the bar across the street and had an espresso by the window, where I could keep an eye on the hotel. The bar was as sleepy as the lobby; the bartender hardly gave me a look. He was toweling off his glasses, taking me for an ordinary hotel guest, I supposed, ready to head out for the red-light district a few blocks over, at Strasbourg–St. Denis. A pleasant Arab woman's voice was moaning from the speakers.

I took a slow draw on my cigarette, tempted to go ask if the red room was available. What if I rented it for the night? It wasn't beyond my means. I had recently added another radio station and a German luxury magazine to my contacts. I could afford my sprawling café life and a few extravagances.

I often find hotel rooms more erotic than private rooms. Private rooms easily chain one's imagination with their clutter. Everything in the red room except the ceiling was red. The walls were covered with crimson damask, the plush carpet was burgundy, and the bed was made up with a comforter, sheets, and pillows in scarlet.

I am sure it was during our first night in the red room that I got obsessed with the mystery of Claude. Onstage, where I had first set eyes on her, her movements had seemed edgy, explosive the way they had to be according to the violent theater style that was en vogue. At the same time, she appeared disconcertingly relaxed, so that I had indeed thought of a wild cat at first—a lynx. When I got to know her, she kept surprising me with her well-trained muscles, the sudden determination of movements I hadn't anticipated and couldn't always follow as easily as a tango step. She also puzzled me with her willfulness when she insisted on some stratagem of costumes or clothes which she would not let me take from her, unyielding as a cat, even in the throes of passion.

That night, I saw her naked on the red sheets. She was lying stretched out on her belly, her face hidden in the bend of her arm. I took in her broad, beautifully rounded shoulders and strong neck. With hardly a waist, her back curved into a small, muscular ass. Seen from behind, with her jaw-long black hair, she could as well have been a boy—painted by the German expressionist Otto Mueller.

We started out as usual, wrestling for predominance. Perhaps she let me win. I turned her on her back, restrained her, and was on the point of conquering the boy. With her half-willing, half-mutinous movements to and fro on the satin sheets she seemed to be passing through a dark red sea. There was no boy or girl. She was a dolphin on my hook. Her sleek body was fighting its way upward to the break of light. This time her face wasn't hidden under a pillow. Her slightly trembling eyelids revealed a small, wet slit of her slanted eyes. And when I saw how she held her breath, when I saw her eyes roll backwards, I crashed, as my German friend Tanja would say, "like Satan into the lilies." This, this I wanted to see. Again. And again.

Where had Tanja found this crazy expression? When the devil crashes into lilies, the matter has biblical weight. Without Claude, I was driven from paradise. How could another woman, no matter who she was, be a match for us? I stared at the hotel entrance, the dim lobby, the dark emptiness of the street. No, I wouldn't go over to the hotel and risk being recognized by the night clerk or leave a trace for Aicha. I wouldn't lose my head after a wasted night of waiting.

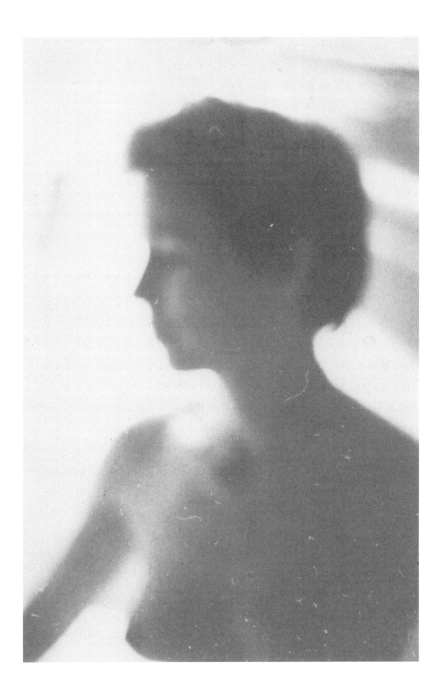

DAWN

I took a handful of spiced Moroccan nuts from a bowl on the counter before leaving the bar. Back home I parked for the night in the courtyard. The building was asleep under a blanket of lead. Not a sign of life. The idea of stepping into the clattering elevator or traipsing up the stairs to my empty rooms was intolerable. I turned back to the street and started walking toward the Luxembourg Gardens.

At 27 Rue de Fleurus, where Gertrude Stein used to live, I leapt up to touch the plaque. It was my timeworn ritual, my homage. How I had strained as a schoolgirl, goaded by Frantisek, to wrap my mind around it: "A rose is a rose is a rose is a rose." Why on Earth was it supposed to be the most brilliant line of poetry written since the turn of the century? Why did it make Gertrude Stein a genius? Why four times, not three?

It came to me little by little when I found my "exile" in Paris, where Stein had found hers. I began to understand that *Paris France* is "peaceful and exciting"; I discovered for myself the paradox that the brilliant Parisian surface doesn't preclude depth; that Parisian women can be intellectual and sexual at the same time. Wasn't the rose an invitation to the dance? An incantation, a spell, a caress? Four times is a paradox. It's a provocation. Four times lifts the mere assertion that a rose is a rose into poetry.

The big trees in the park seemed untouched by the stream of cars still rushing around them. They were waiting, gathering their spring secrets. The garden was out of reach behind its cast-iron fences. The forbidding enclosure

reminded me of a fairy tale from childhood. A girl standing outside a locked-up garden, tearing her heart out to get inside. She doesn't know the word of magic that would spring open the gates for her. I was that girl. There were my roses in full bloom, almost in reach—Claude with her veiled fire and thorns, the stranger in flaming red, all the others still in bud. "Please," I say the magical word.

I turned back. A hungover crowd was lingering around La Coupole and the other cafes, but the lines of parked cars were broken up, people were trouping home. A few steps and the border of Montparnasse nightlife was marked by the dreary station square of Gare Montparnasse.

I continued down Blvd Pasteur, indifferent to the indistinctly modern office buildings, the cheap Prix Unique supermarket, the ugly pomposity that marks most French post offices from the time between the wars. At the railway bridge, I followed my feet into the workers zones of the 14ème, down Rue du Château and onward who knows where, one dead street like the next. My only companions were the chained motorcycles, silent beasts lined up at the front of housing blocks. Every now and then I saw a light in a window, imagining behind it someone like me, unwilling to sleep. Every now and then a taxi forced me to move to the side and squeeze in between the cars crammed onto the sidewalks. I caught myself peering into the cabs as if there were a chance to catch a glimpse of the woman in red. As if I was willing her to cross my path and stop my mulling over Claude.

I strode past the chain-curtained storefronts, wide as dishtowels, and the shabby dry cleaners, *nettoyage à sec*, placed in every second street as if the French had a secret obsession to clean out their closets—from what? The collaboration with the Germans?

The desolate railway tracks reminded me of the abandoned train stations in Berlin, lonely train rides across Europe, Paris–Berlin, when I got my engagement as a dancer in the city of my childhood. Returning to Berlin didn't feel like going home—I had no home in Germany. Long train trips to visit family and friends in the west, stalled hours crossing the Iron Curtain, the train creeping along, bumping to stop after stop, doors clanking to thundering boots, guards with vicious dogs out of a Nazi nightmare.

I knew this mood only too well, set off by ghosts from the past, my early years of loneliness with my family, with Frantisek, then Stéphane, then everyone else.

It's love's illusion I recall, I really don't know love at all...

As a schoolgirl in Hamburg, when I met Frantisek for a concert or theater event, we used to finish the evening with black coffee at Nagel, a bawdy night café. Or we hung out at the waiting room cafeteria of the Hauptbahnhof, the main train station, with its drafty swing doors. I would delay leaving the city, reluctant to take the train back home to the suburb where my mother was waiting. The train that always stank of iron rods and piss at night. I would hang back and search the crowd for someone with the air of a traveler, some intriguing-looking woman who was waiting like me, for what? Sometimes I walked back out into the foggy streets behind a couple of men because I sensed that they were lovers. Lovers from a world a million miles away. I longed to be part of that world that had to be theirs, a world I only dreamt of. Alone, at a distance, I would trail these couples for a while, then turn back to take the last train home.

The illuminated cone of a Tabac attracted me like a firefly in the fog. There was no fog. The dingy café at the edge of the railway lines was the first one open even before the crack of dawn. I was the first customer; a waiter was mopping the floor and taking down the plastic chairs from the tables. I hunkered in a corner near the door, away from the bar where workers would cozy up any moment, warming my hands around a thick porcelain cup of coffee, brooding.

What had I achieved? I was a journalist, not a writer. I was filling notebooks, not novels. I had lovers, easy adventures, not love. I was obsessed with a woman I was perhaps not even in love with. I was in love with a mirage—there, not there, maybe there, maybe never.

The absurdity of my situation hit me. This is what it came down to? Leaving Germany for France, Hamburg for Paris, Frantisek for Stéphane; leaving literature for dance, dance for theater, theater for writing reviews; leaving the Good Girl with her romantic illusions behind—for this?

What if everything turned out to be a failure? My flight to Paris, my freedom—what if it all suddenly collapsed? If Paris vanished and some disaster, some flaw of mine, pulled me back into my mother's orbit, the dreaded cradle of Germany?

Through the open café door came the stink of garbage cans on the sidewalk. The screeching of plastic chairs on the tiled floor had stopped. The waiter or café manager had taken up a position behind the cigarette counter. I heard the first rumble of garbage trucks, the aggressive howling and clanking that marks the division between night and day, between the people who work and those who sleep. I know this sound. In an instant it turns the mysteries of the night into cold dread. I felt the last drop of my energy sucked out of me. Claude would never come back to me. I would never again run into the woman in red, try as I might. I would never have another encounter at the opera, in the lavish darkness of the loge.

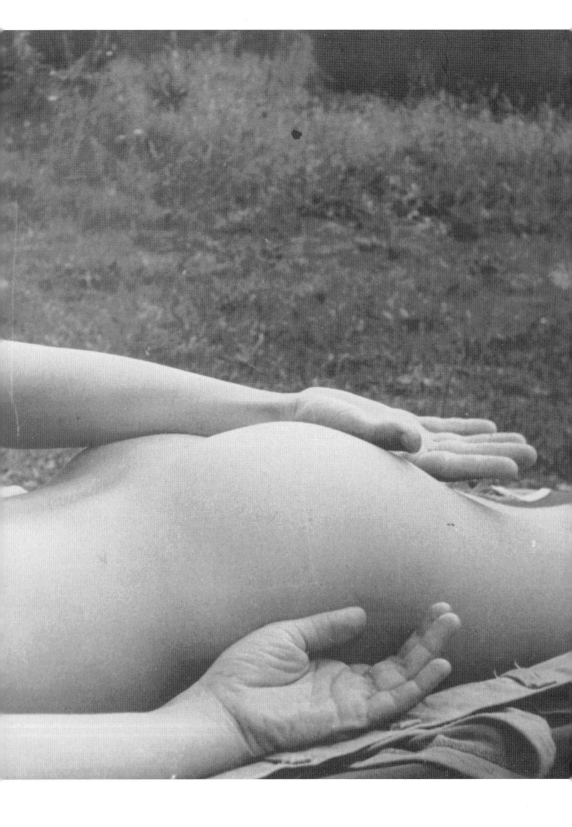

3

SWEET SIN

PLAISIRS D'AMOUR

Wednesday was the day of my *jour fixe*, my regular date with friends and pals. I had recovered from my blue mood; I went. Perhaps someone had heard from Claude or had news about her. Our meeting place was the Péché Doux (Sweet Sin), next door to the Bastille. A shabby bistro, gnawed down by centuries, from a time when it was more important to keep out the cold than let in light through windows. The tasteless wall candles would turn exotic when they were floating in clouds of smoke. It was enough to keep us there for hours. The cluster of small, round tables in our "back room" niche let us observe the traffic in the main room and, more often than not, our laughter drew in new visitors who had been catching the buzz: "Is this a *club privé*?"

It had started with a few friends getting together one Wednesday to rant about lovers. The topic turned out to be inexhaustible. We met again. The topic turned to seduction. Another Wednesday. Then it was exchanging lovers, discussing our latest *folie amoureuse*. Soon someone suggested a name. The "Sweet Sin" of our café inspired "Sinners"—short and *à propos* in a Catholic country. No contrition was our mission. Any overstatement was welcome, whether in words or deeds. New visitors didn't always get this right away.

I was settling in with my glass of wine, getting ready to unfold my list. Like Don Giovanni's servant, Leporello, who keeps a list of his master's conquests in Mozart's opera, I kept my list in accordion folds, with numbers and a brief (or not so brief) resume. I had written up my opera adventure, my sixty-eighth, with the sweet premonition that sooner or later the story would make its way to Claude.

I was about to start, when everyone turned their heads toward the main room. At a little distance from our group, a newcomer had taken off her coat and was leaning against a pillar next to the main room, wearing a tight tiger sweater with a leather belt. From the place where I was sitting, at the back wall, I only saw the sweater, the broad belt, the tall, elegant body, and my mind went into slow motion. But I know her, my mind said, I know her—even before she pulled off her cap and red strands of hair fell over one of her cheeks. What on earth?

I was unable to take her in. Everyone had turned around again to look at me. I was supposed to deliver. The stranger glared at me with the same conspicuous eyes that had fixed me at the opera. Green eyes! Redhead with green eyes like in a *roman de gare*, a novel of sexy clichés. How come I hadn't noticed that the first time? I wanted to stare back at her and be speechless, but I could do neither. How come she had shown up here?

One thing was clear: I would not read my latest entry. Not with her standing there. Call it a case of nerves or sheer excitement. I found myself reading my list from page one. After all, she was a new visitor: shouldn't I give her a bit of a background?

"Lou's *Leporello*," I read the title, not without some misgivings. "From the first, in the distant past, to the latest, but certainly not the last."

"You go, girl!" I got the expected encouragement from our cluster of tables. A repeat reading was always welcome with the Sinners.

"The first one was a glitter-gold angel in the Christmas play and I was a gingerbread. She convinced me that angels have the heavenly privilege of biting into gingerbreads."

"Early does it," Charlie's moon-face beamed at me. I scanned the room, making a quick stop at the redheaded stranger. My number one usually worked.

"The second, my cousin Ulli, showed me how pleasantly one can ride a pillow together. The third, never mind. I'm going to leap-frog here." There were a few grunts of protest. "I wouldn't want to bore you." The stranger didn't look bored.

"The fifth had a birthmark in the hollow of her knee that looked like a tiny sailboat crossing an ivory sea. I couldn't help wanting to bless its voyage with a kiss. And then bless it some more. Already a scamp—"

"No kidding," someone interrupted. The stranger seemed to be leaning forward. Perhaps she didn't want to miss a word?

"I better stick to the essential. Let's see...the thirteenth—" I suddenly wasn't sure where I was going.

"The thirteenth fairy," Sylvie specified, delicately lifting a finger. With her moonstone band across her forehead she looked like one herself.

"—never once took off her green felt hat during the two days and nights we spent in the train from Rome to Helsinki."

"Anything else she kept on?" Charlie asked.

"No rhetorical questions!" That was Marlène, a schoolteacher.

"The nineteenth wore Marimekko dresses, and underneath her dress her skin was like whipped cream, especially where little pools would gather in secret."

"Mm-hmm!" went my appreciative audience. I took in on the sly that the stranger had crossed her arms with a hint of amusement. The thought about my mother hearing me now, absurdly went through my head. *What shall the neighbors think?*

I leapt down my list. "The thirty-first—a quickie behind the counter of the Katmandou—was notorious in the night scene..."

"... a tough kid named Carmen," my pals filled in, in chorus.

"Hey, you're not the only one!" someone pointed out to the general merriment. There wasn't one of us who didn't know Carmen.

I was keeping an eye on the stranger, feigning innocence while I was reading for her edification alone. In my head, I heard the notes of Mozart's Leporello counting out the numbers: "*Ma in Espagna son mille tre.*" (But in Spain, there are one thousand and three.) My list of sixty-eight was a pretty good start, wasn't it.

"The forty-ninth, fiftieth, fifty-first, -second, -third, and -fourth were all at the same party..."

The stranger suddenly left her pillar by the bar. She uncrossed her arms and came toward me as if walking right into my story. I was stopped in my tracks. Everyone turned their heads again. She was towering over the whole room. Her hand raised as if pointing out the obvious, she fired off:

"Believe it if you can!"

Like a gauntlet. Her voice challenging, her green eyes like glaciers. This was not the winged gazelle I thought I had seen at the opera. This was the huntress of gazelles: the Goddess Diana in person! My first reaction was to

be blinded—*comme il faut*. My blurred vision held on to the impression that she let her gaze briefly wander around the room as if we were hardly worth her attention, before she seized her coat. In the stunned silence, her heels went clicking toward the door. Another newcomer, whom I hadn't noticed before, slipped out like a shadow behind her.

Who the hell was THAT? everyone asked on a high pitch. But I know her, went through my mind again. This doesn't make sense. She looks at me for one second at intermission and then finds me here. Have I been followed? Who is she? This oval face with its bud mouth and long, narrow eyes rang a bell, but I couldn't put my finger on it. A Modigliani face. Maybe that explained it. Diana the Huntress, painted by Modigliani. Nonsense. Nothing explained it.

It turned out nobody had invited her. Nobody knew anything.

"Hetero!" one Sinner shrugged, and that was the end of it.

Not quite. The Goddess had shot her arrow. I was struck. I had been hit at the opera and now again. Twice, they say, spells trouble.

T O P   O R   B O T T O M

Later, at home, I was writing in my notebook, a cassette of Mozart arias in my player. The woman in red had walked in on me—a mere apparition, as goddesses tend to be, fast as an arrow, fleeting as a breath of wind. How was it possible? I struggled to remember what exactly she looked like. "Green-flashing ice with a fiery trail of hair," I wrote. I saw her again, flying up the stairs past me in red shoes with glittering heels. I saw her profile in the loge across from me, a tip of hair almost touching the corner of her mouth. The shimmering blouse framed by a chili red jacket. But I couldn't say much about what I had seen today. The intensity of her eyes had surprised and blinded me. Tight-fitting tiger fur, well-shaped, but how exactly? Stripes blur contours. Luscious breasts? Small breasts? Only the belt had stuck with me. The way it curved down, hugging her hips, with a large triangular buckle pointing south. I'd been distracted by my list, my vanity. When she suddenly approached, she got too close.

What did the well-heeled stranger want among my crowd? *S'encanailler*? Like the bourgeois of yesterday who liked to descend into the nightholes of Pigalle to amuse themselves with the uninhibited populace? Then why not be amused by my *leporello*, right out of Mozart's opera? Why not applaud my escape from the coffin of conventional relationships?

We'd seen this more and more often in our circles. We were used to all kinds of women at the cafés and bars looking on and making moon-eyes at us. But newcomers usually weren't as high-handed and trigger-happy as she. This Diana was of a different caliber. I was suddenly sure she had come just for me.

I clicked off Mozart and made a few phone calls. The only one who picked up was Tanja, my friend who came from the same stifling German background. Tanja was a bohemian like me, who placed freedom and sex above everything else. She was a painter in love with transvestites, looking like one herself, with her beanstalk height and wig-like perfection of blond curls around her strong-boned face. She was known to do outrageous things, take off with one of her transvestite darlings, or pick up African "royalty" in the street when her man at home bored her. As a painter, Tanja belonged to several artists' circles.

"Listen—am I interrupting you?"

"*Vas-y*, I don't have a ton of time."

"Did you by any chance notice a new woman about town? Redhead, high fashion, asymmetric haircut?"

"Unsympathetic hair cut? *Non. Une artiste*, you mean?"

"No idea. How would you interpret that: one side short, the other long?" Tanja was my one friend who was enthusiastic about psychoanalysis.

"There's only one meaning, *ma chère*. She can do it this way or that, top or bottom!" Tanja liked to take the tone of an older sister with me, using a clipped German with multiple exclamation marks. "Interesting! Is she good-looking?"

"Would I ask?"

"I'm asking."

"Just as my mother would have wanted me to look—*bon chic bon genre*. You know." Tanja knew only too well.

"And as Claude doesn't want you any more there's an open slot, I suppose? Well, great. It's about time. Mooning about for weeks and weeks!"

"Let's not exaggerate, *s'il vous plait*."

"You know what I think: pining is unfulfilled love for Mama. It's regressive and hopeless to boot."

"Not at all. Claude misses me. She just told me—"

"Remember how you used to carry on when you started out with Mama Oppenheim?"

"You kidding? Papa, if anything."

"Well, right. You got over that one."

"Meret Oppenheim was my Muse. Anyway, Claude said—"

"Asymmetric...no kidding! What did this redhead do to you?"

I told her about following the stranger around at the opera. When I got to her surprise appearance at the Péché Doux, Tanja laughed.

"How dramatic! Operatic! You're going to make up a story. I know you. Another mythic stranger who's come to change your life!"

"Yeah? And why not?"

"Better be careful, operas always end up in disaster."

"Nonsense. They end on a high, in a private loge. Wait until I tell you what—"

"Whatever you say. But watch out, she's clever. That's a trap."

"What do you mean?"

"You're tripped up already!"

With a throaty laugh, she hung up.

Very helpful, I said through my teeth. Tanja's proclamations about me could be pretty *recherché*. Mistaking life for opera! Opera was an inspiration like any great art. Opera could be like great sex—beginning, middle, and climactic ending. If someone was making up a story, it wasn't just me. *Believe it if you can!* What on earth was "unbelievable" in what I had read at the Péché Doux? My *leporello* was my manifesto, so to speak. I was finished with romantic promises—promises nobody could keep. Attachment only as long as passion dictated, and not a day longer.

No matter how impatiently I was waiting for Claude's return, I couldn't get the stranger out of my mind. Her light-footed run. The musical bend of her neck. The rush backstage. An opera fan. Tanja was right. She was fiery, the way she came at me in the café as if seeing right through my game. Okay, my list did embellish truth in the way of any good story. Talk about women and poetry will sneak in. But what would she know about that?

I clicked Mozart back on. Zerlina's touching aria of being torn by Don Giovanni's seduction was playing. *Vorrei e non vorrei*, "I want to and I don't." Temptation of giving in to a dangerous promise of passion; fear of being hurt and fooled. What was the danger for me? What was the trap?

I had been hungry for her applause, reading for her with too much excitement and not enough *recul*—reserve, distance for observation. Instead of applause, the icy arrow struck me where it hurt. Like that stare at intermission that didn't even take me in, just pierced me. None of it had turned me off. That was the disturbing part. I was at pains to explain how she got under my skin so fast.

I remembered a discussion with Christiane about the human need to know. We can't stand not knowing, she had said; we prefer bad news any time to no news. But erotically, I said, not knowing or not yet knowing is the biggest turn-on. Claude would agree with me. I'd never met another woman who cultivated anticipation and delay like Claude. It was a form of *l'art pour l'art* for her—purposefully maintaining a distance, a certain resistance for the sake of passion. I was sure she was doing it right now, thinking of me, *alone not alone*, tempted to start over but holding off, or being held off. It didn't matter if there was another woman. I felt it in my own body—*croce delicia*, the sweet torment of her exercising withdrawal from our heat.

SAPPHO SHOW

There was already a crowd when I shook the April slush from my jacket.
It was the first spring event at the Beaux Arts, where the PATs (Plaisirs
d'Amour Toujours) liked to gather. Something told me the event with Théo
would bring Claude back from the south—with or without her new flame.
Everyone had been talking about it; everyone would be there.

I detected half a dozen ex-lovers in the room. Carmen stood out
because in the midst of sweaters and fur jackets her scrumptious shoulders were bulging out from her undershirt. I heard that Emma, a blonde
with brown eyes the size of dessert plates (my number thirty-three), had
announced a party for later that night, at the Palais Royal, i.e. her parents'
posh apartment. Skylark (who would have thought?) was sitting next to
her Katmandou conquest, waving to me with owner pride. I saw Matou, the
little Algerian with shy eyes who was attached to Claude's theater group.
As she worked at the Crazy Horse Saloon, the fashionable strip club, she
sometimes invited everyone to see the show. I loved watching the dancers,
"painted" by projector lights in stripes and dotted patterns like pretty merry-
go-round horses, the colors pulsing to the rhythm of pop hits. ("Big Spender"
by Bette Midler was an all-time favorite.) Matou, with her little-girl haircut
and chaste white blouse, would sit encased in the glass box of the cash register above the sinful fray, unapproachable like a unicorn. She had become
inseparable from Aicha. I waved to the two of them, but Aicha seemed unwilling to notice me. Aha, I thought, she knows something about Claude.

The unkempt studio space at the Beaux Arts looked like the garret in last year's opera production of *La Bohème*, with dust-blind windows and broken easels piled up in a corner. Théo sat on a raised little step, wearing her trademark black felt hat over her dark page cut. Everyone else was sitting on the floor, at her feet. As usual, she seemed to have a light beam trained on her, and the effect was heightened by the white dancer's shirt she liked to wear. The wide-sleeved shirt, gathered at the wrists, billowed around her slender body and disappeared in a pair of jeans with a rough leather belt. She wore short black boots, as did her young companions, her "bodyguards," who sported boyish haircuts and rarely moved a facial muscle. My occasional lover, Harmony Nayle from California, liked to refer to Théo as a "he/she," but I called her our Prince—a Prince crowned by French literature prizes, who wrote the hottest odes for her amorous sisters.

She sat on that little step as on a throne, receiving our homage, waiting for the microphone to be hooked up. She had a round face with a full mouth that seemed to hesitate about its inclination: would it want to pout or kiss, curl its corners upwards invitingly or downwards scornfully? But her eyes were without ambivalence: big, black, moist, irresistible bedroom eyes. How hard they were to resist I knew from the time I had first run into her, several years ago. I had been meeting some friends at the Beaux Arts when she came down the stairs with a little flock of admirers. She saw me and stopped. She smiled. Her slightly protruding eyes looked at me with a directness, a radiance that stopped my breath. In a single moist-velvety moment they took possession of me. I didn't know what to do. I should have fallen to my knees and adored her, but perhaps I was still carting the Good Girl around.

I sometimes wondered what would have happened had I been faster on my feet. Had I entered Théo's circle and been part of her rising literary fame and the ever-growing circles of women around her. Would it have brought me to a different place, closer to serious writing? I would have met Claude at a time when she was one of Théo's favorites. I might have lived with them in the house in the suburb and travelled to Lesbos with one or both of them...

The evening was getting into swing. Everyone was talking and shouting and not losing sight for a second of the spot where our Prince was sitting, tapping on the tip of the microphone, shaking her head. There also seemed to be a problem with the slide projector and a thickening ring of *garçonnes* was debating the necessary fixes. It turned out the slide carousel didn't fit the projector and no replacement was available. But the microphone finally worked, and Théo raised it up high as if to snatch a spirit from the air.

"We have to imagine what we can't see," she began in her surprisingly high, young girl's voice that vibrated with hidden indignation. "We have to invent what we cannot remember." All heads turned to the studio wall

where she now conjured "The island, in morning mist. An aroma of anise and thyme in the breeze, dawn with gold sandals... Here, on the rock to the left," everyone's eyes swung up with her eyes, "Aphrodite's temple. The graceful grove of apple trees and altars, the scent of smoking frankincense." Her arm with the billowing sleeve swept outward in a beautiful curve. "And there cold water sounds through apple branches; with roses the whole place is shadowed—and from the radiant trembling leaves..."

A hushed chorus joined in: "...sleep comes dropping."

"Who, O Sappho, Was Wronging You?" was a performance Théo loved to repeat for an audience who knew it by heart and lip-synched lines from the poetic fragments Théo had chosen. The highly romantic first part was an homage to "Eros, the melter of limbs," and always ended with everyone reciting together, "The moon has sunk and the Pleiades / and midnight has gone. / The hours are passing, passing / and I lie alone." Many women had their eyes closed, sitting with rapt attention, embracing each other, some lying down, crying. Even the young bodyguards looked dreamy.

The second part held a different spice. Théo would without fail zoom in on her question: Who was wronging Sappho? Everyone among the PATs knew exactly who it was. It was the OWLs (Order Without Lust). The OWLs proselytized that Sappho, the "Tenth Muse," was heartbroken over a man and had thrown herself from a cliff on Lesbos for him. Théo would take them to task. She would scold the monogamous Freudian "Vaginellas," who were hunkered down at the Deux Magots. The OWLs, in turn, scorned the PATs, who were barricaded at the Flore, and called Théo's belief in Sappho's relentless passion for women "clitoridiculous."

In the break, I got hold of Aicha, who was trying to sneak by unseen.

"What's new, pussycat?" I asked in a conspiratorial tone. She made big eyes at me.

"Not much," she said. She straightened an already straight strand of hair in front of her face. She clearly had something to hide.

"You look terrific," I said. "The training shows." There would be no training without Claude. She looked shocked for a second, then broke into a broad smile.

"Really? It shows?" She spun around on her heels like Charlie Chaplin and coquettishly looked over her shoulder.

"Everything shows. Has Claude brought back a new idea for a play?"

"I thought you didn't know..." Suddenly she was suspicious again.

"What everybody knows?" I knew I was out on a limb. "Paris is a village, *dahling*."

"But Claude said she didn't want...well, you can imagine."

"I imagine nothing," I said, my heart beating faster, "because I know everything." As Matou had just come to join us, I declared, "Claude said she'd be here tonight."

"Maybe she'll still come," Aicha said a bit too fast.

"Did you notice how tanned she is?" Matou cut in, her voice both eager and envious. Aicha threw her a look. I wasn't supposed to know about it. Did I have the role of the fool in this comedy everyone seemed to be part of?

"She looks fabulous," I playacted. "To be eaten alive!"

Now they both looked confused.

"I think she's definitely going to the party later," Aicha said with heart-felt conviction. Was she trying to console me? "We're all going. You too?"

"Who knows?" I didn't let on that I was rattled and dismayed. It was a small consolation that they didn't seem to know what to make of me.

Someone grabbed me from behind and put a hand over my eyes.

"Lou, *chérie*," cooed a well-known voice. "Who am I?"

"No idea, Kiki!" I turned around. Kiki Möller, a good-looking woman with a pride of chestnut hair, was a librarian at the Goethe Institute, the German cultural outpost in Paris. She was one of the few forty-something women in the room. Kiki used to assist me when I had to do research for one of my articles. She was married and had only recently discovered the PATs. She often still behaved like a novice.

She hung around my neck. "Save me!" she exclaimed. "Save me from these bewitching women!"

I read blank astonishment in Aicha's and Monique's faces. The women around us turned their heads. In the next moment I understood. I caught the glance Kiki cast at Théo who was striding past us, back to her raised little step. Glued to her was Skylark, who right now had no time for me. The show was going to begin again.

"Could I talk to you for a moment?" Kiki pleaded in German. "I really need to be saved..."

K I K I

I followed her out of the room. "You know I have this panel discussion next Friday, and Théo...Théo has just now cancelled on me."

She gave me such a wild stare, with so many furrows in her brow, that I said, "Come on, let's have a drink and you fill me in." I was glad to leave the crowded room that was suddenly haunted by Claude.

"I'm not going to miss anything?" Kiki asked anxiously. I laughed and took her arm. She unfolded her umbrella and we pushed against the wind.

"I can tell you what you're missing. A flaming tirade against the OWLs, then an incantation of all the girls in Sappho's poems—Eirana, Gongyla, Anaktoria, Mika, and of course Dika! Then a chosen few will recite favorite lines, like, 'Eros shook my mind like a mountain wind falling on oak trees.' Or this one, a special favorite: 'If she does not love, soon she will love, even unwilling.'"

"God, you heard this more than once," Kiki said with envy.

"Finally everyone will deplore the martyrdom of the young brides. That part you know only too well..."

She punched her elbow into my ribs as if I'd told her at mass that the bishop was secretly drinking the wine himself. "And Théo?"

"Gracefully extends her mercy to all those who still serve a husband."

Kiki sounded stricken. "She had no grace or mercy for me today."

We leapt over a gushing river at the edge of the sidewalk and entered the Tabac.

She leaned her umbrella into a corner and squeezed behind a tiny table.

"I'm a mess."

She shook the rain out of her chestnut mane and wiped the drops that had flown onto the table with her coat sleeve. I liked Kiki. Her beautiful, bony face, long nose, and anxious brown eyes reminded me of a fine horse. She was generous and honest and didn't hide the fact that she was quite overwhelmed by life in Paris, by her husband (who had a *maîtresse*), and now, in addition, all those bewitching women. As I was a *Landsmännin*, a compatriot, she had spontaneously made me her confidante, the person she could ask questions about women, men, and sex. She had initiated a successful series of lectures and round tables at the Goethe Institute.

"Hot chocolate with cognac?" I inquired. She nodded absentmindedly. I went to the bar to order.

"I had really counted on Théo," she complained when I sat down. "My guest star! We've announced her, of course. Why first say yes, and then withdraw in the last minute? Without an explanation."

She told me everything Théo had said at first and how proud this had made Kiki of her event on the topic of Temple Sex. Meanwhile, the waiter brought our drinks.

"*Chocolat chaud-cognac?*" he asked with the satisfied expression that always shows up on a waiter's face when anything alcoholic has been ordered.

"*Café serré-cognac,*" he recited for my side of the table.

"*Serré?*" Kiki pondered. "How can coffee and water in a cup be 'crowded'?"

Kiki had a penchant for questioning words, words like *amour* (why is it masculine in French?) or terms like "double standard." She pensively added a bit of her cognac to her chocolate.

"A pretty good topic." I lit a cigarette. "What's her objection?"

"We added a new subtitle: 'Temple Sex: From the Sacred to the Profane'—with a question mark."

"You serious?"

She gave me a pained look. "We wanted to make it, well, a little more piquant. But we added that question mark! I thought she'd like that. She loves controversy, no?"

I rolled my eyes. "You're suggesting that Sappho's temple turned into the first bordello or something?"

"Oh, *mon Dieu*, you think that's how she took it? But it's true that there was temple prostitution—there still is!"

"Kiki, get with it," I clinked my cognac glass to hers. "To men!"

"Okay, okay," she gave in. "Maybe you're right. It's men who always separate us. God, how I admire Théo! I bet she looks down on me because I am still..." She suddenly looked ready to cry. "She's a real intellectual—and not at all mannish."

"But most French intellectuals—"

"Just look at her!" Kiki ignored me. "How she dresses! Boyish, but so romantic. When she's in a room, you can't look at anyone else." She blushed.

"There you have it: Parisian women."

"Why can't we German women be like that?" She saw my expression. "Whatever. I've lost her..." She let her head hang, her hair almost falling into her cup. "How am I going to find a replacement now?"

I wondered who might do Kiki the favor of jumping into the fray of a polarizing debate.

"Couldn't you help me out?"

She asked with such a worried look that I said, "Why not?"

"Really?" She searched my eyes. "You mean it?"

"Women and sex?" I grinned. "I'll come up with something."

Kiki stroked her hair back, still frowning. "So you don't mind the title? Somehow I don't understand..."

"Who else is participating?"

She named Mary Hobbs, an American historian, whom I'd met in the circle at Café Rumpelmayr; Dominique Araki, a journalist I'd never come across; and Angèle d'Albert, an author who had published with the OWLs, whom I hadn't read. All women who wrote. Kiki would be the moderator.

"You can count on me," I said.

In her enthusiasm Kiki seized both my hands and gratefully shook them, knocking over her cognac glass.

"See? A mess!" This time she didn't use her coat sleeve; she pulled an old Kleenex out of her pocket. "You know why this is so hard on me? Théo..." Two tears made their way down her cheeks. "I expected—I don't know. The look she gave me today..." She dabbed at her tears.

"Kiki, you aren't cut out for Théo. Get her out of your head."

She stared at me in shock.

"You don't need a star. Not in your private life. Choose someone like yourself. You can worship her, *bien sûr*. But Théo is—"

"Only for someone like you?" She sounded hurt.

"Not for me either," I set her straight. "Théo is dangerous. Too much power is dangerous. All you'd get is an *affaire fatale*."

"You think she's a *femme fatale*?" She asked, wide-eyed, looking more than ever like a horse. "I don't believe it. Not Théo! There's such softness in her eyes. And her mouth…!"

"Watch out," I looked at my watch. "That's a trap."

I was talking like Tanja. Why was I arguing? Because I couldn't stand that Kiki was eager to be overpowered, as I had been when Théo's eyes first fell on me?

PALAIS ROYAL

The minute Kiki left the café to catch the end of the event, I got a *jeton*, a phone token, at the cash register and went down to the restrooms and the telephone. Damn the French habit of placing the phone right next to the stinking toilets! I dialed Claude's number. No reply. I tried again. I was tempted to just drop by at her place. She was back and everybody except me was in on it. I could hardly restrain my misgivings since Aicha had spilled the beans. Had I missed her calls? Claude the Elusive. No knock at my door this time, but a reunion at Emma's party—for all to see?

Starting over in public suddenly seemed a daunting but thrilling proposition. There had been times when I had almost crossed a line in public. Mathilde, the wife of a German colleague...The two of them were passing through Paris a couple of years ago. Over dinner at the Brasserie Bofinger, Mathilde and I got so turned on that at the end of the evening, I was tempted to throw all respect for my colleague to the wind and rush after her to the ladies' room. We took a taxi, all three of us on the backseat, Mathilde next to me, our thighs pressed against each other, our fingers clutched, digging into the flesh of each other's palm. Her husband had the taxi stop at the drugstore on Blvd St. Germain to get cigarettes. That was the time we had to still our hunger. As our driver was a woman, I didn't care that she could see us, see the way we tore into each other with our kisses, hands desperate to find skin. "Let us know when he returns," I called out to the driver. "Most certainly," she purred. It was an exquisite race against time and the obstacle of clothes.

Nothing like that with Claude. Claude preferred controlled, staged expressions of desire—at least with me. For her it was all about *l'art de l'amour*. My taxi ride with Mathilde wouldn't qualify.

I spooned up the leftover *crema* from my espresso cup, searching my memory. "Love's ruled by art..." We had to translate Ovid in class. We quoted, imitated, distorted him, and mostly puzzled among girl friends what he meant by "Amor, thus I tame you, even if your arrow wounds me." We understood being wounded. That's what we all wanted. That's what I wanted. But taming Amor? What for? Art had to do with control, which we didn't possess, not even in our imagination.

Sex, I used to think not so long ago, was a force of nature. You were overcome by it like by a thunderstorm in an open field. Throw yourself into it, no questions asked. But the lines of Ovid had made their mark. I used to come out of the thunderstorm wet as a dog, blind and beaten, shaking myself and asking: Where have I been? How can it be over? So suddenly over—as fast as it came on?

Coup de foudre—a flash of lightning that would last! That's where the "art of love" would have to make its entrance.

I must have been staring into space. The waiter was hovering near my table. Impatient for another order? I already had a second espresso. No, he was giving me looks from under his bushy eyebrows. What did he think he was reading in my face? Now that Kiki was no longer at my table, I must be in need of company? I pulled my notebook from my pocket, stretched a long leg out from under the table and blocked his passage.

"I'll let you know," I said in a loud voice, "if I need anything."

I checked my watch for the fiftieth time. There was still an hour to kill. Calling up my Teutonic discipline, I went over my notes from an exhibition at the Grand Palais that the German press wanted to hear about. I worked on the side remarks I liked to smuggle into my reports. In this case, "Ramses the Great," I would point out intriguing changes in the presentation of Egyptian couples I had observed. In the earliest period, child-size male figures are seated on the lap of a big mother who is also the queen and goddess. A few hundred years later, the son stands behind her, a good head shorter than the mother. Next, he stands in front of her, still smaller and linked to her by the protective, guiding arm she has placed on his shoulder.

The following epoch shows men and women couples side by side, of equal size (sometimes reflecting sibling marriages). With Ramses the Great, the women have literally shrunk into the background. Should I comment or leave it to my readers to draw conclusions?

I noticed an old couple getting up from their table to leave the café. Both were wearing dark berets. They were walking out into the street hand in hand, as if they had already walked this way to school together, maybe art school. Perhaps a nightcap at their *café du coin* was part of their usual evening round, before slowly walking home together. The idea of such lifelong belonging seemed absurd and yet tugged at my heart.

It was finally late enough to get on my Vespa and drive over to the Palais Royal. Emma's parents lived on the fifth floor in Rue de Beaujolais. Emma herself had her own "atelier" in the fourteenth *arrondissement*, although she had nothing to do with art. Opening the massive, polished entry door, I instantly noticed the "traffic"—the streaming to and fro of women in the hallway and the discreetly lit rooms. In the salon, a few women had already shed half of their clothes, dancing to Joan Armatrading's "True Love." One of them was shouting and swinging her shirt on the balcony where a crowd had gathered to admire the illuminated palace behind its French gardens. It was a pretty sight from the entrance—the silhouette of half-naked jerking, swinging bodies in front of the windows and the illuminated night sky.

Apart from two Louis XV sofas and armchairs, there were pillows everywhere on the floor. A few couples had stretched out to chat; others were smooching in darker corners. A side room, the "music salon" (as one could tell from the Steinway), was filled with a thick hashish cloud. The obligatory group on the floor was lit by candles. It was early; they were still dressed, the chosen one lying in the center. In a guest room, I saw several women seated around Skylark, who was performing Joni Mitchell for them on her guitar, looking like a benevolent lioness. Luckily she had her eyes closed; I could sneak out again unnoticed. I quickly scanned every room and bedroom for Claude, then followed the stream of women into the kitchen where Emma had lined up a battery of wine and a few whisky bottles. Everyone was in

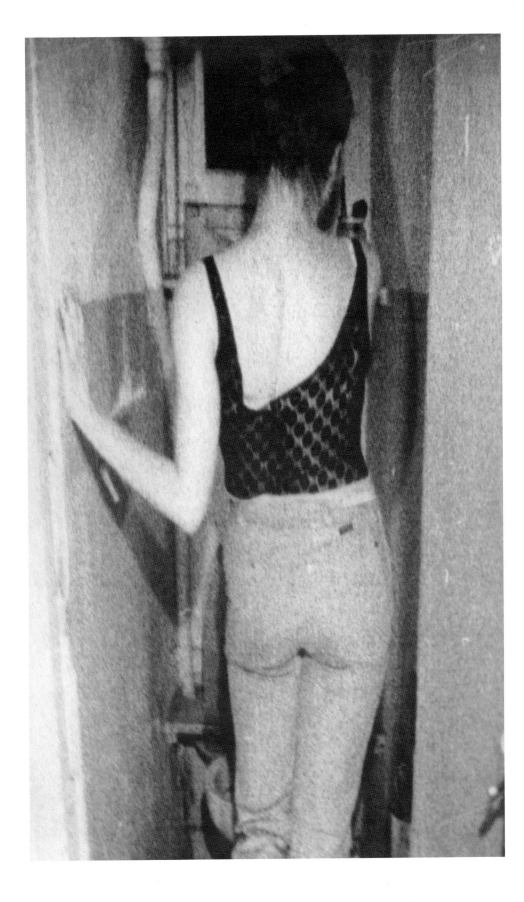

high spirits. There usually wasn't much alcohol at the parties because nobody felt responsible for procuring it. The less there was to drink the more everyone smoked. I was greeted loudly and Emma planted a kiss on my neck. She handed me her glass of red wine and opened a new bottle.

"Who's already here?" I asked.

Théo was expected later, she said. The huge eyes in her doll's face told me she had downed a good deal of alcohol and hash. In the next moment, before I could ask about Claude, Emma had fallen into the arms of a sturdy young dyke and was dragged into a hallway behind the kitchen. I followed them. The hallway led to several small chambers—provision and service rooms, I supposed. The area was packed. Women were standing around talking with a pitch of excitement. Whenever one of the chamber doors opened, everyone nearby craned their neck as if the promised land could be glimpsed in there.

Women slipped into the little rooms, alone or in couples, and some instantly backed out again in shock. As in a comedy routine, doors were torn open and quickly banged shut—and in the flash of light falling in from the hallway, a sock, a naked leg, some sort of divan, a tangle of hair and arms came into view for a second. Every now and then an angry "*Ferme la porte!*"could be heard, but most couples were perfectly oblivious to the doors.

I leaned against a wall, chatting with one of the Sinners about party indiscretions. In the early days, it had been all about greed and timing: getting into the act before any thoughts of consequences or bad conscience could arise. There used to be frequent dramas between couples who had opened a door in the wrong moment. I had once seen Aicha in a *grande scène*: collapsed in front of a locked door. There were noisy negotiations between Aicha's pals and the women in the locked room, while Aicha was hysterically sobbing on the floor. When no agreement was found, we all piled into a taxi and brought her home to the Hotel Violet, holding her hand through the rest of the night.

It had taken me some effort at first to outwit my Good Girl when I was flirting with a woman who was already taken. But the message was clear: everyone knew the hour of monogamous couples was over. Suddenly you notice it all around you, a barrier has fallen, an erotic energy goes rampant, and everyone is on the same wave of desire and permission. The peak of rule-breaking was to turn on the second member of a couple when she already knew what was going on and was supposed to be mad—until she decided there was something more pleasurable than being mad. A few times, the result had been a delightful triangle—delightful because triangles are notoriously unstable; the transient quality of the moment is written in their skin.

Claude wouldn't be part of these chamber games, or would she? Not the Claude I knew. As if by tacit agreement we had refrained from going all out with each other in front of our crowd. Maybe we felt orgies were already a bit *passé*. But who was to say what Claude would do with her new paramour? Maybe they would jump right into a big, reckless scene as a statement to everyone? What would I do in that case? Watch? Or would I join the fray? I might—if the woman in red were to show up with Claude!

My head was spinning. The woman in red? Imagining the impossible because I was getting panicked? And what if the pair acted out the exclusive romantic couple we all had so eagerly abandoned? If they showed off that they needed nothing and nobody else, leaving me out in the cold? Did I really want to stay around for such a thing? An early art object by Meret Oppenheim came to my mind: a pair of old-fashioned, laced-up women's boots standing face to face, their tips glued together, titled "The Couple."

I noticed the flirtatious looks and searching, sideway glances in the crowded hallway. A few more Sinners were pushing through the din.

"What crimes of passion are you up to?" Florence, her sailor earring in her left ear, kissed me three times right and left. "You haven't had a story for us in a while..."

"You're our soap opera," said Marlène, the schoolteacher, drawing on a joint. "We're addicted."

"I got burnt again last weekend because the women just won't give clear signals." Florence let her eyes wander hungrily over the women packed into the narrow passage. "Is it friendship? Is it more?"

"It's always more," I said, taking the joint. Friendship was the last thing on my mind when I expected Claude to appear any moment. "Who cares if you get your fingers slapped?"

"You should give private lessons," Charlie grinned. "Could I be your student?"

"Hey you guys," I said, "has the redhead resurfaced anywhere? You know: *Believe it if you can?*"

"Maybe she's at the Deux Magots," Florence said. "No risk of getting her fingers dirty there."

"By the way, where's Claude?" Marlène peered at me with curiosity. "She hasn't shown up in a hundred years. Maybe she, too, has gone over—"

"Yeah, teaching the OWLs how to go down," said Pierette, who was into martial arts. She was wearing a fencer's vest, her party outfit.

"Bull," Charlie said. "I'll bet Théo's hiding her again in her harem."

"I need a drink," I said.

VENUS IN FUR

I went back to the salon, picked up a half-empty bottle of wine from the floor where a couple was making out, and took a long swig. Waiting was like getting older by the hour. Not a single muscle in me was drawn to the dancers around me. I slid down the wall where I could keep an eye on the door.

Most women were dancing for themselves, at least so it seemed. But there were plenty of virtual spectators on the balcony, on the pillows around the room, traveling by in the hallway. Some couples were shoving along in a tight clasp, ignorant of the beat of the music, entirely concentrated on their rotating hips. Kiki, I discovered, was dancing among all the other half-naked women and had only abandoned her shoes. She was moving with her eyes closed, shaking her chestnut mane from one side to the other. No trace of Claude and her troupe. After some time, Kiki dropped onto a pillow next to me.

"Great African drums," she said catching her breath.

"I can't keep up."

A small, reed-slender woman with a dark, shaggy head of hair came dancing toward me. She was wearing only a skirt with ruffles and a fringed shawl tied around her belly. Her smoothly circling hips and her snakelike arms with many clicking bracelets were beckoning me onto the dance floor. I raised my shoulders with regret, signaling her to continue dancing. With a mischievous smile, she started shaking her upper body. Her breasts and entire chest began to vibrate. Every bit of skin, muscle, fat was transformed into the fantastical geometry of circles and waves. A ring of women formed around her, egging her on. I threw the dancer a kiss and realized that Kiki at my side was speechless. When the cluster of women had danced away, she cleared her throat:

"You know her?"

"That's Mariza. She has gypsy blood. You ought to dance with her."

"I would never dare," she said with indignation, following Mariza with her eyes. "I believe she wanted to dance with *you*."

"Not today," I said. I felt a tinge of regret. Each "belly-dance" on the mattress with Mariza had left me with a delicious muscle ache in my *derrière* the next morning.

"Way past midnight," Kiki looked at her watch and yawned. "I hoped Théo would come..."

Théo usually came late, if at all, watched a while, and then disappeared with her inner circle. There were wild rumors about the small private *partouzes* or sex parties that preoccupied her.

"Apparently she never dances," Kiki said. "She only watches. Strange, no? I would find that somehow embarrassing if somebody was watching me like that..."

"Embarrassing or erotic," I said. When I saw her troubled face, I added, "Depending on your mood."

Velvet Underground was rasping "Shiny shiny shiny boots of leather/ Whiplash girl child in the dark..." Everyone roared out the major lines of the song. "Strike, dear mistress, and cure his heart."

I, too, had puzzled over Théo, the way she usually sat down in the middle of the room, alone or with her dark-haired, boyish lover of the moment, and watched what was happening on the pillows at her feet. She could sit there motionless for a long time, with a wanton and yet closed-off expression on her face, pouting as if her mouth couldn't decide whether the taste was pleasing or not. You aren't going to watch me! I would rebel and withdraw from whatever woman was just unbuttoning my shirt. I envied her position and was jealous of Claude's unknown history with her. Whenever Théo entered a room, the temperature shot up a few degrees. What if Claude came waltzing in with Théo this night?

"I am tired, I am weary/ I could sleep a thousand years..."

The women were dancing with a manic exuberance that looked put on like a costume, everyone a "Venus in Fur." My eye caught sight of a familiar visor cap atop a men's shirt and cravat. It was Katman Cat, steering a PAT woman across the parquet. What was going on? She was now about the only dancer fully dressed. To all appearances she was having a jolly good time in this new hunting ground among the PATs. I was overcome by the same vision I'd had at the Katmandou. Everyone twenty years older, broad in the bottom, sporting tans and leathery smiles, flirting, seducing, and twirling around forever.

Kiki went home and I carried my bottle back to the kitchen. The place looked like a battle field. No, a beehive after a bear has reached in a paw. A lot of buzzing; glasses and bottles everywhere. Women on the floor, half-dressed, swigging from a bottle; two of them on top of each other on one chair, while a third was trying her acrobatic best to climb on, too. Another few were emptying out the fridge.

"Has anybody arrived?" I asked Charlie and Marlène who were watching the scene with interest.

"Only everybody who's nobody," Charlie said with a wink.

Two of Théo's "boys" were leaning against the fridge, oblivious of the eating binge going on right next to them. I was searching for a fresh glass when I heard Claude's name. "Claude? You must be kidding!" I pricked up my ears. I caught the words, "...dominated," and "...new man." "Very busy, the lucky one!" They laughed. "And did you hear what she did with—" In that moment, a trio of tipsy Irish women jumped up from their chairs, linked arms and bellowed the old hit, "Here Come the Lesbians!"

Claude dominated? Very busy? Barely back and already in the gossip mill because of a guy? I felt as much irritation as disbelief.

A sudden hush. Several women stopped in their tracks and turned their heads. A second later, everybody pressed out of the kitchen toward the entry hallway. But it wasn't Claude. It was Théo stepping into the salon, flanked by two boy-girls in black leather. She was wearing her indispensable felt hat over her page cut. She went to the balcony, immediately followed by the two "boys" from the kitchen, and for a moment it looked like the royal procession of five dark knights. The white, open collar of Théo's dancer's shirt was the only brightness, catching the light and reflecting it onto her face as she turned and slowly scanned the room. The smallest, pleased smile curled her mouth. Her big, dark eyes looked moist and drugged.

I surveyed the excited movement of bodies toward her for a moment, and left.

Everything was too much and not enough.

STRATEGIE D'AMOUR

Enough already. Enough waiting around.

I took a bottle of Sancerre from my fridge and poured the wine into a carafe. With the empty bottle in my Vespa bag, I started driving.

The clouds had opened up, flying across a blue sky. I crossed the Pont au Change. The Seine glittered and shone as if someone had given it a bath. At the Théâtre de la Ville my heart took a leap when I saw Pina Bausch announced on the huge program banner. Pina Bausch, the inventor of "dance theater," was about the best thing Germany had offered me ever since I left. Her staged collisions between men and women cut through the suffocating German air with the beauty and ferocity of a knife. When I first discovered her work, a few years ago, my relationship with men, with Frantisek, appeared in a new light. On Pina's stage, our small, private misery—my silence, the violence of repressed feelings, Saturdays with the inevitable missionary position—was turned into an archetypal tale of gender caging and despair. The German public was scandalized, but each visit of the *Wuppertal Tanztheater* was given a huge welcome in France. This spring, not just one, but two pieces were on the program—soon, very soon to come.

I clattered past the Gare du Nord and the Grands Boulevards, a minute away from the Hotel Violet. I stopped to get gas, swung around the Place de la République, up the gray-faced Rue du Faubourg du Temple, and there I was in Belleville, the *quartier* of workers and immigrants. Claude liked the old, decrepit *quartier* whose boulevards looked like Moroccan bazaars. The bustling crowds of people with brown, black, and olive skin, the "flying carpet" salesmen wandering about with one or several rugs on their shoulders, the African vendors of watches and ivory with their suitcases on the sidewalks—to her it all was a sort of street theater. Christiane, who also happened to live in Belleville, did not share this preference. She was hiding out in an old villa surrounded by abandoned gardens that evoked Proust rather than French colonialism.

At a flower stand by the metro station, I chose a calla lily and picked a blank card with an envelope. At the café counter next door, I wrote my message:

> "On my eyelash hangs a star, it is so bright, how can I sleep—
> I always want to play with you. I have no homeland—
> we are playing King and Prince."
> Call me right away, Scheherazade. I want to hear
> the tales of your adventures.   —Lou

I was sure Claude would recognize the quote from a German poet she adored. She would call.

I slipped the card into the envelope, filled my Sancerre bottle with a bit of water for the lily, and walked over to Claude's building. The façade was poorly preserved, the sandstone dirtied with a film of gray, but the windows still had their cast-iron balustrades of a better era. When the massive *porte cochère* (for horse-drawn coaches) sprang open, one had to cross a barely lit passageway to reach a grubby central courtyard. Several staircases led to maze-like side wings and the back building. There was no concierge. I leapt up four flights of *Escalier C* and placed the flower with my card in front of the door, to be discovered, if not by Claude herself, then by some other member of the collective.

But skipping down the stairwell with its spotted, peeling walls, I was hit by doubt even before I set foot again in the courtyard with its garbage cans. What if Claude didn't stay at her place, having moved in with her guy or whoever the lucky one was? I went back up and rang the bell. Nobody answered. My lily in its Sancerre vase seemed lonely like a bottle in the ocean.

I went back to the café to dial Christiane's number. She picked up.

She must have heard in my voice that I was troubled. She had time for a chat.

A winding path through weeds and bushes of a *terrain vague* led to Christiane's house between ramshackle buildings. I love the expression *terrains vagues*, pieces of property that are neglected, forgotten, often of indefinable shape, brooding somewhere, nowhere, between streets and housing blocks. Whatever growth appears on the hard-pressed dirt of these places (where the locals walk their dogs) has an arid, uncultivated charm and is a relief in a polished city like Paris. I used to bring big bunches of summer lilac up to my attics, as nobody minds flower thieves in a *terrain vague*. Parisians couldn't care less what nature offers them in abundance, for free.

I stroked the head of the stone elephant that stood guard at the cobblestone entrance to Christiane's villa, waiting for her to answer the door. I had to get used again to lowering my gaze to take in her small frame in the opening.

"Thank God you don't have a tan!"

She looked puzzled. "Is that out of fashion now?"

It was absurd to think of sunbathing and Christiane's life by night in the same breath. I bent down and kissed her right and left cheek. "Apparently Claude is back and fabulously tanned," I said with a dose of sarcasm.

"Apparently?" she repeated. "Oh dear."

"It seems to be a conspiracy. But Aicha lies so poorly that I've smelled the rat. It unnerves me. I'll end up *parano*!"

Parano, the Argo expression for paranoid, is as inevitable among Parisian women as the café au lait that creates their liver problems. The same way Germans are suspicious of drafts, the French are *parano* about their liver. In addition, of course, my friends, the PATs, had the problem of the OWLs, which made them particularly *parano*.

We passed her kitchen and the big glass door that led into her studio. It could have been a salon in a manor house, a square room with a high stucco ceiling. Every surface, whether the desk or the grand piano, was stacked with books, journals, piles of paper. There were vast floor-to-ceiling bookshelves, stuffed and probably never dusted. The French door that separated the forest of books from the wildly overgrown garden at the back was opened only twice a day when Christiane stepped out to feed the wild cats. The window front, partly closed with dark velvet curtains, let in smoky rays of light, a sort of cathedral light—a perfect fit, I thought, with the work that went on here every day, from late noon onward.

Christiane showed me a bird's nest that had fallen out of a tree at her country house. Of course she had tried to maneuver the nest back into the tree. She opened a book with drawings of bird nests to get my opinion. Too small for a robin, too big for a finch? Then she was eager to hear my story.

"Rumor has it that Claude's suddenly with a guy." I reported what I had overheard as we settled on a little sofa that was relatively free of papers. "Do you suppose that's possible?"

"With men many things are easier," she said, taking off her glasses.

"She'd soon be bored."

"Because?"

"Faking." I saw her puzzled expression. "His."

"I see. Ejaculation doesn't equal orgasm, does it?"

I laughed. How quick she was.

"The best-kept secret," she nodded.

"Men, women, whatever—what I want is the everlasting flash of lightning," I said.

She seemed unsure whether I was joking. When I shrugged she fell quiet. The brightness in her eyes went out like a lake hit by a sudden cloud.

"It was never a problem for me to get a guy, you know," she said. "I would simply pick out the object of my sexual interest and hunt him down. But this mobility is utterly masculine, of course. I stole their role from them—"

"Why 'stole'? You told me you believed you were a boy when you were a kid."

"Although once in bed, the thing would turn around again: there I was back in the ugly old role, conquered, vanquished, fucked!"

This was a topic I usually avoided with Christiane. My liking for her was mixed with admiration rather than erotic attraction. At her age and with her celebrated intellect, she was way ahead of me. There was never the slightest chance of our equality, which was perhaps the reason why I never thought of her as a lover. I'd had the same hesitation with Meret Oppenheim, who also could have been my mother, but with Meret I had been in a continuous battle of sexual attraction and ambivalence.

"With a woman it's different," she continued. "The mere naked sex didn't suit me. Without love, I found it vulgar. Even humiliating."

"But that's only a question of desire," I argued. "If need be, one simply creates the romance, the adventure, love—whatever. At least for a moment. Long enough." I wasn't sure I liked the way this sounded. Was I talking like a *mec*, a guy? And what if I was?

"*Le fantasme*—maybe." She slowly blew out her smoke. "But fantasy runs into reality sooner or later. Making up stories with the help of drugs, booze, orgies—doesn't all that just avoid what could be real between two people?"

Was she speaking of me?

"Maybe one day you'll realize that these fantasy encounters are the stories you should be writing. Adventure stories, if you like. *Tom Jones, Felix Krull*—who knows?"

I found myself leaning back, crossing one leg over the other. "I don't see it that way. If I stopped chasing after women, what would I have to write about?"

"Keep asking. Sexual conquest has an undeniable violence."

I shook my head. "I deny it. Imagine two equally desiring, equally strong women. Women who have no fear of sex, who can take on any role—or change roles at any moment. There's no violence. Quite the opposite: a shared knowledge, a recognition." I noticed her skeptical look and couldn't stop myself. "The roles are only a game, a costume...to kick up the lust."

There was a silence. I wished we'd get out of this topic.

"This kind of balance is a dream," she said gently. "You are dreaming up the twin myth. If it exists, this soul match, you'll only meet it once in your lifetime. Everything else will remain a power game."

Another silence.

"The speed with which you go through women," she added, "sometimes makes me wonder if you'd recognize her even if she stood right before you."

"I've never yet missed an attractive woman," I said and instantly regretted it.

"Of course, my dear." The Cheshire Cat smile.

"Well, you're right," I said because I wanted to agree with her. "Claude plays a power game with me."

The room seemed to be listening. I heard the cats fighting in the garden.

"And you play along, and you even like it, don't you."

"I want to understand her game. Stay in until I see her cards." Even if

I lose, I added for myself.

She drew on her cigarette, her eyes narrowed. "Perhaps her game is simply theater," she mused. "An intermission between the acts, giving you time—"

"—to prepare myself for the next act?"

"—which she is already directing, keeping you in suspense."

It sounded almost too good to be true.

"I've just left her an irresistible message."

"So you're attempting to do some directing yourself?"

"I think I'll hear from her any minute." I suddenly believed it.

She didn't look convinced. "You've got something to offer her?"

That hadn't occurred to me. I looked at my watch. "I mustn't be late."

I remembered how hard it could be to separate from Christiane. She was a master in delaying conversations she didn't wish to end. I just had to say something like, okay now, it's late, I've got to get going, and in an instant, she would produce a new idea that would captivate me. This time, too. I got up and worked my way backwards as usual, step by step to the big glass door and back into the hallway. I was already approaching the heavy, black entrance door when she launched into her latest project of establishing an international campaign for children's rights. When leave-taking threatens, I thought, she turns into a child herself. She doesn't want me to go. Her eyes say, *Couldn't you stay a bit longer? Don't leave me yet.* And I am generous because I am fond of her, but tonight I can't wait—not if right now Claude is preparing the next act of our theater play.

M O N S T E R

I raced into my building and was almost up one floor when the concierge
called out after me.

"*Mademoiselle! Votre courrier! Un pneu!*"

I hate being called Mademoiselle. I stopped, snatched the light blue
envelope and a stack of mail from her hand and took two steps at a time,
easily outrunning the old clatter-box of an elevator. At my doorstep my
heart was pounding. Don't let me be too late, I pleaded with the telephone.
I downed a glass of water. Eyeing the phone like a snake charmer, I took my
letter opener from my desk and sliced my "pneumatic" telegram open. It was
from my old pal Harmony Nayle from San Francisco, the only person I knew
who was still faithful to the arcane Parisian speed post system. I loved to
imagine the little metal tube shooting through some underground labyrinth
from one post office to another. Whenever Harmony had business at the
Unesco she shot me a *pneu* and usually suggested a rendezvous at her hotel
the same day. Tomorrow, I thought. I distractedly thumbed through a stack
of newspapers, magazines, bills. A postcard from my mother, the usual kind
about the weather, the last tennis tournament, the next trip to some beach
resort...without me. The tug of loneliness I felt—was it hers? She did not
ask about me, not really. She didn't know how to ask about me. I pressed the
bitter feeling back down, out of sight.

The phone rang.

I took a deep breath and lifted the receiver.

"*Comment ça va?*" Tanja's animated voice. "Any news from the asymmetrical haircut?"

"Not right now," I said quickly. "I'm expecting a call from Claude, any minute. I'll call you back later, okay? Sorry..."

"Can't wait to hear about that one! Okay, until later then!"

I had hardly recovered when it rang again.

"Yes?" I said. "Anything else?" But it wasn't Tanja. An odd silence at the other end.

"Lou?"

"Claude! I just hung up with Tanja. And you are calling—fantastic!

I almost thought I'd never...." Get a grip, Lou.

A small laughter like rolling marbles.

"Claude *chérie*, I don't know what got into me. How are you? Tell me the news. No—first of all: welcome home!" I was unable to control myself. This confirmation of my intuition was too much for me. It felt like a victory, a sense that I could foretell everything that would happen between us.

"Thanks," she said. I heard her take a long breath. "I've been far away..."

"I noticed. But you were close, very close, the other night..."

"The other night...?" She sounded clueless. Was this a game she was playing?

"Yes, when you called me—that night, with *stars all over your skin.*"

"You're not going to over-interpret my call, are you? I was stoned out of my mind. You know how I can be."

The rise in her voice and the clipped tone were a warning: if I kept this up, the call would be over in no time.

"You got my message at your place?"

"Exquisite, your calla lily. Made me think of Tamara. *Mille merci*, Lou."

Just as I intended. Tamara de Lempicka's erotic painting of calla lilies was what I'd had in mind. Her voice was dark and mellow again. Her cello voice.

"My pleasure, Scheherazade. So, the news?"

"Lou...I am in love."

I waited, skeptical. "And?"

"I hope you don't mind too much..."

Not mind? What a cute expression for the feelings tormenting me. I took a breath. "Come on, Claude. You know me better than that."

"I know, I know. But listen, I see us—I see the whole thing with different eyes."

"Of course, and so do I. I needed some time to think. But now—"

"Now everything is changed, Lou." A snap of scissors in her voice.

"What do you mean?"

"That we weren't always on the same page is irrelevant now, you know? I'm in a new place..."

I played my cooperative part. "Yes, tell me."

She paused. "Lou, all my dreams have come true."

Good God, I thought, that sounds horrific. Does she have to put it that way? "You mean we can't see each other anymore?"

"No. Of course we can. Just not like before." It was what every woman said when it was over and the outdated lover had to be consoled and a Band-Aid applied. I wasn't going to be the discarded lover with a Band-Aid.

"I see. The other night you wanted to dance with me. You remembered our interview. Stoned as you were, you remembered! You talked about giving each other a chance again—and now you're telling me there's no more desire between us?" I had to laugh at the thought. "We're supposed to bite it all back? That's not so easy, is it?"

A suppressed sigh. "Exactly. Alas."

I instantly picked up hope. The honesty of her stoned phone call was still there, after all. She was laying it on with her new dream lover, but she was torn.

"I've been thinking a lot about you," I said with feeling. "Our favorite games...the red room..."

"I know, I know. You mustn't think of that now."

"Not think of our unbearable erotic attraction?" I, too, could lay it on. "Not think of—"

"Believe me," she cut me off, "the other is even stronger. It's more than enough."

I felt a stab in my back. "Come on, Claudine—there's never enough! You always said it yourself: when we're freshly turned on, we have the greatest capacity to love. We both know this by heart."

"That's true..." Was there a small flutter in the cello strings?

"So there must be a little bit of space left for the two of us, no?"

"I don't know. I just want to concentrate on this right now. Body and soul, you understand?"

"That's not what you wanted with me." I felt hurt. Was she doing it on purpose? *Body and soul!* Right out of kitsch-land.

She hesitated. "Maybe I did want it, maybe not. I can't pull that apart right this moment."

"Yes you can. Go ahead."

"In any case, I know something was missing..."

"And what was that? The one and only *lovey-love*? You aren't going to end up at the Deux Magots, are you?"

Her laughter was mocking. "I can't explain it to you," she said. "I think it best we don't see each other for a while."

"You're that scared of me? I'm not supposed to tempt you—that's what you mean, isn't it?"

Silence. "If you like, Lou. Whatever."

"But which one of you is more scared of me? Tell me the truth!"

"It's got nothing to do with her. Just with myself."

I bit my tongue. So there was no man in the picture.

"You don't want your freedom anymore?" *Are you insane?*

"Exactly. I think freedom is overrated. The more women, the better." The snip-snap scissors. "But it isn't better, it is..."

"With us, it was better, much better," I cut in.

"It doesn't fit me anymore. I want to be her slave!.... Lou? You still there?"

I was too shocked to speak. "Who is she, after all?" I brought out. "You said I don't know her."

"It's better that way. I've already said too much."

"...with few words," I murmured and fell silent.

"Lou?"

"Are you going to Pina Bausch?"

"I've been trying forever to get a ticket. I'm too late...because of my trip," she wailed. "I could kill myself for not having thought of it while I was away."

"Be my guest." I knew the envy eating at Claude because she had only seen bits of Pina on TV.

"What?"

I repeated my offer.

She swallowed. "You...you've got a ticket?" What she meant was, *you're not taking some other lover to Pina Bausch?*

Merci, Christiane, I thought. "Friday in a week. But as you are so scared of me you'd rather not go with me, right?"

"Lou, you're impossible!" Her voice had risen by an octave.

"Afraid so." I punched my fist in the air. "Well then—Friday in a week, half past seven, you know where."

"Théâtre de la Ville," she said as if reciting a prayer. "I can't believe it..."

"And not to worry: I promise to be on my very best behavior." I blew her a kiss through the ether.

After hanging up I sank back—Phoenix, wiped out.

Was I supposed to believe what I just heard? Claude had swept me off the table; no question of another act. Now it was entirely left to me. She didn't want to be disturbed or distracted—a shocking piece of news. *All my dreams come true.* How the hell could someone have taken possession of her, *body and soul?* I was alarmed by my ignorance. What kind of a monster was this woman? *I want to be her slave...* Who was she? And who was Claude?

I saw the reflection of our history in our phone calls, each of us finding ways to distance ourselves when we got burned or bruised. But that night when I thought I'd seen her at La Coupole, I must have called her up, so to speak. She must have caught the vibe of my adventures at the opera and decided to remember me. It wouldn't be the first time. She used to have the fine sense of a hunting dog whenever I got distracted or took a step backwards.

Was this really what I wanted? But why dream up perfection? Claude was as close as I'd ever come to the flash of lightning I was after. Everlasting because the cold air gathering between us always led to the next thunderclap. This time she had imposed a veritable ice age—but how much sweeter the melting would be...

Never mind her way of turning the screw on me. She was fighting her own attraction. We were still talking. We weren't supposed to see each other, but we were going to meet in a week. Eye to eye—and after Pina—everything would change again.

4

THE STRANGER

TEMPLE SEX

I almost arrived late for Kiki's panel discussion, having doodled away an hour in the tangles of one of my dreams.

This time I was running after a suitcase. I knew what was in it—the prize possessions of my childhood. A small net of colored glass marbles, a doll in a Dirndl dress with a white apron, and a kaleidoscope. I was making painful efforts to catch up and get hold of the suitcase. I woke up sweating.

I was sure it had to do with Claude. That doll had a head of dark hair and a cloth body easy to dress and undress. The glass marbles had to be about winning—winning the competition for her favors. But the kaleidoscope? If Claude had taken my pleasure away, maybe she had also robbed me of some childish views I still hung onto.

The little group gathered in Kiki's office turned around to greet me when I rushed in. I stopped short. Among the faces in the circle, the red-haired stranger was looking at me, her eyes almost blinding me.

"Meet journalist Dominique Araki," Kiki introduced her. I reached out my hand but she only performed a short bow. The longer side of her hair went over her cheek like a silk fan.

"We almost know each other already," she said, as if this made a handshake unnecessary. She spoke in a cool, low-pitched voice with a slight accent. At least she remembered me. My hand was seized and shaken by Mary Hobbs instead.

"We also know each other," Mary said, her splendid American

teeth flashing.

"*Enchantée*." Angèle d'Albert touched my hand with the tips of her fingers. She had watchful eyes and dark, chive-like hair down to her shoulders.

Kiki put her arm around me, obviously grateful that she had all her little sheep under her roof. She led us into the conference room where about fifty women were already waiting in stiff rows of chairs. The long speakers' table was set with microphones, note pads, freshly pointed pencils, water pitchers and glasses in Teutonic rank and file.

Dominique Araki, I kept repeating, raking my memory for any hint, as if the repetition of her name could calm my nerves. *We almost know each other already...* Was it really happenstance that Kiki knew the mystery woman? How was she connected to this scene? Perhaps Théo had something to do with it. While I was thinking fast, I noticed that Mary and Angèle d'Albert were veering straight to the chairs at the center of the table. I wasn't sure how to find a position. Kiki aimed for the free chair at one end of the table and with one quick move I took the spot at the opposite end. This way I had Kiki—and next to her, Dominique—in my field of vision.

While Kiki introduced her panel I had time to collect myself and pursue my observations. Dominique Araki was honoring the occasion with a knit ensemble in night blue. It set off her hair like lightning, and her mouth, like a cherry dipped in red liquor. Her single-slit skirt was tight; the jacket edged with white piping at the pockets and lapels. I had already stumbled (metaphorically speaking) over the silk stockings with a blue seam when I followed her from Kiki's office to the conference room. No wonder, with her getup, the eyes of the audience were glued to her. I took in Mary's bulky briefcase and Angèle's Moroccan reticule. Dominique had no handbag; she carried a black French note folder tied with ribbons. I was listening with half an ear to Kiki's effusive apologies for Théo's absence while I registered that Dominique, Kiki, and Angèle were wearing makeup. I was pleased with my own attire—washed-out jeans, jeans shirt, studded belt, and short, supple suede boots.

"Dominique Araki," Kiki said and got my full attention, "here at my side, is just back from Japan. She has been a research assistant at the Sorbonne, has written for a number of journals, and her latest essay, fresh off the press, is a new interpretation of Ingmar Bergman's *The Silence*." French intelligentsia, *très chic*. I'd have to get my hands on that article. *The Silence*

had made an indelible mark on me in my late teenage years. Was she married to someone Japanese? The man with the ponytail?

I noticed several familiar faces; a number of them belonged to American-English circles. Charlie sat next to two other Sinners. She signaled with a head jerk and wink what a whopper it was that "the redhead" was on the panel with me.

"For starters," Kiki said. "I think we are all aware that we've been discussing women's sexuality forever and we still don't have any conclusions. Is sexuality gender-specific, immutable, or transcendable? Nature or culture? Sacred or profane? So let's go back to the earliest sources and see what we've got." Kiki paused and cleared her throat. "I want to thank everyone for attending our discussion today. It proves to me—with all the partying going on everywhere in town and country—that we are still..." her voice caught and she had to pause again, "...still remembering our intellectual pursuits!"

"In the temple of amorous pursuits," Dominique added, looking straight ahead, poker-faced. Just in time, I thought, to keep Kiki from getting sentimental.

"Indeed!" Kiki joined the friendly laughter and shook herself into gear. She cut a historical arc through our topic to the popular notion of a "sacred marriage" between a priestess and visitors to her shrine, which was seen as the universal root of temple prostitution in the Ancient World.

Almost instantly, discord rumbled. There were sniggers when Kiki mentioned the "big whore" of Babylon from the Bible.

"Sacred marriage sounds fishy to me," I threw in. "Just the thing male historians would make up."

"But we know that every spring Persephone returned from the underworld," Angèle argued, "to assure fertility with that sacred rite."

I looked over at Dominique. "She's just back from her abduction and rape by Hades, and that's celebrated with another rape, called 'sacred marriage'?"

"Barely veiled pornography, you mean?" Dominique looked back at me with a glint in her hard-to-read eyes. There were appreciative chuckles in the audience. Was she making fun of me? After her provocative reaction to my reading for the Sinners, I expected her to contradict everything I said.

The discussion got bogged down over the questionable historical sources. Kiki, Mary, and Angèle battled back and forth over Herodotus and the like. The room was growing restless. The fact was, we didn't have any facts. Finally Kiki raised the question: what were the women in the temple doing if they weren't sexually servicing men?

"Practicing parthenogenesis," I suggested for fun.

"Right on!" someone called out.

"Ridiculous!" someone else countered.

"Believe it if you can," Dominique remarked, cutting me another glance. Was she throwing me the same gauntlet?

"Well, we can't say what sexuality for women was like." Mary swayed her curly head. "We always end up with what we already know, and can't get beyond."

"But we can still detect our natural sexual voice within us," Angèle declared. There was a murmur and shuffling that told me the PATs were on their guard. "We just need—"

"Good ears?" Dominique proposed. She bent her ear toward Angèle, and her hair fanned out over her cheek again. I grinned to myself. I wasn't her only target.

Angèle ignored the joke. "We need to go to the bottom of our suppressed drives." She was leaning forward as if to eat up her microphone. The murmurs got louder.

Kiki nodded eagerly. "Gender is a fantasy, as Simone de—"

"Aren't we all a fantasy?" Dominique stuck a silk-stockinged leg out from under the table. "I know I am!"

The audience laughed. Was she trying to keep things from sliding down a slippery slope or speeding them in that direction? I liked her daring. Go for it, I thought. Drive it to the bottom!

"I think we are getting a bit off track." Kiki nervously moved her glass to the side. Her years in Paris still hadn't accustomed her to the hotheadedness of French women. "Let's get back to imagining the temple before..."

"Why don't we have the temple right here? Right now?" came from the corner of the Sinners.

"This is a serious discussion," Kiki turned to us for support.

"We must take an analytic view," Angèle demanded. Mary nodded encouragement.

Was that a look of cross-eyed, comic despair coming at me from Dominique? I stopped listening and rummaged through my memory files, going over a list of paintings. Which Modigliani? Or was it a Matisse after all? I was probably in the wrong file cabinet. Was it some long-eyed actress? Dominique Sanda? Charlotte Rampling? Which face had imprinted itself on my memory to make her seem familiar? But eyes of such icy intensity?

I heard Dominique say: "Japanese men think the sex they get from a geisha is better than any other." I pricked up my ears. What had I missed?

"*D'où tu parles?* Speak for yourself!" the audience reprimanded her.

"Nobody here has spoken for herself," Dominique countered, "except me." She stretched out her leg again. I felt like applauding. She clearly knew the rules of French debates and was mocking them. "If everything we say here has to be a personal confession, why don't we start—"

"Let's do it! Let's start!" A pink-headed woman leapt from her seat. "Let's do it in the road!" She pretended to pluck away at a rock guitar. Some women applauded, others tried to shush her. I would have preferred to hear what Dominique had to say.

"Nothing is gained if women turn into men and have sex like men!" Angèle shouted, her chive-hair flying.

"Outdated!" "Nonsense!" "Speak for yourself!" I noticed that some women in the back were getting up.

"I think we are aware that all of us come from very different positions to this topic," Kiki raised her voice to control the agitation. She was sending an alarmed glance in my direction. Angèle looked miffed; Mary nodded.

"I find it interesting," I said to help Kiki out, "that nobody today has yet said the word lesbian."

I heard an American voice amid general approval, "You go, girl!" Dominique was leaning forward, one elbow on the table, to get a good look at me, and I suddenly had no idea where I was going.

"These women, or priestesses, were clearly practicing with each other in their temple. They had to be the best lovers around!" I read in Kiki's expression that this was not exactly helping her.

"How can you prove that?" Angèle asked and was promptly booed.

"Desire doesn't care who the best lover is," Dominique said as if to herself. We all looked at her, perplexed.

"Proof?" I couldn't stop. "Women just know what's what. Eros wins! Our passion wins out through the sheer force of desire, with unpredictable consequences!" I had to shout the last words into the microphone in order to get through the eruption of mirth. I hoped for Dominique's applause as well, but she sat there with a pensive, vulnerable expression.

There were debates in every row, as if the line between the panel and the audience didn't exist. Kiki tapped on her microphone to call the room to attention, "Please! Would you please—ladies, please!"

"Ladies please, ladies please!" Two women in dungarees started to dance in the aisle. A few others joined them at the back of the room. Three women stormed up to the seated panel. One of them took hold of Dominique's microphone.

"PATs! Down with the traitors of the OWLs!"

"Kiki!" I called out and gestured for her to shut off the microphones.

Kiki waved to the technician. He didn't react. Angèle still had time to shout back. Mary tried to convince the three intruders to leave the stage but was forced to use her briefcase to defend her own microphone. Dominique suddenly tore off a strip of paper from her notepad, scribbled on it, and held it up to me in between the struggling bodies. She turned her silver-ringed fingers against each other to propose exchanging phone numbers. I nodded, grabbing my notepad and pencil, signaling her to wait a sec. I first had to rush over to Kiki, who had stepped to the edge of the stage in a panic to get the technician's attention. I put my arm around her.

"Terrific!" I exclaimed. "You'll be in the paper tomorrow."

At this moment, the microphones were shut off.

"Why don't you just tell them goodbye?" I said.

Kiki swung her arms like a tarmac guide. As she had long arms and her mane of hair looked wild, the women began to leave the room, excitedly pursuing their discussions. Angèle was surrounded by a cluster of OWLs who approvingly tapped her on the shoulder. It struck me, not for the first time, that they all looked alike—long hair and long skirts with high-heeled boots. Mary and a little troop of Americans tried to calm down the *parano* PATs. I was relieved to see Kiki being addressed by a group of young admirers, while Charlie and company were pushing up to me with broad grins and thumbs up. I quickly wrote my phone number on a page I tore off my notepad, but when I turned to hand it to Dominique, she had already left.

THE SILENCE

Kiki and I went to lunch at Café Wolfgang, a German place near the Goethe Institute that would soothe Kiki's nerves. I wanted to assure her that her panel was a success, that the skirmishes of the day had made an impression on everybody, myself included.

Café Wolfgang was the ultimate in *Gemütlickeit*, German cozyness—carpeted in beige, the walls in rosewood silk with little rosy lampshades, dense muslin curtains at the windows. The menu proposed expensive versions of traditional German dishes, like *Kassler mit Sauerkraut*. A glass case displayed towering buttercream tarts. Ever since leaving Germany, I had felt liberated from petty curtains and hefty tarts, but the chocolate monster on the top shelf was undeniably sexy with its wet frosting.

A few lunch customers had taken newspapers from a rack, turning the pages around stiff wooden holders. My left-wing German papers weren't on that rack. *Stern, Die Welt, Die Zeit*—conservative papers only. We settled in little upholstered chairs far enough from the curtains, but in easy reach of a waitress in a stiff apron and cap that made her look like a nurse.

Kiki told our nurse-waitress how to take care of us, clearly relieved to be in a safe place.

"Look at those Loden," she nudged me. Two couples were getting out of their long, elegant coats, dark blue for the ladies, hunter's green for the gentlemen. "Haute couture Loden," she whispered. "Several thousand a piece, I've seen them in Munich last fall." While the coats were heaped onto the arms of another waitress, we talked about our mothers' unfulfilled desires for such high-end Loden. Then, finally, I was able to sound Kiki out about Dominique Araki who hadn't waited for my phone number.

Kiki had no idea if Dominique was married to a Japanese man. Mary had introduced her as someone with "unusual ideas." Kiki had done some research and found a few of her articles, which she liked. Dominique's Sorbonne connections had naturally weighed in her favor.

"She does look fabulous, doesn't she?" Kiki said. "That Chanel ensemble was a dream! But I found her a bit cold. And provocative." She picked the endives from her salad and moved them aside.

"Without her, Angèle would have babbled us to death with her 'women's true nature.'"

"But she has a point..."

"'Aren't we all a fantasy!' She's quite the player, no? Really cocky." I forked up a few of the endives from Kiki's plate.

"That was pretty original. True. But what a pity things weren't a bit more serious. I would have liked to hear what she meant by 'human desire doesn't care who the better lover is.' If you hadn't interrupted right then—"

"Kiki! You'd never have managed to get a German discussion going. Not with these women. You know that."

She looked stricken. "But why?"

"Come on, we happily went into battle, and your audience was thrilled. That's what counts."

"Maybe you're right. I've got to let go of my German ideals." Her eyes wandered around the café and I knew what she was taking in—the quiet. People politely leaning in at their tables to keep their voices low. Even avoiding the clicking and clacking of their cutlery. Everyone so considerate of the social space that none was left, just isolated islands of good behavior. Nobody jumping out of their fauteuils with excitement and holding forth, arms rowing and cigarette ashes snowing to the floor.

"Our cursed perfectionism," I said, thinking that half the stifled people at these lunch tables could have been my family.

"Why do we still cling to it?"

"Because of our less-than-perfect past?"

Kiki sighed. "Anyway, what do you think she was saying about desire?"

"I was wondering, too. Desire is one thing, reality another?"

"No, I think it means one can't help it if one likes men."

I laughed. "*D'où tu parles*? Does that console you?"

"Oh, sometimes it unnerves me, this eternal *d'où tu parles*! Before one can make any kind of statement, one has to start with Adam and Eve and justify what one intends to say! That's also perfectionism. But tell me, please: what is one to do if one can't overcome one's heterosexual inclinations? Always feel excluded?"

I lit a cigarette. "Look around. I can see any number of women managing to be included."

Kiki looked around. I grinned at the idea of Café Wolfgang's rich expatriate women going wild with each other, turning the place into a lesbian den.

The nurse-waitress was guiding a tea trolley with desserts to a table. Kiki tried to get her attention with a little wave.

"I've never longed for, let' s say, poppy cake because I just prefer banana cake," she laughed at her Freudian metaphor. "So how am I supposed to long for poppy cake all of a sudden?"

"My friend Tanja—she's in analysis, you know—would say: if Freud was right, we've all been polymorphously perverse as children. Ready for any cake."

Kiki frowned. After a while, she said, "Still, Dominique Araki is a riddle to me. She looks as if she's into men, but her article about *The Silence* contradicts that. It's pretty sexy, I tell you." She blushed and fanned herself with her napkin.

"You've got that article? Could I see...?"

"Hold on." Kiki rummaged in the document case she had brought along. She pulled a photocopy from a plastic folder. "Here."

"'*Broken Silence*,'" I read the title out loud. "'Ingmar Bergman's shocking film seen from today's perspective.'" I eagerly scanned the first page and quoted a few words that stood out. "'Alienation as a hallmark of modernism... European police controlled the age of moviegoers.'"

"Police! Remember, *Lolita* was censored, too! Can you imagine?"

"Sure," I said, "Bergman broke every taboo. That nymphomaniac sister and the crude sex scene in public, and the other sister, a lesbian who masturbates—" I stopped as Kiki cast a worried look at the nearby tables. "And the dwarfs who dress up a little boy as a girl to have fun." I remembered how avidly I had taken in every detail of the film, thrilled by the fact that all good Germans must be falling out of their seats, while I was falling head over heels in love with the actress who played the lesbian sister. "Aha, here goes," I continued. "'From today's point of view the good father-identified sister and the bad, rebel sister are trapped in the same cage, longing for the love of the patriarchal father.'"

I wondered if Kiki was still trapped in such a contradiction. Good Girl and Rebel Girl. I was neither one anymore. I was free, wasn't I?

The trolley of cakes came rolling up to our table.

"*Eine Tasse Kaffee, die Damen?*" The nurse-waitress must have overheard our German conversation, addressing us as compatriots.

"They only serve filtered coffee," Kiki said under her breath.

"*Guter deutscher Kaffee!*" the nurse-waitress assured us, raising her white porcelain coffee pot. I accepted with dismay. "Good German coffee" was one of the many things I had luckily escaped. Kiki chose a twisted puff pastry filled with sweet cream, a Schillerlocke, the baked equivalent of a corkscrew lock from the head of our classical poet. I opened my mouth to say, "A slice of your chocolate tart for me, please, with whipped cream," when I realized this was the Good Girl at my mother's Sunday coffee hour, always producing an ecstatic appetite where there was none. I stopped myself in time. Enough already. I sipped the sour-tasting coffee and hastened back to Dominique's page.

"Where were we? Oh yes." I read, "'Bergman preempts the sexual revolution, but the two sisters repeat the traditional dichotomy of Madonna and whore, here in the variation of the intellectual and the whore.'" I looked at Kiki. "All good and well, but not exactly new or sexy."

"Further down. You'll see."

I leapt over several more paragraphs. "'Anna, the sex-crazed rebel sister, witnesses the brutal honesty of sex right next to her in the variety show she has wandered into. She exits with disgust. Unconscious of her self-loathing, she goes to pick up her next anonymous lover. Unable to face herself, she can't leave her cage...'" I pictured hordes of women in Paris and beyond, breaking out of their father-dominated cages, storming the citadel with their desires. "'The era of Bergman's morality landscape is long gone.' Excuse me: The era of a landscape?"

Kiki waved off my question and urged me on.

"'As a filmmaker today,'" I read, "'if I wanted to show a contemporary Anna, I would not place her in a somewhat pornographic Punch and Judy show.'"

"Was that what it was?"

I shrugged and went on. "'I would show my modern, liberated heroine at the opera. A sexy opera like *Don Giovanni* or *Così fan tutte*. Anna would notice two shadows in a seemingly empty loge. The shadows turn out to be two lovers. The young woman with an afro is hardly visible in the loge because of the dark color of her skin.'" I stared at the page. "Beg your pardon? When did she write this?" I stubbed out my cigarette, tipping over the ashtray and spilling ash onto the white tablecloth.

"No idea." Kiki helped slap at the ash with her napkin. "Why? It just came out."

I scanned the next few sentences and made a quick decision. I wasn't going to reveal to Kiki that I was personally affected, to put it mildly. I swallowed and went on: "'But her exposed legs contrast with the dark pants of the person she is straddling. Her skirt has ridden up. Intrigued, Anna raises her opera glass. She observes the couple with avid curiosity. Like in a regular lap dance—'"

"Right, what's a lap dance?"

I was glad for Kiki breaking in just then.

"An erotic dance on the lap of a client in a strip club."

"Who is on the lap of whom? Oh, I see...but that's called a dance?"

I ignored Kiki's bewildered expression. I took a breath, determined to stay detached and find the whole thing amusing. *With avid curiosity....* Was this Dominique speaking for herself?

"'Like in a regular lap dance,'" I repeated, "'the two bodies move and circle, rise and sink, following Mozart's music. Anna is enchanted, turned on.'" I couldn't help feeling my heartbeat rise. This wasn't amusing after all. It was "strong tobacco," as the German language would have it. I gulped a drink of water. "'But just like in Bergman's theater loge, the woman throws herself backward as she climaxes, and for a second, her partner—a woman—comes into view.'" I stopped and stared. Blindly.

"See what I mean? Don't you find this sexy?"

"This sounds too bloody real for my taste!" I blurted out. "How dare she?"

Kiki looked at me, taken aback. There was a hush in the café. Every movement had stopped around us. Some people eyed us, but nobody turned their heads. A whole café full of Good Girls, it struck me, all frozen in place.

"It sounds as if she really saw this and now commits the indiscretion of making it public!" I was unable to control my voice.

"No way!" Kiki snatched the article from me, shaking her mane as if to shake the German customers back to life. "How can you take this for real? She just transposes Bergman into a modern scene, nothing more!" She kept her voice down and I heard the discreet rustling of newspapers and the murmur of voices picking up again. "She's got imagination! Don't tell me this is too sexy even for you?!"

My perplexed face must have given her enough of an answer. Kiki had no idea how little imagination Dominique Araki had used for this scene. That she had observed it in such detail put me over the edge. I automatically reached for Kiki's untouched Schillerlocke and wolfed down a good half. Kiki smiled approval at my enthusiasm for the pastry of our homeland. Should I be embarrassed or gratified? Dominique had noticed me, spotted me with her opera glass, and somehow tracked me to the loge.

Anna is enchanted, turned on…

I let Kiki have her victory. Delighted, she took her turn reading Dominique Araki to me. She let her hair hang close to the page as if to draw a curtain around us.

She read now, "'Anna is not sure: is it a man? With hardly a break, the same dance begins again, and Anna is not going to rush from her opera loge with revulsion. The co-option of culture for sexual pleasure is an obvious concept for her.'" Kiki raised her head. "I love this! 'The co-option of culture for sexual pleasure.' This really says a lot, if you ask me."

I wasn't asking, so Kiki let her hair fall down again and continued, lowering her voice, "'Anna feels invited to watch. She can't turn her eyes from the couple. She waits for the moment when the lover becomes visible again. The act is long; drawn into this melting of music and eros, Anna melts. She lets her opera glass sink. A tear rolls down her face as the young woman with the Afro gets up, rearranges her dress, and leaves the loge.'" Kiki's voice caught in her throat. "'But now Anna, the modern heterosexual woman, asks herself: is it possible that she is aroused by the coupling of her own sex?'"

I was speechless, at a loss. What did this mean? Was Dominique Anna, was Anna Dominique? A woman who had not yet discovered women? I didn't know what to think of her. All I thought was, I need to get out of here. I've got to go. I can't keep up this charade and hide from Kiki how troubled I am and how thrilled.

"See?" Kiki said. "You're impressed! You wouldn't have expected this from Dominique Araki, right?"

I had to laugh. "You're absolutely right," I said, giving in. "I would never in the world have expected this."

Kiki gathered up the papers, satisfied.

"Do you happen to have another copy?"

"I can copy it for you at the office, if you have time."

"Great. But then I'll have to get going. My old friend Harmony from San Francisco is in town."

With the copy of Dominique Araki's voyeur confession in my Vespa pocket, I hurried to my rendezvous. Driving fast, fast...

HOTEL LUTETIA

The moment I saw Harmony's kind beaver face with its little crow feet of laughter, I relaxed. I kicked off my shoes and joined her on her bed. Harmony was eager to tell me about her latest affairs and ask about mine. As an expert in business mediation, Dr. Harmony was notoriously curious. She wouldn't do with vague answers; she demanded details. At a women's film festival in Amsterdam, where I'd met her, she had approached everyone in the hallways to find out which sex toys they were already using in "backward Europe." Most women had never heard the old adage that "independent orgasms guarantee independent thinking." Hammie (I'd given her the nickname because she had a charming way of showing off) should have become a sex educator. She was convinced her Californian origins predestined her to be avant-garde. No matter what she heard from European women, Hammie's comeback would be, "In San Francisco, that's already old hat, dahling."

Hammie showed me "the latest" from San Francisco: silver spheres, big as dove eggs, that fit into any body opening, and of course Hammie had a story about one such silver egg that had given rise to a wild chase after going missing in action. Hammie's pneumatic missives and our ad hoc trysts were dear to me, but truth be told, after the recent events and Kiki's revelations over lunch, my thoughts were somewhere else. I distractedly embraced Hammie's luscious, almost fifty-year-old body and kissed the white strand of hair that fell in a jaunty wave to her eyebrow, reminding me of an Oxford boy. She proudly introduced her "double-horned goddess"—a vibrator of gigantic dimensions, but when she saw my doubtful look she stopped.

"Where are you, honey? Far away, I'd say."

"I know, I've been in a funny mood lately. Sorry to be so boring..."

"Nonsense!" She stuffed the double-horned goddess behind a pillow. "We've known each other long enough. Anything goes. I can tell your head is filled with trouble. I noticed it the minute you came in. Is it still Claude?"

"Claude again," I said guiltily. And now Dominique, I added to myself, but how was I going to explain all my mixed feelings in one short afternoon? Tell Hammie about Dominique Araki's journalistic homage to my opera escapade? She would insist on seeing the essay and make me translate every word. There was no way. I needed to talk about Claude. I needed to complain.

"She's driving me crazy."

"Wait, I'll order a snack for us and then we'll have your confession."

Hammie slipped on a striped robe and insisted on placing her order with the concierge in French. I went to the bathroom and threw some water over my muddled head. Where to start?

It took time for Hammie to get her rudimentary French to the other end of the phone line. Her order of Champagne with *jus d'orange* was misunderstood as "just oranges." She had to repeat it a number of times. Then, undeterred, she ordered Waldorf salad, but I could have told her that her "wooldur sellahd" wouldn't stand a chance. I knew better than playing prompter or taking the receiver out of her hand. Hammie had no greater passion than the French language for which she was as deaf as a mule. After a while (I politely closed the bathroom door behind me), a fully laid table was rolled into the suite. We lolled in bed with the Champagne, orange juice, and Salade Niçoise. I told her about my jealousy after the ice age Claude had imposed for no reason I could think of, unless it was to take some sort of revenge on me—in short, my "Claude complex."

"Dahling Louise," Hammie said and stroked my wet hair. "Such a dramatic change of heart doesn't come out of nowhere. I'm speaking from experience. I don't see a revenge in any of this, honest. If anything, I see hurt feelings. You somehow managed to upset the poor girl, and that's why she backed out and jumped so readily into her new *amoureux*. Moreover, with someone who is your exact opposite: possessive and butch and—"

"Hey, you saying I'm not butch?"

Hammie teasingly took hold of my chin. "You are an in-between, a *garçon-fille*, an eel of the slippery sort—the worst. You won't commit. Your Claude, however, seems eager to be under lock and key."

I grimaced. "But Claude and I were both known—should I say notorious?—for wanting anything but."

"Ha! Being notorious can be quite exhausting. I speak from experience." She swung her salad fork like a piece of evidence. "Once I even...but never mind. Lust doesn't go AWOL all of a sudden, with no warning. What happened? What crime did you commit?"

I slid deeper under the covers and pulled the sheet over my nose. "It's all my fault?"

"Jewish-Christian guilt is at least an appeal to reflect a bit." She put her glass on the night table, leaned back, and tapped on her shoulder. "Come here to big mama and out with the truth."

"I haven't done anything to her," I protested and greedily inhaled the warmth of her skin. I tried to snuggle my face into the fold between her arm and breast. She gave me a smack on the back of my head.

"Concentrate! I want to get that story. Now. When exactly did the climate change?"

After the red room, I wanted to say, but I couldn't speak. My throat suddenly clammed up. A wave of pain rose from my belly. Before I knew it, tears poured from my eyes. I hid in Hammie's arms, shaken by sobs.

"Yeah, yeah," she murmured every now and then.

I was in the grip of something I couldn't name. What had happened in the red room? Why did I recoil from going back to those feelings? Had I fallen in love and let my hopes go wild? What had Claude done to me? What had I done to her?

"It's all over," I brought out. "I'm not cut out for love. I give up."

"What's underneath all that? You can't mean that everything comes apart because of Claude?"

"Yes, it's all a mess. I'm no match for Claude. I'm no good in Paris. Not anymore. I'm bored with everything. The Katmandou is dead, dead as a rat. The damn parties are a bore, women are a bore—I can't stand it. I mean, what's it all for? What is Paris for, after all?"

"Paris? Honey, you want to go back to Germany?"

I was shaken by another wave of despair. "Have I ever found what I was looking for? Do I even know any more? Freedom, sex, sex, sex, and so what? Am I ever going to be a real writer? I am just repeating myself, nothing new, all old. I was always supposed to be the muse for everyone—my mother, Frantisek, every guy, Stéphane, of course, and even Claude, with her troupe and always her need for new ideas! But what about me? Why can't I—"

"Dahling, this is way bigger than Claude! It can't be that the world comes to an end because—"

"You've no idea what it was like, always being turned on, even when we were mad at each other." I had to come back to the cause of my tears. "I thought I had it all with her, but now I have nothing and I can't go on, I can't. Nothing feels real." I looked up at Hammie who dabbed at my cheeks with the edge of the top sheet. "I can't explain it..."

"There's always an explanation," Hammie said consolingly. "It'll come to you, don't worry. It always does, it always comes through tears."

"Okay, it's all my fault," I said miserably. "She got back at me because I rejected her...more than once." I pulled a bunch of Kleenex out of the box on her bed stand.

"See? I told you. You are a very naughty, slippery eel and you deserve to get your ears pulled." She tenderly plucked at my earlobe.

I blew my nose. "How can one be so hot one day and so put off the next? I am always torn, always running after her or running away. My friend

Tanja says there has to be some old story behind it, but there isn't. Unless it was our trip to the south of France..."

"Your trip to Nice? You didn't say much about it last time we met."

"She had to look after her mother, so I went down with her. I thought it would be a really sexy trip, but it wasn't." I fought down another sob. "She got on my nerves because I wasn't used to being around her from morning to night. But it wasn't that. She was suddenly different."

"Different?"

"I don't know—in a romantic daze all of a sudden, making dog eyes at me all day long, you know? Always waiting for something, something huge, gargantuan, that I was supposed to be feeling for her..."

"Oy vey," Hammie said and yawned.

"Tired?"

"Nah, just a bit of jetlag."

"Listen, you don't have to come to the ballet with me tonight. Maybe you'd better get some sleep?"

"I have to be in Brussels tomorrow morning, but don't worry. Go on."

I lit a cigarette to stop myself from getting teary again. "I wanted to have sex, be blown away, you know? Have sex in olive groves, in lavender fields, in—"

"I can see that. With a burned backside to boot! Here, have another glass of Champagne and get it out. Don't sidetrack!"

I obediently drank. "How to describe it? I was in love with Nice. The crazy crickets all day and night... And the Corniche, you know? That steep road at the edge of the rocks, with the fog blasting up from Morocco or Gibraltar. It was like a drug, watching this fog melt into the heat, turning blue..."

"Ah yes, *la belle Midi*," Hammie sighed. Gender confusions of French nouns were a specialty of hers that usually cracked me up. Not this time.

"*Le beau Midi!*"

"I know," Hammie consoled me. "Go on, dahling."

"We were stared at. When we walked along the road, our arms around each other, women waved to us from their cabriolets and shouted something…"

"Very romantic!" She gave me a loving, skeptical look. "Is that the story?"

"Yes. I don't know. Every time she visited her mother she was in a weird mood. Clingy like a wet sweater. But then she didn't want to have sex because I was 'just greedy.' One night we went down to the beach. There was a little cove, in the dark, and I really wanted her. She was indignant: 'Here? In public? Are you kidding?' As if her mother was there on the beach!"

"Mm-hmm!" Hammie said.

"It didn't make sense. We got into a fight, but she wouldn't or couldn't explain it. Finally, I let on that I needed some breathing room. 'No problem,' she said, 'why don't you leave—I should really take care of my mother.'"

I heard Hammie's soft snoring. So what? My story didn't explain anything. Maybe my friends were right. I was hiding something from myself in this obsession. How else to explain that by the time my train reached the Rhône Valley and was heading back north, barely an hour after my departure from Nice, I already felt the relief, the freedom…and immediately longed again for Claude?

D É J À   V U

My radio deadline was kicking in. I drove over to the
Rostand first thing in the morning, dredging up my
Teutonic discipline. I had to pull off a review of a dance
performance that had swooshed by me almost unnoticed the previous night. Hammie hadn't shown up at
the theater, but sent a morning *pneu* to say goodbye.
My eyes still felt raw from crying. Why break down
over Claude when I was going to see her so soon? All
night I had been running in my dreams. All around me
walls were crumbling, arcs buckling. There were whole
streets—German streets—in ruin. But I had no time
to wonder what the hell was the matter with me. My broadcast was
scheduled for the late afternoon.

After a double espresso to get me going, I forced out a first draft,
then, relieved, cleared a corner of my table for breakfast. A corner wasn't
good enough for Pierre. He waited disapprovingly for me to clear newspapers and notes out of the way and make room right in front of me. What a
French waiter serves is of central importance, *s'il vous plaît!* I liked to resist
the tyranny of French waiters, but Pierre just humphed as if to say, "See? I
could have told you."

Three hours later I scanned my review one more time, preparing to
read my scribbles in the recording studio without stumbling over my words.

Nobody familiar had shown up to interrupt me. I noticed a young couple at a nearby table; students, perhaps. The young man was not addressing his girlfriend; he was holding forth to the space around her. She was hanging onto his every word. The longing and childlike hope in her eyes pained me. I turned my gaze back to the window. If there was one thing I could take from my meltdown with Hammy, it had to be this: stop fanning my hopes in some childish way like this girl with her naked face. Much better to be a cynic than any shade of a naïve dreamer. Expect nothing, especially from Claude, especially now.

It was another typical April day—windy gray with few breaks of sun. I saw people hasten through the Jardin, shivering. A few joggers were doing their rounds, most likely expats. Pink-white petals from the chestnut trees were hurtling through the air before getting stuck on the wet pavement. If I didn't watch out, my leather jacket would dissolve under the onslaught of this weather. I folded up my papers and drove over to one of the better secondhand stores on Rue d'Alésia, in the fourteenth *arrondissement*.

Déjà Vu was owned by two middle-aged ladies of standing: Mme Marie, with her silk turban in multiple shadings; Mme Mathilde, with her black, lacquered (faux) hair bun. Both with a weakness for rouge on their cheeks. I had bought my aviator scarf from them, my suede Robin Hood boots, a motorbike cap that recalled Amelia Earhart (perfect for a day like this), and my theater jeans.

When I parked my Vespa at a lamppost across the street I was struck by a familiar redhead emerging from the store. Dominique Araki was walking up Rue d'Alésia with long strides, hair flying in the wind. She was dressed in a belted trench coat, carrying a big, apparently empty travel bag. I wasn't quite ready to meet her after the revelations of her essay. But how could I let this occasion slip by? I almost called out to her, but the flash of a thought stopped me: she had just unloaded her stuff at Déjà Vu. That I had to see first.

Indeed, a large and a small pile of clothes—one glance told me it was couture fashion—were heaped onto the counter. Mmes Mathilde and Marie, with red faces and even redder cheeks, were already busy arranging the new clothes on hangers and stapling price labels onto them.

"Has this just come in?" I asked, taking off my cap. "Could I have a peek?"

They both nodded mildly, perhaps because the piles promised excellent business, or because they recognized me as a customer. Usually new ware was untouchable until it was on the sales racks. Between the elegant feminine ensembles and blouses, my eye fell on something black, made of leather. I pulled it out from under the pile. *Ça alors!* A black leather jacket. My heart beat faster. The jacket was longer than my usual style but the leather was like silk, had a slate-gray lining and was almost as light as a dinner jacket. A Japanese designer, according to the label. The form was classic, almost military, with a short stand-up collar. I slipped it on and turned in front of the mirror.

"Do you know how much this jacket is going to be?" I asked over my shoulder, smoothing down my hair. No matter how much—I had to have it.

"The jacket is not for sale," Mme Mathilde said. "Sorry."

I turned around, astonished.

"It's damaged."

"A tear at the pocket," Mme Marie explained, a safety pin pressed between her narrow lips.

Startled, I fingered the pockets. True, the left one had a long rip at the corner.

"No problem," I reassured them. "I'll take it anyway." My concierge took on sewing and would manage to repair it.

The jacket was both sensuous and austere, striking and understated. I looked different in it. My battered old jacket was forgotten. A new person had suddenly emerged, sure of herself, ready for anything.

"How much?" I asked.

"We aren't selling this jacket," Mme Mathilde repeated sternly. "We only take impeccable quality."

"But as you already have it here—" I couldn't possibly separate from the jacket. I had just discovered that the collar could be folded up: ideal for the Vespa.

"The jacket only happened to be here because the seller—"

"Mesdames, couldn't you make an exception, just once?" I pleaded, unable to tear myself away. This had to be my new courting jacket. Out into the world, out to conquer Paris all over again!

"You have to understand that we can't—"

"It's okay," a voice I recognized interrupted, and Dominique Araki appeared in the mirror right next to me.

"*Salut.*" We grinned at each other, a bit awkward. Should I feel somewhat caught out?

"Suits you perfectly," she said and let her green gaze wander over my reflection. "Better than me."

"Impossible."

I assumed the right to examine her reflection in turn. She was an inch taller than I, even with flat shoes. She was wearing pants. Diana the Huntress with her trench coat and wind-blown hair, and I in my sexy military look were quite a pair. It didn't hurt that her mouth was once again cherry-red. For a moment we stood there, wordless, facing our image.

"Made to order," she finally smiled.

I had to agree. I took off the jacket and handed it back to its owner. "Unfortunately I can't buy it here. *Mesdames* won't have it."

"I know, the tear."

"I couldn't care less." I felt the dread of having to renounce my desire, being left with the old image of myself.

"Let's do this outside," she said under her breath. "One moment."

I felt a warmth in my blood and face. Hadn't she just come very close? I had caught a whiff of her perfume, a veiled, dusky scent. She had already turned back to the owners and was emptying another bagful of clothes onto the counter. What to make of the fact that Dominique Araki was selling her clothes at a store, my store? I kept "leafing through" the jacket hangers, trying to keep my cool.

For a moment I was struck by a doubt. My jackets were my second skin. Back in my days with Blue I sometimes slept in my jeans jacket. My old leather jacket had been a *trouvaille*, a lucky find from the flea market; it had marked my freedom from Stéphane and now, finally, was at its last seams. Did I really want to walk around in something owned and worn by Dominique? The usual pleasure of secondhand shopping is anonymity, but this was new. It was a challenge. I thought about the chili red ensemble in which I had spotted her first, the tight tiger sweater and the leather belt with its suggestive buckle, the slit, knitted skirt in night-blue. I had sought out the form of her body, the warmth of her skin through these extravagant clothes. I took a deep breath.

While Dominique concluded her business I had time to check out every jacket in the store and even try on a few just to confirm what I already knew: no comparison with Dominique Araki's leather wonder. She finally winked at me and left, the bag with rejected clothes over her shoulder. I thanked Mmes Marie and Mathilde and followed her.

"It's only a few steps to my car," she said. "Next block." We started walking. "What an unexpected meeting."

"Another one!" I faked astonishment. "I can hardly follow up any more. How many is it by now?"

She laughed and I pricked up my ears. It was the first time I heard her laughing. I wanted to hear it again right away—a burst of merriment that held nothing back.

"Is that a rhetorical question?" she wanted to know.

"Do you believe in coincidence?" I asked back.

Her green eyes flashed and narrowed as if trying to pierce my mind. "I find it more amusing not to believe in coincidence."

"But if it's not a coincidence—?"

"Then it's really amusing, no?"

I opened my arms into a cosmic invitation. "Kismet!"

I saw that she was having fun with me. I danced a few steps ahead of her as if Rue d'Alésia were Broadway and I, Bing Crosby. "All lost in wonderland, I'm a stranger in paradise..."

Again she laughed her infectious laugh. I wondered what had taken hold of me.

"If I didn't know you're a journalist I would have taken you for a photo model," I said.

"That's what I once was. I was young enough to be persuaded."

"Any regrets?" I was thinking of my own follies.

"Not at all. It was a fascinating world. Here we are." She opened the door of a glossy gray Citroën, threw in her bag, stood again next to me, and handed me the jacket. "Voilà. A little damaged, but—" her gaze wandered over my old jacket, "it'll hold up a while."

I stroked the smooth leather. "Is it from Japan, like your name?"

"A designer here in Paris. A friend." Not exactly revealing.

"What do you want for it?"

"What do you propose?"

I wasn't fooled by her poker face. Her mouth could hardly hold back her amusement with my dilemma. "I'll invite you to a coffee."

She erupted in laughter. I joined in.

"Agreed," she said, looking mighty pleased. She stuck out her hand as if to seal a contract. "When?"

A pleasant, cool handshake. No joke, I thought, she really means it. Should I delay in order to gather my wits? Invite her to the Rostand some other time? Or perhaps to a more sophisticated café like La Coupole?

"Right now," I heard myself say, already looking around for the red double cone of a Tabac. "I have a radio broadcast scheduled nearby, at five."

"How about afterwards? The cafés around here are pretty awful, aren't they?"

"True." But I was suddenly in a hurry and didn't want to allow us any time to prepare. She might end up changing her mind or once again disappear through some door.

"Rue des Plantes," came to my mind. "Across from Villa d'Alésia. There's a little bistro in the old style, quite tolerable. Just two blocks from here."

"Let's walk," she agreed. "Would you like me to store the jacket for now?" She pointed to her car.

"No thanks. I don't want to let it out of my sight."

"Is that how you feel about everything you have?"

Something in her teasing made me think of Claude. "Only if I'm not sure to have it."

"You aren't thinking that I am going to trick you?" In her flat moccasins she was walking with the same long stride as I. *Vorrei e non vorrei*—Zerlina's ambivalence toward Don Giovanni crossed my mind. "You don't trust me, do you?"

"We almost know each other already, right?" I quoted her ambiguous greeting at Kiki's event.

She laughed again. "But that will now change, won't it?"

I looked at her. She had said it ingeniously, as if wanting to shake hands and make a contract again.

"Now that we have excluded coincidence," she added with apparent merriment.

We had turned onto Rue des Plantes.

"Café Kismet!" I said, holding the café door open for her. She threw me a sideways glance. Again she didn't carry a handbag, a fact that for some reason intrigued me. The café was small and smoky, but one table by the window created a small illusion of air and space. She placed her coat on the chair next to her; I did the same with my two leather jackets. She shook her hair into place and leaned back. I would have loved to stare at her. But now that we were not walking side by side, her challenging gaze was trained on me. It was high time for a cigarette. I dug into my inner jacket pocket for my tobacco and lighter. Dominique pulled a pack of Gitanes filter from her coat and offered it to me. I took one and lit hers and mine. She was holding the cigarette between her middle finger and thumb, which looked *très chic* with her long, groomed, silver-ringed hands. I wondered if one of her rings was a camouflaged wedding band.

A young woman took our order: a Kir for Dominique, espresso and cognac for me.

"Upper and downer," she commented. "For balance?"

"A bit of both," I nodded, noticing that with her, everything except her haircut seemed in balance. A long, narrow waist but also long legs. Slender arms but a well-formed bosom. She was wearing a dove-gray angora twinset and gray corduroy pants. Before sitting down I had stolen a glance at the slim curve of her hips and buttocks.

"Honestly, I still think you can't be serious about the jacket," I said in order to say something.

"No, truly. I was going to get rid of it anyway. The style is a bit too severe for me."

"Exactly right," I stroked the leather admiringly. "Rough and silky—a bit of both."

"The *both-and* jacket." It sounded like good-natured mocking.

"The *both-and* haircut?" I used the same tone.

Like a shadow, a quick expression of discontent passed over her face. "I don't see why one's exterior has to be interpreted as a reflection of the inside."

"No? Soft shell, hard core?" I teased her.

She made a little moue. "What would happen to you if you'd put on something feminine for a change?"

"Nothing," I lied. "Why add on to what I have anyway?"

She laughed briefly and looked down as if she had her own thoughts on the matter. I used the moment to study her face, her mouth with its little upswing in the corners, the oval lines of her cheeks, chin and eyebrows. A shade of tiredness around her eyes that I hadn't noticed before. Something in her face resonated like a song that was on the tip of my tongue without revealing its name. "*La fille aux lèvres de cerise*"—wasn't there a song by that name? "The Girl with the Cherry Mouth"?

I turned to look for our waitress. Our drinks arrived. I lifted my cognac.

"Thanks for the smartest jacket I ever owned."

She clinked glasses with me and smiled like a cat who has just made a good catch. "The pleasure is all mine," she said in English.

Hadn't I made the catch?

"You speak English without an accent," I observed, "but in French I hear something, I don't know what, if I'm not mistaken?"

She bent her head backwards to exhale the smoke sideways over my head without turning her eyes from me. "Family mish-mash," she said. "I didn't grow up in France."

"But?"

"Everywhere and nowhere. My father's a diplomat."

"Japanese?"

"French-Italian." Aha, Modigliani. "My mother is Swiss."

"So you speak Swiss French. And also German?"

"I used to be fluent, but now it's rusty."

I put my hand to my ear to get her to speak.

"Okay," she conceded. "*Ich habe fast alles vergessen...*" It sounded like a poem about forgetting almost everything. Then, with a theatrical flourish of her hands she added the opposite, that nothing had been forgotten: "*Doch nichts, nichts habe ich vergessen!*"

"So much the better," I said. She did sound rusty. I ignored the twitch in the corners of her mouth. Should I care about how much she had or hadn't forgotten? We didn't have much time.

"Where does your Japanese name come from? Are you married?"

"Long ago. In Japan."

I almost asked: and do you regret it? But I was certain I would again only hear that it was "fascinating."

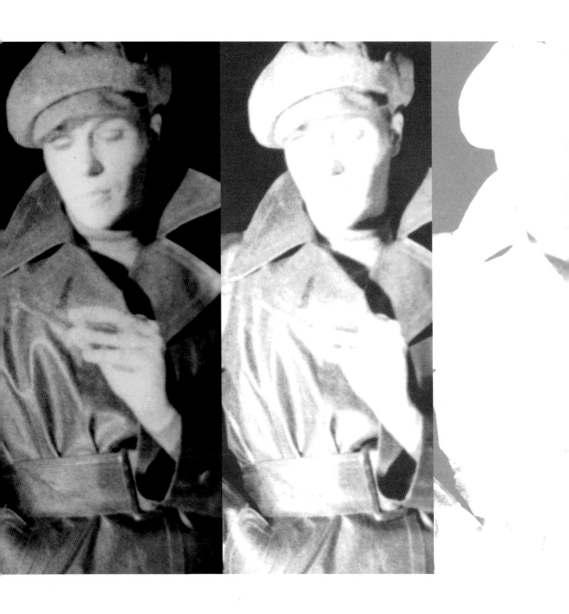

"And now?"

"Now?"

She knew perfectly well what I was after but was stringing me along. Surprisingly, I wasn't irritated. Was her mouth a padded rose? A candied cherry? I couldn't decide. I was fascinated by this mouth, the way it thickened when it closed around the cigarette or the rim of her glass of Kir, or when it hesitated over a word as if hesitating over a kiss. When it wasn't stretched into a smile or laugh, it seemed to hold back all kinds of secret inclinations.

"Are you with women now?"

She rolled her cigarette back and forth between her fingers. "It's got nothing to do with now. But usually—" she seemed amused by the idea, "not in plural."

Well then. We were speaking the same language after all. I wanted to ask about the man with the ponytail.

"I'm never sure," she continued, "why this question of men or women seems so important."

"At this point in history, men are dinosaurs compared to women."

"What does that have to do with desire?"

"I don't deny the certain charm of the dinosaur. To each his or her own."

"That's just ideology—that women are better, or women are better lovers. Women have always tried to look down on men, that's pretty old hat."

"Oh dear, we are back to our panel discussion," I said. "Let's not go there."

"That was hilarious, wasn't it?"

"You didn't laugh a single time!" I heard the reproach in my voice. If she had laughed just once...

"But the audience laughed." As I didn't respond she added, "So it's a taboo subject..."

"Just not particularly fun."

"Oh?" She acted surprised. "It has to be fun?"

"Why repeat? Déjà vus are rarely a turn-on, if you ask me."

She grinned to herself, looking out the window, and said nothing. What did she have to grin about?

I stole a few more looks at her proud neck, the dove-gray angora hills of her breasts, her pale skin, and the brash color of her hair and eyes. I was "editing" her like a text, a bad habit of mine. I can't help shortening or lengthening noses, straightening teeth, or erasing a fringe from a low forehead, according to the aesthetic emergencies of the moment. Dominique's eyes were supposed to be warm, even dreamy, instead of shock-green. At the very least they ought to be a Modigliani color, transparent turquoise, for example.

"Let's talk about opera instead," I said. "Your essay on Bergman was outright flattering."

"Really?" Again her look withheld any information. "Tell me."

"'Anna feels invited to watch. She can't turn her eyes from the couple,'" I recited by heart. "So you felt invited?"

"In public one is always invited to be a voyeur, no?" She watched the ringlets of her cigarette smoke.

"I take that as a compliment," I said.

"My pleasure. I counted on it being flattering."

What a sly, self-satisfied air she had taken.

"I like seeing my reflection in such a mirror." I had no trouble keeping up with her. "Naturally, a good performance depends on a good audience."

She laughed her irresistible laughter. "*Fräulein* Neumann," she shook her head, "you should be writing a *Roman*!" She used the German word for novel. "Are you writing a *Roman*?"

I was baffled. How did she know my name? I wasn't used to hearing my birth name pronounced in stark German. Even less in the tone of my schoolteachers. She was making fun of me. *Roman*, with its echo of "romance" or romantic pursuit, seemed to imply that I was making up stories of a questionable sort. How could she know such subtlety in a language she had more or less forgotten?

"I wouldn't mind some inspiration." I leaned forward like a good student, my elbows on the table. "We've already got the opera scene. What's next? What do you suggest?"

She searched the ceiling while she let her hand with the cigarette twirl around a few times. "In any case a 'both-and' leather jacket. A jacket with an unknown past..."

"*The Secret of the Indefinable Leather Jacket*!" Not bad, inventing a romance together. "And then?"

"Ah, I shouldn't interfere with your creativity. A jacket with a secret can lead to impossible possible developments."

"Like another rendezvous?" I looked at my watch. "One that's not coincidental?"

"Absolutely!" We smiled at each other. She extinguished her cigarette. I felt she was going to say something, but she just watched me while I paid the bill.

"And can we now exchange phone numbers?" I asked. "Before you disappear again all of a sudden, like after the panel discussion?"

"Oh, that..." She was searching her coat and pulling out a pen.

"Why disappear on me like that?"

I could tell she was reluctant to answer me. She avoided my eyes. For a second, I saw her face vulnerable as if a mask were torn away. Two little red spots showed on her cheeks. "You were pretty busy, I thought."

I was puzzled by her embarrassment. While we were writing down our numbers, I explained that I had to rush over to Kiki, who was in a panic. I went a bit overboard, which Dominique signaled with a skeptical, but also, I thought, grateful glance.

On the way back to her car, she suggested I join her for a seminar by a new star of the analytic intelligentsia. I had heard his name, Lacan, from Tanja, who never missed anything new concerning psychoanalysis.

"The avant-garde of dinosaurs?" I asked.

"The dinosaur has something interesting to say about seeing one's reflection in a mirror..." She waited to see if I would take the bait. I grinned and proposed she join me instead for a slide presentation about the women of Surrealism, to be given at a salon.

"Fun guaranteed?" she asked in English, one eyebrow raised. We had arrived at her car.

"Well, maybe not at the level of *Così*." I automatically played along with her language switch.

She pulled her keys from her coat pocket. "*On s'embrasse?*" Back to French. Without waiting for my reply, she quickly kissed me on both cheeks in the French way.

I was left with the feel of her skin, silky tips of hair, and a second whiff of her dusky, veiled perfume.

LAST YEAR IN MARIENBAD

My radio program went well enough, but underneath my controlled voice I felt the agitation. A brief discussion with my "station master" about the events of spring that we might cover, and I hurried off. I was impatient to be alone and make a semblance of order in my mind. Driving down Rue Losserand, I stopped at the Entrepôt. My stomach was clamoring for attention. Leni's Restaurant inside the cinema was empty; the afternoon show was on. I ordered a croque monsieur at the bar.

I was half mad at myself and half pleased. The luxurious jacket hung next to me on the bar stool, a leather-silk companion I could hardly wait to meet. I wouldn't be wearing it before it was repaired, but on the ride I had draped it around my shoulders, not wanting to hurt it on the tight Vespa rack. The leather at my neck and face had felt like the touch of skin. It had been a folly to insist on an ad hoc rendezvous with Dominique, curtailing my chance of finding out more about the stranger who wasn't a stranger any more. The stranger had a husband's name and knew my birth name, probably from Kiki. I didn't like my German details to be known.

Everything I thought about Dominique Araki was instantly contradicted by something else. Her face was familiar; her eyes disturbing, alien. Her laughter was close and inviting. The polished rest of her—hair, clothes, lipstick—created a distance. She was smart and cocksure, then out of nowhere suddenly wounded. I recalled her miffed reaction at my repartee about her "both-and" haircut. Why on earth would she ask if I was writing romances, in that challenging, personal way? The question had left a sting like the gauntlet she had thrown me at the café: *Believe it if you can.* Her provocations raised my desire to challenge her in turn—and carry off the better line of flirtation. Because that's what it was, a flirtatious battle, like two fencers in a courtly ballet.

I hadn't found out much about her. I'd been in a rush, surprised by her strangeness. How could my question about her sudden disappearance from the panel embarrass her? It was I who ought to be embarrassed. Getting caught in front of the mirror, in her jacket, admiring myself. And exchanging a designer jacket for a glass of Kir. It made no sense.

Our image in the mirror, however, had made a lot of sense. I in the jacket, she in her trench coat with her wind-swept hair. The way she looked me over. The way we both took in our reflection. Seeing what? Why hadn't I suggested we continue our date after my radio program? I didn't understand my hesitation. It was like slipping backwards in time, into my teenage habit of hedging because I was unable to risk getting close to people who fascinated me. Afraid of getting what I wanted; afraid of not getting it. Until one day I decided that it was always worth the risk.

So how about now? Was Claude holding me back? One more day! This time tomorrow I would finally see her. No wonder I was on edge. I had to keep my cool and not get carried away, which was easier said than done. My victory over her new principles of abstinence jolted me every few minutes with its sweetness. I couldn't stop trying to imagine what she must be feeling right now, on the point of breaking her rules for Pina...and me. But I also told myself every few minutes, *don't be too sure. Remember to eat, chew your croque, think of something else...*

I looked around. The foyer next to Leni's Restaurant with its tall potted trees was filling up with people. The Entrepôt was an art house, playing classics and underground hits all day long. I grabbed the program from the counter. *Last Year at Marienbad* by Alain Resnais was scheduled for 7:35 p.m. I rarely went for evening shows at the cinema. I preferred the quick in and out of matinees or early afternoons, a casual approach I had adopted when I became a journalist and had to attend night performances. Theater, opera, ballet seemed to set higher demands and often leave deeper imprints than movies.

But the opposite had been true when I was very young. Films—Bergman, Fellini, Antonioni—gave me the intense fantasy close-up with women and men I wanted to meet and fall in love with.

Seeing *Last Year at Marienbad*, on my first visit to Paris, as a schoolgirl, was like walking through a thick curtain of dreams. The camera-travels along empty hallways of a luxury hotel, the nostalgic murmur of the voice-over, forbidding geometries of a French park—everything seemed a metaphor for a loneliness and longing I recognized. A man who mastered a mathematical matchstick game held the power over a woman who was as beautiful and passive as a marble statue. Was there even a story? I didn't grasp the story but felt it was somehow about Frantisek and me.

The crowd in the cinema had suddenly thinned out. I followed some latecomers into the auditorium just as *Marienbad* started, and sat through it, stunned. This was not the film I remembered. It was like watching a train wreck, the crash of a romantic vision of "life as poetry" that had upheld me throughout my youth. Had I made up a fairy tale in my inability to follow the text?

I walked out in disbelief, back into the foyer. Students, artists, film buffs in high spirits from Alain Renais's "masterpiece" were rapidly filling up Leni's restaurant. Near the exit, Dominique Araki was saying goodbye to a chic-looking couple. She was already turned toward me, not looking the least bit surprised. Had she been following me?

"Not again?" I said, coming up to her.

"A coincidence twice in one day?" She had an impish look on her face.

"You don't seem surprised."

"After *Marienbad*? Anything seems like a setup, no?"

"Artificial for sure," I said with some emphasis. "Honestly, did you make this happen?"

"You mean, did I follow you around? Why would I do that?"

I was thrown off by her directness. I wanted to say, you've spied on me before. "It's just too unbelievable."

I expected to hear her gauntlet line again. But she only laughed her merry laugh.

"I agree. It's surreal. Maybe we've also met last year in Marienbad?"

"Exactly. Maybe we have." My tone of exasperation seemed to take her aback. She studied me for a second. "Why did you wish to see it—see it again?"

I was torn. "To tell you the truth, I'm in a bad mood. I hated it. It was nothing like what I remembered."

"So you have changed? I enjoy it more every time. Memory, repressed memory, invented memory—*mein Leibgericht*." Her "favorite dish"? She must have seen the doubt in my face. "Let's compare notes. Let me invite you to a glass of wine!" Apparently she was alone. There was something infectious in her enthusiasm. Or maybe it was her slight accent, her relish saying the German words. I scanned the crowd milling in the foyer. She slipped her arm under mine and moved us toward the restaurant. "I know Leni. She'll find a spot for us."

"But I want a short evening," I protested meekly, not sure that she heard me.

Leni, a small, sturdy person in a chef's apron, hugged Dominique and got a waiter to maneuver an extra chair into the corner of a long table at the furthest edge of the café. Not a place to make an easy escape from. A carafe of wine appeared with two glasses. We had our private corner in the hubbub, edged into the forest of Leni's potted trees.

"To Leni," she proposed. "Tell me why you hated it now and didn't hate it then. When was then?"

I lifted my glass. "To being followed—and then interrogated!"

Instead of laughing she gave me a funny look. "Maybe you didn't notice that I changed clothes from this afternoon." Indeed, now that our coats and jackets were off, I noticed. She was wearing a bottle-green sweater and skirt. A charming sweater, in fact, with buttons on the shoulders that stood guard by her graceful neck like little soldiers. Red tips of hair were side-swiping that neck as she shook her head at me. "*Marienbad* has really upset you."

"I'm sorry, it's true. I can't understand what I saw in it when it first came out. This time I found it disturbing. I almost walked out."

"I would have walked out with you—to make sure you knew you were followed."

I didn't know what to think. I felt sheepish having taken her presence personally when any Parisian could revisit *Marienbad* just as I had—especially someone who wrote essays on films.

"I know the movie by heart," she said. "But I see a different story each time. The woman does remember having met the man, but she can't admit it.

No, they never met, he makes it up, and she's seduced by his story. No again. He's right, but she didn't want to remember, she forced herself to forget. No, she promised and convinced herself it never happened..."

I watched her mouth spilling out the words. Who was writing a *Roman* now?

"You are romanticizing it completely," I said. "The whole thing is a male fantasy about hunting down the elusive female and dragging her away from her present owner. A rape fantasy, in fact. Cloaked in all this ethereal beauty blah blah—totally empty. And that woman—Jesus, dead as a plank."

Her eyes had widened with curiosity. "I see your point. From this perspective it's outright necrophilia." We both laughed.

I half-emptied my glass.

"Pathetic. And this organ music droning on..."

"But fascinating in its cinematic perfection and philosophy, no? Don't you like the theory that life, or love, or memory are just narratives—changing narratives? Something in it must have caught you, before?"

"Oh, what caught me was simply that it was French. I can see that now. I was seventeen, my first time in Paris. It all sounded like poetry." I was aware of the loud clanking and nasal honking of French voices at our table and beyond.

"You already had an ear for the language?"

"I was in love with my French teacher, a young bohemian, a real charmer."

"There's nothing like love when it comes to learning a language." Her graceful hands marked her statement with quotation marks.

"Like Japanese?"

She cocked her head as if that went without saying, but her expression said, are you sure you want to know? I wasn't sure.

"Love—and drama," I kept going. "That teacher was eager to leave wife and kids and marry me. It would have been a scandal. I was sent away to France in order to get over it."

"Ah, forget him, like the heroine in *Marienbad*. Did it work?"

"Yes and no. The whole thing was absurd and had to end badly."

"So back then, you saw something in *Marienbad* that you knew?"

I looked at her. "I guess." The green of her eyes had softened—was that possible? Or was it a softness in her voice? The way she was attentive, tilting her face toward me? "I'm not sure what I knew. Something merciless—the French park without shadows. Those endless hotel corridors..."

"A castle, no?"

"Afterwards, I always liked hotels. Any hotels. Being unmoored, in-between, on the go."

Our fencing ballet had stopped, our foils been dropped. From the din around us I caught the words Resnais, Surréalisme, Delphine, Nouvelle Vague.

"Maybe I saw *Marienbad* as a dream of getting away," I said. "Not just from my teacher, from everything."

"Is that why you moved here? To get away?"

"You bet."

She pensively drew on her cigarette. "How did you manage to stay? Did you get a *carte de séjour*? Are you legal?"

"I'm a German enemy alien," I said, "I'm undercover." I enjoyed her puzzlement. "Not really. Legally, I'm a 'both-and'. They invited me into their system. Halfway."

"You mean you got an employment?"

"I got a French bank account."

She raised her eyebrows as if she had an inkling of the story that was to come.

HAUNTED

A waiter reached a long arm across our table and placed a plate with *amuse-gueules*, bits of salty cheese pastry, between us. Dominique rose up to search the crowd between the kitchen entrance and the bar. She waved a thank-you to Leni, who was standing there, nodding at Dominique with a broad smile.

"Leni never forgets a treat," Dominique said. "I often have a glass of wine after a movie." In the company of the guy with the ponytail?, I wanted to ask. Your husband? Or do you often go alone, as I do? "It's the perfect night food," she added, pouring another glass of wine and making the little pieces of pastry disappear between her lips without messing up her lipstick. I agreed. It was a pleasure to be taken care of as if by magic.

"Now, your story?"

"You know how it is. They don't give you a *carte de séjour* unless you have work and don't let you work unless you have the *carte de séjour*. I had to stand in line for hours year after year to get a student card in order to stay. I was tired of doing odd jobs, getting paid under the table. But there was no alternative—until there was. One day, my bank account showed a ten thousand francs credit. Out of the blue. I didn't waste a moment."

"Bravo! You believe in miracles?"

"I didn't want to believe I'd have to pay the money back. Although my father warned me. He works at a bank—an expert in penny-counting. And sure enough, six months later, a letter arrived from the Credit Lyonnais: We are so sorry about our mistake. We expect a prompt return of our money!"

"Money well spent, I imagine?"

"Six months of happy living! But I'd learned a few things from my dad. I went to the bank and said to the clerk: 'Too bad, I assumed the money in my account was mine.' 'But Mademoiselle...' 'If the bank had discovered this mistake right away, it wouldn't be a problem now.' The clerk got upset, so I asked to speak with the manager. I put on some charm and good grammar. 'I am certainly eager to pay it all back, *Monsieur*, but being a poor student, I wouldn't be able, alas, to afford more than 100 francs a month.'"

"Well put. A poor student—most unfortunate!"

"He contemplated this for a moment. Then he said he'd give me a loan of 10,000 Francs, to be paid back from my account in monthly 100-francs increments. I thanked him and said, 'I trust I won't be charged any interest on this loan? I wouldn't have to pay for the bank's mistake, correct?' That was the moment. I'll never forget how he studied me, as if to read who was outfoxing whom. Then he said, 'Correct.'"

She was studying me in the same way. "But only a French citizen can receive a bank loan in France."

"A detail the manager took care of in no time. Overnight, I was no longer considered an alien. I was the owner of a legitimate French bank account, on equal footing with the rest of France."

"An illegal with a legal bank account." She understood perfectly.

"Why be more popely than the Pope? If the Credit Lyonnais, the second major bank in France, didn't give a fig about my *carte de séjour*, I didn't have to bother with it either, did I?"

"Do I get the impression that you like to court risk? As I noticed at the opera?" She cut me a look.

"It's my German background. You wouldn't know unless you were German. I mean it. It's in your bones. You can't break away unless you refuse to obey. You've got to break major rules. My Hamburg friends all wanted the same thing. We all wanted an exile, but none of them made it. They stayed. Got settled. Married with kids."

"Yes, kids," she said, somewhat ambiguously.

"Do you have kids?"

She shook her head as if to say she had other worries.

"Paris is made for exiles," I went on. "Gertrude Stein made me aware of it." I tried to remember her exact words: "'That's why writers have to have two countries, the one where they belong and the one in which they live really. The second one is romantic, but it's really there.'" I added, "Something like that."

"I like to think Paris isn't real but is really there."

"If it were real I wouldn't love living here as much. I mean, if I were French and had to obey French rules and regulations. But I don't have to. I'm German by my passport and French by my bank account. *Both-and.*"

The corners of her mouth went up while her expression remained pensive. "Paris isn't real," she said, "you aren't real, but you're free."

"Never enough."

She smiled but her eyes still unnerved me.

"Want to hear my ode to a French check book?" I said to distract her scrutiny. "That check book was all it took to get a driver's license, no further questions asked. And a phone line—that used to take a year if you weren't legal. I could finally get 'real' jobs while I was doing experimental theater. I did disco-dance fashion shows—that was the latest back then. Horrid. Bit parts on TV. Embarrassing. Or playing tour guide in churches and museums—getting school kids excited about the Mona Lisa. Hard. I loved that. But the best was being Girl Friday for a famous artist. Anything rather than a career in Germany. Of course, with journalism I'm sort of settled now."

"To the little mistake that could." She raised her glass.

"Paris wanted me," I clinked my glass to hers, "as much as I wanted Paris. Without asking too much. How about you?"

"My father's French passport, as a diplomat. We spent two years in Paris when I was a teenager. I knew I had to come back one day, live here... Which famous artist?"

"Didn't I say? Meret Oppenheim."

"Man Ray's photo model? I don't know her work."

"She started out as a Surrealist, in Paris, in the thirties, and then dropped out. Now that she's doing amazing work again, it annoys her that it's still called *surrealist*. There's no category for her kind of work. Or her kind of person. But it's not easy for me to talk about her."

"Try?"

I saw she was serious. "I felt like an idiot most of the time I worked for her."

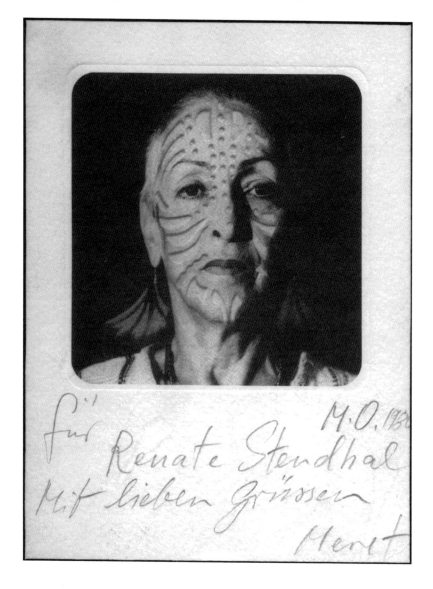

für
Renate Stendhal
Mit lieben Grüssen

M.O. 198_

Meret

"Meaning, you were young?"

"I wanted to understand her art. I saw her working day after day; she had me ground her canvasses for her, and she'd start. Some of the things she made were so beautiful that I...I can't describe it. I was like a teenager with a big crush, writing poems about paintings that obsessed me."

"Did she know?"

"No way. But there was a lot of what she made that I couldn't understand, and that was another torment. One time I asked her. She was working on something abstract, all geometrical shapes a bit like planets, and I didn't understand what it was and why she would want to paint this thing. So I asked her, Was it a dream? She often used dreams in her work. No, not a dream. So how do you get there, I said, how do you know what to paint and how to do it? I was thinking of writing, of course, wanting an answer for myself. She said, 'Something tells me: do some gray Dot-Dot here and then do some white Stripe-Stripe there.' That's what she said. I puzzled over it. I had no clue how to apply it to myself."

"Was she talking about intuition, you think?"

"She said she learned not to interfere, to do exactly what she was told and not question it. That shocked me. Such obedience, really. It stopped me, made me mute."

"A form of listening perhaps, to some larger unknown..."

"She's been on my mind these days for some reason. A nostalgia, I guess. Something about missed opportunities."

"And now? You mean, it's not just about her?"

"I feel I missed just about everything because yes, I had to be young."

Her silence didn't separate us; rather, it seemed to separate us from the rest of the café.

Two more plates arrived at our corner, handed down the long table from one customer to the next with outbursts of envy and approval. One with *quenelles*, the other with slices of *boudin*.

"Leni's specialties," Dominique said. "She's from Lyon, from a long line of women chefs. Did you know? When the aristocracy lost their money in the First World War, they had to let go of their cooking staff, so the women started their own eateries. Simple bistros with home cooking, but looking at Leni, they must have been artists, too."

"I'm not yet French enough for blood sausage," I said with regret, savoring the creamy egg taste of a *quenelle*. "A lot of French food is lost on me."

"But getting away from Germany you could have gone anywhere. Vienna, Rome, London?"

"I had a romance with France. I had it—I don't know, from birth. Not with *foie gras* or frog legs, though. Paris was literature, art, poetry. Culture with a capital C. Paris was Jewish."

"Jewish?"

"Another long story, I'm afraid." I hesitated, but felt compelled to go on. "I'd only ever met two Jewish people in my life. Of course, there weren't any Jews left in Germany. But in Hamburg, where I lived, there was Herr

Katz, who had survived. We were friends. He had the Jewish bookstore right in the center, where we got our books and records."

"We?" She was playing with her lighter, a simple Bic lighter, orange plastic. A lighter one would pick up to quickly replace a lost or forgotten one.

"The same group of friends. After such a disaster you are haunted, you want to get at the truth. Get anything Jewish you can put your hands on, know every detail that's been silenced." I suddenly couldn't stop talking. "It's like a fever you can't recover from. You even want to become Jewish, convert...we all studied Yiddish at the university."

"I am Jewish."

I was stopped in my tracks. We looked at each other in silence. There was nothing challenging in her gaze. Her face had taken on a darker, brooding expression. She, Jewish? It would never have occurred to me with her Japanese name. I felt flooded with a million questions. What does it mean? What does it mean to you that I am German? Is this the end of our conversation? The end of everything? I felt overwhelmed. Dominique Araki Jewish! Her provocative sense of humor, quick wit, and verbal panache. Her no-holds-barred laughter. The absurd thought crossed my mind how Frantisek and our circle would have taken to her...

"Really? You studied Yiddish?" she broke the silence, taking a long draw on her cigarette. "At a German university?"

"It was the first Yiddish course taught anywhere in Germany, two decades after the war. At Hamburg University, by chance."

She, too, seemed on the verge of asking questions.

"But now I mostly just remember the songs."

She cupped her ear the way I had when I wanted to hear her German. I combed through my repertoire of Yiddish songs.

"*Ich ken mul nicht fargessen majne mame's shabbes licht,*" I recited.

"I can't forget my mama's Sabbath light," she translated. "It sounds like a sad story."

"As sad as can be. A favorite of mine."

"I don't know Yiddish, but I can tell from German."

"Yes, with German it can be quite easy. Most of Yiddish is medieval German, which I had to study for my literature degree. To my ear, Yiddish is the most tender form of German." I paused, aware of the potential minefield

I had entered. The minefield of Germany. Once you had set your foot in it, it wasn't easy to get out. You had to move on and hope for the best. Hope for some form of permission. "I'll never get over it. A language born in a country that did everything to destroy it. Wipe it off the earth." She didn't seem alarmed or embarrassed, so I went on. "The most musical German. Words that sound like they are small things that are loved—*Margaritkalach, faigalach, oigalach...*"

"Little marguerites? Little—?"

"Birds. And eyes—*Augen.*"

She smiled. "Tender like talking to a child." When her face lit up, I had no problem with her eyes (although they could certainly never be *oigalach*).

"I was invited to an American seder here, a couple of years ago," I said, "and we sang Yiddish songs. Everyone ran out pretty soon, only I could still go on. Small irony—the one *goy* at the table!"

"You didn't convert?"

"No, I lost the desire after the '67 war. Not that I ever recovered from being German. The first time I got to Paris, it seemed a miracle to find Jewish people alive. I had no idea. To discover a whole *quartier* where Jewish people lived and worked. Streets with Jewish names. I didn't know how to take it in." Her look seemed to give me permission. "I went many times, in a daze. When I found Mohnkuchen and Apfelstrudel in the Jewish bakeries, it made me cry. The same cakes the Germans have always loved."

"Yes. And they bake them the same way..." She said it in the present tense but seemed lost in a time and place I felt I recognized.

"For a while I couldn't think of anything else. This was what Paris was to me then. For a year, maybe two. I looked up synagogues, out in the suburbs. I wanted to feel what it was like to be among believers." It struck me that I had never spoken about any of this since leaving Frantisek and Hamburg. "It dawned on me that they were all survivors."

"Survivors," she repeated in the same stricken way.

"I still see them coming down an alley of Linden trees, old men with long coats and hats, walking slowly, with little steps. Think about being chased everywhere in the world, being homeless, in hiding. But here they were coming out of the synagogue, looking like they belonged, whereas I was the alien who would never belong, didn't deserve to belong." I had a knot in my throat. I had crossed through the minefield to another place, a place where I had no *Heimat*, no homeland, any longer. This had been sitting inside of me forever, waiting.

"I also needed a sort of exile. Mine was Japan." She moved in a bit, leaning her elbow on the table, barricading us from the others. "Don't you think there's always more than politics? Something entirely personal about chosen exiles?" She fingered a filtered cigarette out of her packet. "Wanting to get away from…" She nervously flicked the wheel of her Bic with her thumb. "From one's own story. In order to rewrite that story." Her lips closed around the cigarette. Her Bic didn't light.

"I suppose." I was thinking of Frantisek. I lit a match. I felt her warmth as she came even closer, her silver-ringed hands cupped around the flame. Her perfume seemed to be sifting out of her hair. Our hands touched ever so lightly. "Rewrite it? Because it's too painful?"

She exhaled slowly. "I was quite young. If that man, X in the movie, had given me a story like that, like in *Marienbad*, I would have believed it. I would have followed him. Anyone." Her hand with the cigarette waved a negligent circle toward the restaurant.

"But we only have our own story. Even if—"

"Do we have it?" she challenged me. "Broken pieces, forgotten bits, memory lapses, denied truths?"

"Maybe not…" I was startled by her vehemence. "But even if we did. You can't edit a bad story into a good one by running away. Or running into whatever next story you are going to invent."

"We can't? You ran away from a bad story to find a better one, didn't you?"

Someone further down the table was laying out rows of matches, beginning the game played in the movie. People were getting up to watch.

"I found a million better ones after Germany," I admitted. "But that doesn't mean…"

"Isn't all that just to make sure one has survived what almost killed one?"

Again I was struck by her intensity. "You mean…your family?"

She laughed, but it was not a merry laugh. "Sure, family, country, God, and love! Being Jewish. A million stories." She leaned back and watched her smoke drift into the potted trees.

"You got married in Japan? I happened to get married young, too."

She looked at me, brooding.

"But not because I believed in it," I added.

"X didn't convince you?"

"If you put it like that. Monsieur X came along and convinced me for a little while."

"But you dislike the story, you don't like the memory of who you were then."

Two spots of color had appeared on her cheeks—the same spots I'd noticed before, puzzling me. What did she know about my memories? I usually didn't touch upon my muddled youth. I avoided revisiting my story with Frantisek too closely.

The players at our table were exclaiming, "See? You lost. Let me try. My turn!"

"It took me a long time to know anything about myself that I could like," I said. I wanted to add, I had nobody. Even with Frantisek and the friends, there wasn't anybody there for me. Something about how lonely I felt when I was young pulled at me as if to sink me. "Maybe that's part of why I had such a sour reaction today." I tried to get hold of myself. "It's disturbing to see right through those nostalgic dreams like *Marienbad* that once were my lifeline. It was all I had to cling to." I couldn't look at her. I was drawing circles in the ashtray with the butt of my cigarette.

She turned her face away, leaning her cheek on her hand. I caught on just before she closed her eyes with a frown. She was holding back tears. I was shocked by the sudden intimacy. What were we sharing? Which story? Marriage and delusion? Survival? Exile and liberation? What reason did we have to be sentimental about it in unison?

"I don't know why I am talking about all this," I said. In fact I wondered what had got into me, revealing my past to an almost stranger. "This old stuff still gets to me. But look, I warned you. I'm in a funny mood. *Marienbad* is a run-in with old dinosaurs!"

Her half-smile was hard to read. Was it dismissive? Regretful? Maybe my dinosaurs were getting on her nerves.

"I think I need to go home and sleep off this mood," I said, not quite truthfully. The memory of Claude had leapt up again. It was late. Another half hour and I could say, *today!* A few more hours… I suddenly didn't know what to do with myself.

"Maybe we both had a déjà vu," she said studying the empty glass in her hand. "It's nothing, and at the same time, that's why one goes to old movies, isn't it? To revisit ghosts." She sounded shut down.

"And chase them away with a good glass of wine," I said, trying to stop myself from fidgeting. "I have a big night tomorrow."

"Professionally? Personally?" She picked up the bill that was stuck in a water glass, and with a gesture refused my automatic movement for my wallet. She didn't wait for my answer. "Next time, another coffee or drink, your turn again?" She placed what seemed a generous amount of money under the edge of the plate.

"Maybe next time you can tell me more about your getting away," I said as we left the cinema. "I'd like to hear about Japan."

I had a guilty sense of having talked too much. I shook it off with an operatic gesture, flinging my new jacket over my shoulder like a cape and bowing to her like a chivalrous page. She stood on the sidewalk, head slightly tilted, the corners of her mouth slightly raised, watching me.

5

THE LEATHER JACKET

PINA BAUSCH

I waited for Claude in the foyer of the Théâtre de la Ville. It would be a
work-free night for me. Pina Bausch's program had already been reviewed
in Germany. My article, later on, would only have to sum up the French
reactions to the German *wunderkind* of dance theater. What would Claude's
reaction be?

The audience was streaming in. I recognized a few ballerinas and
dancers from the Paris Opera Ballet. As usual, a number of *"jeunes rats,"*
ballets students, were strutting around with stiff legs and turned-out feet.
Kiki's chestnut mane appeared next to her husband, a good-looking, burly
giant with a blond hunter's moustache. They apparently were part of a whole
group from the Goethe Institute. Kiki waved to me excitedly and indicated
with a turning motion of her finger that she would be calling me. Liane
veered toward me in a white silk Mao jacket, her half-long black hair ironed
into a shiny curtain. She always came early to chat with the innumerable
people she knew on and off stage.

She told me she had been at the rehearsal this morning. Too bad I
hadn't thought of that. I could have accompanied her.

"I can' t wait to see your photos of Pina. How is your own work going?"

"Formidable," she said, her Vietnamese features unstirred. "I still do
my own settings of film scenes, but lately I've got more assignments for my
Live Environments. Last week I had a photo shoot for a young bride and
groom. She wanted to set her veil aflame for their wedding album."

"In your atelier?"

"No," she laughed her throttled laughter. "That would go a bit far. In a private park. I prefer to work in my studio, of course, where I control the lights. It took a whole day but the results are fabulous."

"A real theater scene."

"That's what I thought. But wait until you see Pina's scenes."

"Could I see those Environment shoots some day?"

She nodded to a colleague from *Le Monde* and embraced me. "Come by any time. Ciao!"

I smoked a cigarette, expecting at any moment the shock effect of Dominique's hair and chili red ensemble in the midst of the mostly black-clad crowd. Would the man with the ponytail accompany her again? Would I be introduced? I was still wearing my less and less glamorous old jacket as the new one was in the hands of my concierge.

"*Salut*, Lou," a well-known alto voice greeted me. My friends Hélène and Berthe were smiling at me from ear to ear. Hélène and Berthe were the most long-standing lesbian couple I knew. They had been together for eleven years, "almost from the cradle," I used to tease them. Hélène was a gynecologist, and most of my friends went to her. Berthe was a chemist working at a government research institute.

"What's new?" I asked. "I haven't seen you in a hundred years."

"Too much work," Hélène said. "Not enough time to hang out, isn't that so, Bébé?"

Berthe regretfully straightened her hair back from her temples. She was a beanstalk, slightly bent in her shoulders and hips, as if her skeleton were too thin to hold her up straight. Hélène was the exact opposite: round and solid like a Breton peasant.

"The only study group I still keep up with is cloning," she said.

"And? Any closer to parthenogenesis?"

She laughed. "Step by step," she said in her pleasantly dark voice. "In theory, we are absolutely sure. But we are lacking lab time and money. When do women ever see real money? How about you?"

"The usual—trying to catch up with events."

"And with the women." Berthe grinned atop her glasses.

"Exactly. Tonight I am going to have fun."

"Is it going to be good? We ordered our tickets months ago."

"Because Lou forced us!" Hélène threw in.

"It's going to be good," I assured them. "Unbearably good."

They hugged me and wandered on. Berthe, the epitome of the "knight of the sad countenance," guiding Hélène, the Rock of Gibraltar, delicately by her elbow to the orchestra.

Claude didn't show up. I was getting nervous when I saw the last little groups of spectators rush in, cursing about the Metro and being hustled inside. It was 8 p.m. Was there a sudden Metro strike? I knew that Claude would rather die than miss Pina. Somehow she was delayed; somehow she'd manage to get here. I was sorry to miss part one, *The Seven Deadly Sins*, Pina's re-creation of the song and dance piece by Brecht-Weill that had premiered with Lotte Lenya in Paris, in 1933. I was even more sorry for Claude's sake. I wanted Pina's full-throttle impact on her.

I waited at the doors, scanning the Metro exit stairs and the square with its column. The golden Victory on top, holding her laurel wreaths out to the city, didn't want to include me in her gesture. Preparing myself for disappointment had not included outright defeat. I began to curse Claude, suspect her of some incurable malice. Perhaps she had faked her exuberance over the ticket. Letting me down again, staying out of reach, rubbing it in. I should have kept my companion press ticket and offered it to Dominique. If I had, I would now be watching *The Seven Deadly Sins* with her, looking forward to another intense, mystifying conversation. It was odd, in fact, that Dominique wasn't in the audience. She wasn't, as far as I could tell. Not interested in Pina Bausch?

Was I thinking of Dominique Araki because I was angry at Claude? But I still hardly knew Dominique. I had talked and talked and left abruptly and then regretted it. The suddenness of things with her made me uneasy. Everything came without a warning—her provocations, laughter, disappearance, sudden distance. Then the closeness, out of the blue, troubling me most of all. Would I ever get used to her eyes?

I lit my fifth cigarette and still didn't leave my post. When the intermission started, my heart sank.

Just then Claude came rushing in, her coat already over her arm.

"Damn Metro!" she raged. "I thought I'd never make it."

"You'd never forgive yourself for that," I said, unable to hide my dismay. She frowned with irritation and kissed me hastily right and left. A second later I knew what I'd been waiting for during the last forty-five minutes—or rather, what seemed like forty-five weeks. She looked ravishing with her tan and the heightened flush of her face from the trot up the Metro steps. She was wearing an elegant, ankle-long black dress.

"Someone jumped or fell on the tracks! Instead of my fifteen-minute ride, I had to get off at République and go all the way around to Concorde and change there," she continued with fury while I took in the contrast between the elegant dress, her boyish body and nonchalant strands of hair. "Everything was jammed. You can imagine!" Her dark eyes were flashing. "It was useless to take a taxi; I would have been late anyway."

"You look splendid," I said and took her hand. "You only missed one half. I bet the best is still to come."

"They never let latecomers in at this place—even if the world breaks down." She greedily soaked in the foyer and the people still milling about with their drinks. She rushed ahead, pulling me with her to get into the auditorium.

"What a fantastic dress," I said when we were at our seats. "Don't say you fished this out of the theater rummage?"

"Oh no," she laughed, looking around the orchestra rows. "What a seat! I've never been so close to this stage." She turned to me and proudly stroked her dress. "Who wouldn't go to any length for Pina Bausch?"

"You mean, that master thief of yours?"

"Rachel?" She looked at me for a second as if I were coming from the moon. "From a Karl Lagerfeld boutique? Not even Rachel would manage that."

"And how does one manage to get a Lagerfeld dress when one is a struggling *bohémienne?*"

She gave me a haughty look. "Connections, connections," she sang.

The dress, made of a light, flowing crêpe, seemed to be sown to her body. The low-cut princess shape flattered her hardly existing curves and fondled her thighs. The deep golden tone of her dolphin shoulders gave me a stab at the thought of her elopement to Nice. Too bad there wouldn't be another intermission, no occasion to devour her image and register the little waves of excitement that our appearance together usually stirred up in

public, especially at the theater. She never minded that everyone, including me, was staring at her.

"I can't believe I'm here," she said and granted me a long, excited look from her almond eyes. Unfortunately, the lights went down just then.

"When I am laid, am laid in earth," I recognized Dido's lament from Purcell's *Dido and Aeneas*. The voice of Janet Baker, with its shroud of darkness, went through my heart and bones.

"Is that she? Is that Pina?" Claude whispered and grabbed the opera glasses from my hands.

"The second one, at the wall," I whispered back. She audibly took in her breath. We were both marveling at the long, slender figure with a low, dark ponytail, the sinewy, trance-like movements of her body, seemingly naked under a long silk slip. Her deep-set eyes were closed in a state of pained sleepwalking. Her body smashed into the wall and fell, hovering on the ground as if suspended in rigor mortis. She rose for another attempt to sleepwalk away, only to smash back into the wall again and again.

I whispered bits of information into Claude's ear, touching her skin with my cheek and once with my lips. I played the Pina expert. It was not for nothing that I had been at the Theater Festival of Nancy the previous year and had heard a live interview with her. Claude sat more and more tensely at the edge of her seat as if she couldn't get close enough to the stage. After a while, she seemed to have all but forgotten about me. I kept glancing at her from the corner of my eyes, trying to guess what she was taking from Pina, how she was taking her in. I was watching with her eyes, comparing, taking notes, judging the brilliance of the piece.

Halfway through, it occurred to me how differently I would be watching if I were alone. I would let myself be swept away by the despair and alienation, the unrelenting violence between men and women. I would sink into my own German story, that airless space where any reaching for love was blocked by tyrannical order, loudness, and brutality.

This was the way I used to feel growing up: stuck to the wall like Pina and the other women, making blind attempts to escape. *Café Müller* could have been called Café Germany. Everybody trapped in this café could have been Jewish as well as German, with no way out. Would Dominique have seen it this way? What we had touched on at Leni's came back to me with

renewed unease and wonder. I had let her in on things I never talked about with Claude or anyone.

At one point Claude sank back into her seat. I turned to look at her. She had tears running down her cheeks. I took her hand, surprised when she squeezed mine tightly and wouldn't let go. At the end, she sat there unable to move, while the entire orchestra section rose and burst into applause. Finally she jumped up. "Brava! Brava!" she cried fanatically, her face wet with tears, as if she had just seen God onstage, while Pina bowed with questioning, doubtful eyes. When the final curtain came down, Claude still seemed to find it hard to leave. We were among the very last spectators getting to the doors. I put my arm around her.

"Time for a drink," I proposed. "I need something strong. How about you?"

She nodded. Outside, she pulled me past the Café Mistral toward the Seine. "Not here," she said. "Too many people I know."

On the way to Ile St. Louis, along the quay, she took my arm and pressed against me. We were silent until we reached the pedestrian bridge between Notre Dame and the bistro at the tip of the island. Claude stopped and gazed at the illuminated cathedral, her eyes still moist.

"This is religion for me, such a piece of theater, you know?"

I squeezed her arm.

We found a table away from the draught of the door; I ordered two gin and tonics. Claude blew her nose like a child, then emptied her glass in one gulp. I stroked a wet strand of hair out of her face. She looked down at her crushed handkerchief and took a deep breath.

"*Mon Dieu*...I didn't expect that, in spite of all..."

"That's why I wanted you to see it."

She brushed a grateful glance past me. "One simply has no idea..." She stared at the table in a daze. "In spite of it all," she repeated, shook her head and suddenly laughed. Then she was fighting tears again. "How incredibly beautiful she is," she whispered. "Almost unreal. These long, long arms and hands..."

"Gothic hands."

"Like a Madonna, with her hooded eyes."

"Gothic eyes. She's an old soul."

"Where does all this come from?"

"Didn't I tell you that I saw her dancing before she became a chore- ographer? I was still a schoolgirl. I wrote her name in my diary because I'd never seen anybody dance like that. With such soulful intensity. That was religion to me."

Claude looked at me with hungry, burning eyes. "How on earth is she doing it? These chairs! How does she get such ideas, kicking and tearing down a whole roomful of chairs for a whole hour?"

"Her parents had a pub. It's somewhat autobiographical, I guess."

"It's so brilliant, I can't stand it...where does she get this violence from?"

"You're asking? Growing up in our beloved fatherland?"

"The women are slaves. They're trained, their pitter-patter steps, trained animals going to the slaughter."

"The marriage slaughter," I said. "But the men in her pieces are also trained..."

"She's my wildest dream come true!" she shouted and drank from my glass. "I'll give up my company and audition with her..." She erupted in laughter again.

"A few lessons of classical ballet and off you go to Wuppertal!"

Claude leaned against me. "Lou, that you made this possible! I'll never forget this."

"I sure hope so." I waved to the *garçon* to bring two more drinks. "I deserve better treatment from you, don't you agree?"

"Of course," she said, a bit tipsy.

I took her hand and kissed her palm. "Do you promise? I miss you terribly..."

She pulled her hand away. "That's your own fault," she said, her face suddenly edgy and hard. "You ask for too much. And...and you don't give enough in return."

"What do you mean?"

"I always wanted to tell you this. Your perfectionism is a killer. Always criticizing something. Nothing's ever good enough for you!"

Was that true? The stab I felt had to be my answer. I wanted to de- fend myself, but it would be useless. Defend myself against being German? Against the murky guilt and drivenness that were my inheritance? She was brooding over her glass with the angry stubbornness I knew only too well.

If she was referring to the way I'd left her in Nice, she had a point.

"I know I am flawed," I said as remorsefully as possible. After my confession to Hammie, I could admit as much. "But if anything as perfect as Pina can come out of Germany, there's hope for me, too, no?"

She frowned at me as if to say, don't think it's that easy!

"You, however, in this dress—you're a dream. You are perfection —Parisian perfection *par excellence*."

The bad mood was forgotten in an instant. Over our new drinks Claude didn't seem to notice that she was leaning against my arm on the back of her chair.

"So good to talk to you," she said with her warm cello voice. "You understand theater. You understand that sometimes I think I'm not good enough..."

"But your ideas are not so different. Your image of the five tied-up women was in fact—"

"No, Lou. I had symbols on my stage, stereotypes. Nothing like this— this raw emotion. In a piece like mine you have time to think, but this takes your breath away."

"But it's also symbols. As you said yourself: sheep caged for the slaughter. And not everything she does is great. Frankly, I found the figure of the tottering bar lady unconvincing. Annoying."

"On the contrary, she's funny. A lot of it is so funny you want to cry because it's so sad, in fact."

"I sense more rage, German rage underneath everything. And bitterness."

"In any case, the tipsy bar lady is there to interrupt and create a counterpoint—

which is what I tried to do with the chansons."

"To Pina!" We clinked glasses. We tried to imagine the spectacular stage sets of pieces we had only heard about—the whole stage floor a pile of dirt and smelly peat moss, the next time covered with water, dry autumn leaves, or thousands of carnations. After more drinks, an order of pommes frites and a few cigarettes, we had analyzed every moment of *Café Müller* and rehashed every moment of *Acharnelles* as well.

"Do you remember how we used to have fights over who is avant-garde and who is passé?" Claude nudged me with her elbow.

"Fights? We?" I played along. She sounded as if our story had happened decades ago. "We only fought over those who never admit being gay, like Peter Brook. Or Robert Wilson, who is hiding out by getting more cold and abstract by the minute."

"Of course, you always had to be right. But I really miss that."

"My being right? Me too. Why don't we see a little more of each other again?" I lightly brushed my hand along her neck and shoulder.

"You are too dangerous. I know you. You're the Big Bad Wolf!" She bared her teeth and growled like a mischievous child, bringing her face so close to mine that I wanted to grab her.

"I won't eat you alive, Little Red Riding Hood," I protested. "I am quite harmless and only want to nibble a bit—" I bent over her dolphin shoulder, "where there's something too delicious."

"No, you're dangerous," she insisted but didn't push me away. "Little Red Riding Hood is not supposed to play with you. That's forbidden now."

"But who's forbidden it?"

"The granny, of course," she giggled. "She told me: don't you dare go into the forest where Lou, *Lou Garoud*, is lying in wait..." She eyed me to see if I'd catch the double entendre of *loup garoud*, making me a "werewolf."

"Granny's just envious because you're having a little fun in the forest..." I gnawed at her earlobe.

"That tickles," she laughed. "Stop it!"

"I'll tell you why it's forbidden," I said. "Because nobody bites like *Lou Garoud*, isn't that true?" I placed little bites on the curve of her neck and felt her slight tremor; her neck went pliable. She emitted sounds somewhere between protest and agreement while I gnawed my way back to her earlobe.

From the corner of my eyes, I noticed the sensuous expression of her mouth. She had closed her eyes.

"It's so good one can't stand it," I said into her ear, pulled her toward me and brazenly kissed her.

She drank me in as if half-dead with thirst. Seized by a wolfish greed, I pressed my other hand on the sweet, swelling flesh over her heart. You are mine, mine, my own heart hammered, and my tongue (glutton!) couldn't get enough of her.

We both stopped and stared at each other. It wasn't our usual style to kiss with such lack of self-control. I was stunned that she let me get away with it. How could she be so parched—with this super-woman in her bed?

"Lou—" she pleaded and covered her mouth with her fingertips. "See what you do to me if I don't watch out?" Was there a spark of glee in her eyes? "Now I am really in trouble," she wailed.

"That makes two of us," I consoled her. "Time to drive you home…"

It was a quiet ride through the night. The streets up to Belleville were empty. Claude was riding "sidesaddle" behind me, her dress raised and wrapped around her calves, her arms clasped around me. She leaned her head against my neck and shoulder, and I made sure my rider didn't fall asleep after having one too many drinks. I parked the Vespa at her house and pulled her toward me. She hesitated.

"It's got much later than I thought…" She sounded guilty.

"Too late? I'd love to…"

"It's not easy for me either," she said in a pouting voice.

"Make it easy for us, Claudine!" I brushed my lips along her cheek and drank in the scent of her night-fresh skin. "*C'est tout simple, l'amour,*" I imitated Arletty from *Children of Paradise.* I saw her smile and kissed the corner of her mouth. She paused and waited, as if she, too, at this moment recalled our first rendezvous in her boudoir. Our first kiss. She didn't kiss me back.

"We must say goodbye," she said with a mournful crease on her forehead.

"Must we? I don't want to say goodbye." I covered her face with panicked little kisses. "One more time, just once. Once doesn't count!" Damn, I could think only of clichés.

"Lou!" She turned her face away and looked over her shoulder as if

expecting the apparition of her lover in the doorframe. "Don't you get it?"

I let go of her. "You're not alone at home?" I had to laugh at the absurd thought. "And you are home this late! Little Red Riding Hood, I feel sorry for you." Her face shut down. "Come, come, don't be offended. *Lou Garoud* is simply besotted. You know how I am. It's okay." I hugged her, and this time she didn't withdraw. "We'll find another occasion to play in the forest…"

She hesitated again.

"No need to say anything. Just a kiss and I'll be gone…"

She gave in, reluctant, passive, slid out of my arms and rushed off. I heard the horrid clicking of the heavy door when it fell shut behind her. For a moment I stood on the sidewalk staring up at the building. Even by night the stucco walls looked dirty. Then, with a resolute turn, I started my Vespa. When it came down to it, I didn't care what went on in her boudoir. It was beside the point. All that counted was our kiss at the café, how starved she seemed, how close I'd come.

SLEUTH

In the morning, however, I cared very much to know what was going on in Claude's boudoir. I remembered my fitful sleep with half-awake dreams and wishful fantasies about how the night could have ended. In one dream, I seduced her under the cover of the café table, then pressed against a wall on the quay of the Seine. Suddenly she had red hair and vanished behind the thick hedge of a park, but I knew she was only hiding; I could smell her perfume. Then she escaped, and I ran after her up the four floors to her apartment. Just as I arrived at her doorstep, the automatic light went off. I peeled the elegant dress off her body in the dark while she was fighting with the keys, unable to decide whether to resist me. Her new flame opened the door, took it all in and, with the aplomb of a *bon vivant*, said: "Come on in, sweethearts, the bed is a bit more comfortable after all." The picture of this person didn't stay with me once I was awake. Try as I might, I could only come up with a stage dominatrix—some leather version of Zizi Jeanmaire as Carmen.

I made myself a coffee in my hexagonal espresso pot. My plotting with a little help from Pina Bausch was promising (with due understatement). And yet, I still heard the unforgiving click of the door in the night, shutting me out, leaving me in the dark. A single evening and once again, everything seemed possible, while nothing was real.

It didn't help my morning blues that I had nothing to do. The reviews of Pina would begin to appear earliest in the late afternoon, starting with France Soir. Altogether it would take two or more days before I had to

get to work. I went to the *Papeterie* next to my baker for the morning papers, and on the way back fetched my leather jacket from the concierge. The repair was almost invisible, as I had hoped.

I had a chat with Madame, who told me all about the factory in her hometown in Spain, where the best leathers were used and where most of her sisters, aunts, cousins, and second cousins were working.

"Good leather," she acknowledged, fingering the jacket. "But lining, no good. Torn here and here. I fixed. And this I find down at seam." She held out a business card. "Lucky. You forget appointment, no?"

Photo Studio Liane Cao, I read, puzzled.

Back upstairs I inspected the card. On the back side, a handwritten note said, "D.A. Photo shoot April 29, 5 p.m." That would be Wednesday next week. What could it mean? Was Dominique back to working as a photo model? For Liane? Doing some journalistic reportage about Liane's photography? Or was she one of Liane's chic new clients who had booked a private shoot, one of those "Live Environments"?

Another mystery of Dominique. A faint scent of her seemed to be hanging in the jacket. The same dusky perfume I had caught when she suddenly embraced me at her car, when she leaned in with her cigarette at Leni's. A "dangerous jacket with an unknown past." Had she said that or had I? I turned in front of my mirror and dropped my hands into the pockets at just the right height. I folded up the collar, stretched my arms

forward and hummed the noise of my Vespa: there was nothing to be wished for. I threw my aviator scarf around my neck and imagined my next appearance at the opera or night club. How was it possible that a jacket reaching down to my thighs could be so light? I stroked the slate-gray silk of the lining and discovered a discreet inner pocket, the kind usually found only in men's jackets. The jacket with the unknown past was made to order for me.

I decided to give Liane a call. We first exchanged our enthusiasm for Pina, then I slyly asked if it would be okay with her if I came by next Wednesday afternoon?

"Hold on…no, that's not a good time. I am doing a photo shoot for a client."

"Could I watch?"

She was silent for a few beats. "These Live Environments are very personal. Otherwise you could come watch at any time. I don't mind, in general."

"Nobody's supposed to be present? Not even the press?"

"The press?" She gave a husky little laugh. "This is strictly private. It can get quite intimate, you know."

I pricked up my ears. Intimate? This meant that Dominique was not invited as a journalist. In fact, it could only mean that D.A. had booked her own studio time.

"I am asking about the press," I said, quick as a thief, "because I want to discuss a new idea with you. My German luxury magazine, *Die Waage*, is interested in an article about your work."

"Really?" Liane's throttled voice sounded pleased; one could almost call it excited.

"They would like me to send them some information right away, if possible. Some copies or prints."

"Sure."

"If it works out they may want it already for the next issue. The theme is multimedia—you would fit in perfectly."

"Mmm."

"The only problem is time. I don't know if I can make the deadline with this project." A nice little lie, but it was only up to me to transform my lie into truth. It might turn out to be fun to write this article. Liane's work was sexy, Liane was sexy, and her clients were probably *très* sexy. The magazine was sure to snap it up.

"What exactly do you need from me?"

"They want me to follow you in the studio for a day or so, observe what's going on. I see the article as a portrait of your work. Next Wednesday would be really ideal for me."

"You're welcome to come by in the morning. Just not in the afternoon, okay?"

I would have to find a way to be there. "But first let's pick a few sample photos for the magazine. We should get together very soon."

"Fabulous," Liane breathed. "Come right over. I'm doing a pretty perfume ad."

I contentedly chewed on my ball pen. My chance discovery of Dominique's photo shoot made me feel like Mata Hari. Dominique still hadn't told me much about herself. She seemed to evade questions while getting me to talk. Maybe, possibly, this time I would find out something about her. It would be thrilling to pull even, watching her on the sly as she had watched me at the opera.

The phone rang: Kiki. Another round of raving about Pina was due. I mentioned that Claude was tempted to give up her company and join Pina's "scandal-kitchen."

"A member of our Goethe Institute group knows her from Wuppertal and says she doesn't like scandals," Kiki reported. "We had a debate whether her work is feminist, but apparently not at all."

"Are you sure?"

"And she is with men. She thinks men are victims, too." Did I hear relief in Kiki's voice? "He also said she doesn't believe in women's art."

"If Pina did 'women's art,' she'd be considered second-rate. She wouldn't be able to provoke her audiences and hit them over the head the way she does."

"You say this as if it were a sport! I think she really suffers. She's incredibly sensitive."

"Maybe she needs our support. I ought to interview her. Let's go to Wuppertal, all of us!" A brilliant idea. Get Claude out of the claws of her dominatrix...

"You won't have to go that far. This colleague from Germany brought us a video tape of her *Bluebeard's Castle*—the tale about the seven forbidden doors."

"What? The piece where the men smash the women against the walls? I've read about it. Kiki, you angel! Claude's got to see it, too. When?"

Kiki promised to organize a showing as soon as possible. I sent her a dozen kisses through the ether and decided to instantly tell Claude. The occasion was worth a *pneu*. I sent off my new irresistible bait on the way to Liane's studio, a big space in one of the old Montparnasse artists buildings with high metal-frame windows and tile decorations from the Belle Epoque.

At the studio, Liane had built up a nest of black velvet below several projector lights, bedding a stark naked nymphet. As the model had her eyes closed one could unabashedly contemplate her body. It was a fine-limbed body with bee-stung breasts, smooth and glowing in the lights like fresh magnolia leaves. An assistant (from the perfume company, I assumed) arranged the blond curls of the model, gathered up or smoothed down the velvet cloth around her body according to Liane's husky commands. A second (male) assistant exchanged gelatins in the projectors. Liane, in her usual workers-blue Mao suit, tigered back and forth between her tripod and her victim, seemingly dissatisfied. I couldn't imagine what displeased her. The effect of the magnolia-white body and golden hair on the saturated black was like the birth of a teenage Venus from a starless night. Every tiniest spot of skin from the little toe to the fingertips was made up and flawless; cheeks and lips were only slightly blushed for a "natural" look.

"Isn't she charming?" Liane asked, audible to everyone. "Only the feet, that's always the problem, and we can't put heels on her, can we?" Everyone laughed. The little nymph opened her eyes and smiled shyly. She had the broad, flat look of a child.

"How old is she?" I asked, taken aback. I wondered why film and photo jobs weren't considered child labor.

"Fifteen," Liane said. "From Sweden. A rookie, but gifted."

The assistant and Liane together tried to conceal parts of the feet in folds of velvet. The nymph had to turn her upper body forward, her legs backward. I was reminded of Manet's "Olympia," a good hundred years back, resting on her sheets and pillows scandalously dressed in nothing but a dainty pair of slippers.

"You okay, chérie?" Liane asked every now and then, and the girl nodded gratefully. The assistant powdered her forehead and her light-blond bush as if it didn't make the least difference. Poor little nymph. She was certainly not a day older than twelve but was already trained and apparently comfortable exposing her body for a lot of money. Liane would make sure that this body would glisten on the page of the fashion magazine like a jewel of luxury dreams. I thought of Claude as the Girl onstage, in her thin, sweat-soaked summer dress. The paradox of innocence and explosive energy in her portrayal had caught me with a jolt, whereas this tamed, perfectly exposed beauty didn't do much for me. Perhaps the perfume was going to be called "Lolita." I roamed around the studio, admiring the patience of everyone involved, trying to remember the scent of Dominique's perfume.

Liane's restaged film scenes filled one wall with poster-size photos. Her *Belle de jour* wasn't convincing. The model or actress showed too much vulgar fun at the game. The classic-cool perfection of Catherine Deneuve's face stirred by desire would always be tough to imitate. I had to grin when I detected a new version of Antonioni's *Blow Up*. When I first met Liane, during my theater times, she had spontaneously proposed to restage a scene of *Blow Up* with me. I was supposed to writhe on the floor. Not like the fashion model in the film, however, but (with the peroxide haircut I wore at the time) like a David Bowie clone. She had dressed me in a crumpled men's shirt and hung a loose tie around my neck. It wasn't clear to me how David Bowie would writhe on the floor beneath a woman photographer. I felt blocked. My outfit made me think of Patti Smith, and Patti Smith was even less likely to writhe on the floor—in short, it was one of those misunderstandings that happen between women.

Instead of me, a black-haired Punk girl was now on the floor, the roughed-up shirt unbuttoned beneath the loose tie, and the rider kneeling on top of her with the camera was a lion-maned blonde in a mini-dress. Had Liane become less imaginative? What kind of sexual adventures had she had lately? Was she planning one with Dominique?

Photo studios were certainly the place for mind trips. Liane could have found a better term than "Live Environments," even if environments were still in. Something more erotic—"*Fantasmes privés*," for example. Although that would be untranslatable for a more international clientele. "Fantasies" (in English) carry a different, more playful mood; the obsessive sexual energy of the French *fantasme* falls flat in translation, whether in German or English.

I itched to step into the glass box of Liane's "office" and thumb through her calendar to make sure that the Wednesday date with D.A. wasn't another misunderstanding. I saw a big mock-up on her desk of Meret's "Déjeuner en fourrure" framed by several people pretending to drink from the furry cup or stir it with the furry spoon. The cup they used had to be an imitation; I couldn't imagine that Meret, who of course knew Liane through Ruth Henry, was in on this all too literal idea. Apparently everyone, not just me, had Meret Oppenheim on their mind, puzzling over how her creations unhinged the real. Liane's literal scenes seemed to weaken the object, take the power right out of it. But why? Maybe interpreting or acting out the meaning was like explaining what was self-evident. One had to experience the paradox oneself, be on one's own with that cup and receive the shock of taste and distaste, sexual attraction and horror, beauty and beast. Nothing in the photos conveyed the appeal of the golden antelope fur, its softness like a summer meadow, and the imaginary nightmare of its function.

I turned away and continued to meander through the studio. Photo shoots were even more tiresome than film shoots if you weren't an active participant. I already saw myself condemned to a long day of boredom when I noticed that the technical assistant was carrying an additional projector light in from a hallway by the kitchen. There had to be a back door to the courtyard where his car was parked. I followed the hallway, turning a corner past the tiny kitchen to an exit that had never caught my attention. This delivery door was the unofficial entrance I needed.

I quietly pulled the key from the door.

"I need a coffee," I said to Liane a moment later. "I'll be right back."

DEADLY VIRTUES

My mission with Liane accomplished, I recovered at the Rostand. I had spent a whole glorious spring day moseying through a dark, projector-lit studio. Moseying productively though. Every time my hand wandered to my trouser pocket and felt the shape of the copied key, I sensed the stir of adventure. During a break, while the nymphet was freshly coiffed and beautified in the dressing room, Liane and I had paged through her dossier, choosing photos to be copied for my magazine.

I chatted with Pierre, who served me a *ballon de rouge* and a *crudités* salad. For the first time this spring, the café windows were open. The late-afternoon sun bounced off the lacquered wicker chairs on the terrace where Parisians and tourists were relaxing elbow to elbow. The chestnut leaves had begun to thicken into the pruned walls of foliage that I took as a cultural statement. Green-tailored walls of nature set against the stone walls of the city. Country of balance, of the golden mean. I sighed my usual sigh of relief at not having to endure the culture of my "homeland." *Heimat*, homeland, in my vocabulary meant Nazi-kitsch, a sentimentality of gigantic, deadly proportions, pulverized into nothing by Allied carpet bombing, followed (resurrected?) by the "economic miracle" of the post-war era I'd grown up in, an era of pomp and klutz—German steel and concrete squatting in all the best locations like fat daddies in their club chairs, puffing on mean cigars.

Paging through *France Soir, Le Monde, Le Figaro* and *Libération*, I marked the reviews of Pina's performances. As expected, the French critics were enthusiastically puzzled by the "new version of German expression-ism," unable to come up with a better label. Then I tried to jot down some notes for my potential article on Liane, but Claude and Dominique were interfering with my concentration. Would I get a second Pina-moment with Claude after *Bluebeard's Castle*? Apparently Pina had hacked and sliced the music of Bartok's chamber opera like acts of murder. The impact of the stage violence together with Bartok's dark, glittering music might fling her back into my arms, this time perhaps for good. I was wearing Dominique's jacket for the first time. Perhaps she had put a spell into the leather. I hadn't failed to notice how Liane's sickle eyes repeatedly wandered from my jacket to my face as if she were taking new measure of me. Perhaps she was seeing me in another staged movie scene or planning to offer me a Live Environment.

What kind of private obsession was Dominique planning to capture in her photo shoot? Something Japanese? Luck had played the little card into my hands, slipped into the seam of a jacket she must have worn when she made the appointment with Liane. I imagined still feeling the warmth of her body in the silk-lined leather. If I were tempted to stage a fantasy scene, who would be in it? Claude? A Metro scene at night, a car filled with workers, a young woman in a schoolgirl's beret, leaning her head against the window, dreamily unbuttoning her cardigan? Another vision interfered. An elegant woman in an opera loge, dressed in gleaming white and chili red, looking over at two lovers in another loge, her opera glasses held in her lap, a tear in her eyes.

Back at home, I felt an impulse to check on Claude. For once she picked up.

"*Salut, ma belle.*"

"Lou!" Apparently thrilled to hear my voice.

"Did you get my *pneu*?"

"I did. I was going to call you, too. Tonight."

"Ah, you're alone?"

She laughed. "I am, right now."

"Want me to drop by?"

"Hold on! What would the granny say? She'd give me a spanking!"

I was astonished that she remembered her tipsy joke and resorted to it in an instant.

"Lucky you. I wouldn't mind meeting that granny." The dominatrix Carmen… "Maybe you'll introduce us one of these days?"

"Listen, Kiki's invitation is fabulous," she sidestepped. "Thank you! I can't wait to see this *Bluebeard*. The seven locked doors with their terrible secrets…based on Perrault's fairy tale? I can't believe I missed *The Seven Deadly Sins* because of the stupid Metro accident. I could still tear my hair out!"

Her talkative mood surprised me. "Well, you almost missed Pina altogether, remember? You didn't get a ticket because you were so…distracted? That should really give you pause. If I hadn't saved you…"

"I deeply repent, believe me."

"I'm glad to hear it. Such negligence ought to be one of the deadly sins."

"You're right. I'll walk in sack and ashes from now on."

Sack and ashes would be a ravishing contrast to her golden shoulders.

"A sin against the artist in you." I couldn't stop needling her.

"I know…" A tone of dark contrition. "Did I ever tell you that I always wanted to stage that piece myself? I'm glad I didn't because now I would probably have to die of shame from the comparison. I read the reviews."

"Exactly, such sins come back to haunt one. But now that we are into forgiveness: you promised me something."

"I did?"

"You did. When we were very close to the magical forest, Little Red Riding Hood."

"It was really a magical night." There was her cello voice. "I still walk around in a trance and hear Dido's lament…"

"*Remember me, remember me…*"

"And Pina—I still see her with her closed eyes. Like a sleepwalker, *La Sonnambula*…"

"And I still see your closed eyes, when you forgot the granny for a moment." She was silent. A good sign. "Do you miss me?" I asked.

"Of course I do. There's nobody I can talk to about my work like you." So I still occupied a number one spot somewhere. "Tell me," she went on. "Do you really think I would have embarrassed myself doing the *Seven Deadly Sins*?"

"Now that you are so monogamous, you ought to do something about the seven deadly *virtues*, don't you think?"

"Well, it's not that bad," she protested.

"You want me to believe that?"

"I thought you'd noticed." Did she say that without any coquetry? I hardly believed my ears.

"I did notice. And it took my breath away." The silence played like several celli to my ears. "I just wish the evening had been longer." Was that a sigh of longing? Or impatience? "I wish I could talk you out of virtue." Kiss and bite it out of your mind.

"You know, these 'deadly virtues' are really a great idea, Lou." What an actress she was. The cello was still there but now the tune was, *Let's rather stick to work, shall we?* "What would they be, by contrast to the sins?"

"Let's start with obedience to rules (the absurd rules of monogamy, I thought). Smiles when there's nothing to smile about. Saying yes when it's no. The obvious virtuosities..."

"Virtue-osities..." She tasted the word. "I like that. I can almost see the piece already."

"A continuation of your *Acharnelles*. No, a deepening. Going down to the bone, the underlying psychology..." I was pretending to be her dramaturgist.

"Say more: what else do you see?"

Aha, she had tasted blood. "I see it all, but..." I couldn't help wanting to see a few drops of that blood. "I can't go into it right now. I just wanted to make sure you got the news about Kiki's Pina plan."

"Oh, you've got to get off already?"

"Sorry, I've got plans for tonight." There it was. I was paying her back.

"I thought a moment ago, you wanted to come over?"

This was what I wanted, wasn't it? Making her notice. *Virtuosities!* Where did that come from? I wasn't exactly proud of this pretending, but how eagerly she had grabbed it. How quick she was turning a conversation into something useful to her.

"We're both quite busy these days, aren't we?"

She didn't respond. Was that regret or was she miffed?

"But why don't we have a bite together soon," I said brightly, "and brainstorm about virtues?"

"When?"

Suddenly I wasn't in a hurry. I watched my feet propped up on my desk, rocking up and down. The fortress was certainly crumbling. Another little push and it would come down. And then?

I had a sinking feeling. Could there ever be another night like Pina's performance night? A magical night where we were transformed? For one evening there had been no games, no stings, no competitive arguments. Just a closeness, excitement, a depth of feeling I had always wanted with her. How was it possible that she had let this night slip away instead of seizing the moment? As if she hadn't even registered what was suddenly given to us without any effort. It was all there that night—at least for me, perhaps only for me. There and gone.

PHOTO SHOOT

I paid Liane a calculated visit just before the ominous Wednesday to get the photos for my magazine proposal and take down some notes on her work. She showed me a few of her Live Environments. One of them was the bride dragging her veil aflame behind her at an unsafe distance. Another showed a gay couple seated in front of a wedding cake, both in leather, one of them crowned by a wreath of white camellias. Liane described—but didn't show me—a bondage scene in a truck on a country road. I tried to find out as much as possible about the protocol, especially how long it usually took until a "scene" was in the box. Liane was unable to specify. Everything was "it depends." She counted three to five hours per session. Often a revision was needed. To cover my tracks, I told her I had forgotten to show her some older photography issues of the magazine that were a must-see. I would drop them off tomorrow.

"But not after 3 p.m.," she reminded me. "I won't be available then." Obviously she was dead serious about the intimacy of her photo shoots. I felt a murmur of nervous anticipation in my stomach.

Did I really want to do this? Break into Dominique's privacy? Back at home I settled into my Thinking Chair by the window. I was perhaps crossing a line, doing something *unkosher*, of poor taste. Or was I scared of getting caught with my hand in the cookie jar? The discovery in the leather jacket surely was a message meant for me. The proverbial offer one can't re-fuse. Why then the doubt, the pull of resistance? I felt torn with excitement and misgivings, unable to make up my mind. The longer I sat with it, the more my mood of indecision puzzled me. I kept staring at the gray sky, its cloudless emptiness.

The dream! I had almost forgotten that I had another dream last night.

I was running in a mounting panic. I wasn't fast enough. There was the old urgency to reach someone. A danger. I was sweating, every step seemed more leaden. I heard a voice, "What did you do to her? What did you do to her?" It was my mother's voice. Not her critical, reproachful voice. She sounded worried, and somehow this was about me. Something had been done to me. I had to find out what it was, and the answer lay right ahead of me, if only I could reach it. I had been running out of a city, a German city—Berlin? Hamburg?—and was entering the countryside. All of a sudden, the road was gone. There was nothing. Everything a shapeless, empty gray.

It took me only a moment to make the connection. If I didn't get up from this chair and do something daring, I'd never find what I was after. To my shame, the Good Girl was still interfering with my desire. Still holding me back even when I was running. But not again. Not this time. No argument would stop me now. Why would I protect Dominique's privacy when she was sharing it with Liane?

Wednesday afternoon at 5:30 p.m., I got ready.

There was a stir in the air. Everyone in the evening rush to the metro, cars, buses, seemed to be hurrying to some urgent rendezvous. As I drove toward Liane's studio, an invisible sunset was flaming up a suite of windows in the Montparnasse high-rise like a promise, a secret signal for me.

I parked my Vespa a few blocks away at the Alliance Française and approached Liane's back door. Armed with my magazine copies, I listened and heard music inside. I gently unlocked the door and was glad for the sound volume in the studio. Liane was playing Yoko Ono. Telling myself that I had every right to my journalistic mission—even if I got the time wrong—I went past the kitchen to the end of the unlit hallway. The studio was darkened like a theater during a performance. When I stopped and peeked around the corner, I jerked back as if bitten by a snake.

On Liane's studio "stage," in the shine of a red projector light, stood not Dominique, but Claude. She was leaning against the prop of a street lantern, wearing the dress of the Girl in her theater play. Her head was tilted back and her pose suggested yearning—some exaggerated form of it, chest forward and hands behind her back.

A wave of outrage shot through me. Why Claude? What was she doing here? Why had Liane invited Claude to be part of Dominique's Live Environment?

"Go!" I heard Liane's hoarse command. Liane was outside my field of vision. And here, "by the barrack gate," sauntering into view, came Dominique Araki, dressed in a white sailor suit, a strand of red hair bouncing from under her sailor's cap. She walked with long steps, hands in her trouser pockets, until Liane shouted, "Now!" Dominique half-turned and looked over her shoulder back at Claude.

"Pretend you're walking on," I heard Liane, "so we can't tell if you'll stop for her."

I watched Dominique's stride as she rehearsed her nonchalant shoulder turn. The intention seemed obvious. I couldn't deny that Dominique in her sailor suit had the cool, natural ease of a sailor on the prowl. But Claude? What was this silly, passive pose? Lili Marleen in a flimsy little dress, swooning as if she heard the angels sing?

The darkness of the studio and everybody's focus on the shoot made my hallway corner the perfect observation post. I noticed the red cord attached to the lantern, wound around the post. Claude pulled it to her and let the end of it snake around her throat like a necklace. It was the prop from her play, the cord that had been holding the women back. Claude's untamed Girl had been the only one to break free. Now, going back into her position of swooning, she looked like a kitschy Saint Sebastian at her lamp post, eager for the arrows to strike. What the devil did it mean?

Between takes, Claude and Dominique clowned around. Claude wrapped the cord around her head into a thick turban, undulating her arms like a silent-movie odalisque. Dominique exaggerated her prowl, pretending to pant after Claude. I felt enraged again because this change into a sailor seemed so effortless for her. Was she an even better actress than Claude?

Liane called a break to readjust the lights. She said something I didn't catch because Yoko Ono's "Will You Touch Me" was drowning her out. I watched her and Dominique go up to Claude to fumble with the folds of her dress. Apparently the thin summer dress could be draped more suggestively over her thigh. While Liane disappeared (back to her camera, I presumed), Claude raised the seam of her dress and for a split second let it flip up. I couldn't see if she was wearing anything underneath. All three were laughing. Then Dominique bent over and kissed Claude's neck. The scene froze in front of my eyes. I saw Claude's sensuous smile, the flattered, amorous look in her almond eyes, fastened on Dominique.

I must have leaned my head against the wall. I felt a weakness in my knees; I almost gave in to the temptation to go down, knocked out cold in Liane's studio. Somehow I managed not to let the magazines clatter to the floor. Before I could do something I'd most likely regret, I backed down the hallway to the exit. I forced myself to breathe and lock the door behind me without dropping the key.

The cold April air beat on my face. I went down the twilight alley onto Blvd Montparnasse where I dumped the magazines into the nearest trash bin. It was good to walk in the stream of cars and people, past the brightly lit cafés set up for dinner. I forbade myself to think, refused to think. I drifted in the direction of the Seine, anywhere but home. At the modest Tabac near the Institut Catholique I downed a double cognac and blindly continued. At St. Germain I followed my usual tracks to the Pont des Arts. On the bridge, facing the illuminated front of the Louvre, I stopped to smoke a cigarette, staring at the black, rushing river below.

So that's what it was. Claude and Dominique. Dominique and Claude. When and how did they meet? Perhaps through Liane. First Claude took me to the south of France—without the expected success—then she went down with Dominique. For how long? I still had her sigh in my ear over the woman who "fulfilled all her dreams." She even had to act it out in front of Liane's camera for all eternity, while I didn't have a clue.

Impatiently I flipped my cigarette butt into the river and marched on. Not a clue. Not a clue. The heels of my boots drummed it into my brain. Walking was my protective coat against the jealousy that was licking at me with a fire tongue. I felt no hunger. The cognac and my stride triggered the warmth I usually felt on my night walks. I would have liked to smoke a joint but didn't want to lose control over my emotions.

I still felt the heat of the blow, the vertigo in my body. Claude and Dominique. What the hell did this Dominique manage to do better than I? Something about her, no, everything about her was unnerving. She'd stolen my role and snatched Claude away. She'd stolen my opera scene for her article. She'd tried to take away the credibility of my Leporello list. Thievish spy, sneaking up on me and drawing me out, but keeping all her cards to her chest. This street lamp kitsch, however, wasn't from me. If that was her idea, I could only shrug. Unless Claude had come up with it. In fact, the scene had Claude's theatricality written all over it. Draped around a lamp post! Perhaps Claude had found the lover who was equally enamored of play-acting, happy to suffer her masquerades, costumes, caprices.

A vexing idea. The sexuality of that scene was so banal, so obvious, and at the same time I'd been surprised. Seeing Dominique on the prowl disturbed me not only because she was after Claude. I couldn't say if I was more envious than jealous. That cocky sailor act had seized me with an alarming attraction. I wondered how Dominique Araki was in bed. Had she turned Claude into her slave? Why had she picked Claude instead of me?

I felt like a fool, not knowing what was going on, unable to "read" clearly what I'd seen. Feeling left out touched a place of confusion and pain so deep that I had to recoil. The cigarette I took out of my silver case fell out of my hands and rolled into a puddle.

Cut it out, I ordered. Stop being hysterical. What was I left out of? Certainly not Claude. I heard my mother's voice: "New brooms sweep well!" One of her choice sayings, reflecting what she knew about the half-life of passion. She had a point though. Claude and the woman of her dreams? That woman also had her eye on me.

I managed to light a fresh cigarette and strode on, entering the little alleys north of Les Halles. Hardly anyone was in the streets. I saw the bluish flicker of TV screens behind the shutters and blinds, heard the clatter of dishes and kids' screams. When had I last felt such turmoil? When I lost Stéphane? But with that loss I had got my life back. My life without romantic illusions. So what, if I got knocked about every now and then and my vanity suffered a blow? Let them have whatever they liked. From a neutral perspective I could hardly resent Claude's fascination with Dominique, nor Dominique's with Claude.

A neutral perspective?

Voyeur, you got your comeuppance, I told myself. You saw more than you bargained for—a well-kept secret, cracked open. Mata Hari had just unmasked a double agent: Claude the Treacherous. Claude toyed with me—and perhaps not only with me. Perhaps Dominique was also in the dark. Did she even know Claude's ongoing story with me? It would be amusing, at my next rendezvous with either one of them, to know what I knew.

My mood was lifting. Jealousy, I spelled out for myself, jealousy only means feeling excluded. I was anything but the weeping third. Dominique was courting me in mysterious ways, in spite of her success with Claude. Claude had just hungrily kissed me. It was a triangle of hot pursuits, open on all sides. A twist of fate had played a lucky card into my hands.

Night, you belong to me, I breathed, unvanquished.

GIRLS IN KILTS

For the first time since my panicked exit from the studio, I looked around.
I'd reached the Grands Boulevards where crowds of people were out for
pleasure, cars bumper to bumper. The next day was a holiday, and people
were set to *faire le pont,* "bridging" the Thursday-to-Monday weekend span.
I caught the smell of fresh crêpes. Suddenly starved, I stopped at the Porte
St. Martin. It was a Breton crêperie; I could tell by the blue-eyed, pink-
cheeked faces of the vendors that they were the real thing, fresh from the
countryside. I got in line, greedily watching the process, the way the ladle
was dunked into the bucket (not exactly clean on the outside) and the pure,
milk-white batter poured onto the hotplate. The quiet sizzling, the speed
of the little stick-tool that shoved the mass around, smoothed out splatters
and blotches. Another quick round and the batter was spread in a perfect
circle, all seams glued together evenly while the heat was raising a quivering
bubble here and there. I got lost staring. Something about the thick batter
being poured and spread and manipulated reminded me of lovemaking.

While I wolfed down my *beurre-et-sucre* I watched two couples
peeling from a cab: the men tall like Ethiopians, in violet and purple-colored
silk tunics with white kepis, the women in gold lamé evening gowns and
stolas that flattered their cacao skin. All four of them sparkled with gold and
jewels. Everyone turned their heads. *Paris when it sizzles...* I started to follow
them to see where they were headed, when a familiar motorbike roared past
me. The plump black-leather butt on the narrow seat was unmistakably my

pal Charlie's from the Sinners group. She was wearing a helmet and didn't hear my whistling. She must be headed for a date.

I felt a pleasant stir of possibilities. Crossing over the Boulevard at Metro Strasbourg-St. Denis, I entered my old haunts, where I had spent a good year in an attic room. I ordered a gin and tonic at "Chez Paul & Pierre" and stood a while at the bar. The air was thick with beer and cigarettes. I lit my joint, watched the customers, and let myself be looked up and down by a group of transvestites who were crowded around a table, craning their beautiful, strong necks and spreading their feathers. I lifted my glass to them. With the last of my drink, I popped a pill of speed from my cigarette case. The speed would curb my getting obsessive from the joint, and the alcohol, in turn, would nicely round out the speed.

Entering Rue du Faubourg St. Denis and its side alleys, I was hit by

the high pulse of the night. In almost every doorway a woman was posing for the stream of men who were searching, scanning each body for their fetish-fantasy. I stopped and took position at a discreet parking meter, as was my habit for my night watch: observing the fluid contact between the women and the johns—the brief stops, chats, laughter, bursts of giving each other hell. I soaked in the lascivious way the women waved their feather boas, propped up their corsets to present their goods, stilted to and fro on their platform shoes, swung their asses, negotiated coldly and haughtily, their arms crossed in front of their chest.

"*Elloh, mon p'tit,*" one of them said as she stilettoed past me, "in need of a Mama?" She smacked me a kiss, winking at me with tiny, swollen eyes. With her rust-brown curly wig she looked like my concierge, an aging housewife, but dressed in a tightly belted patent-leather coat that left her décolleté exposed.

"Not tonight, Mama," I replied, enjoying the low register my voice automatically took on. I dove into the stream of men. My heart beat faster. I registered my high, the ease and recklessness of my disguise. It had been a while since my last night walk. I sent the ladies my admiring, inquisitive looks, and frequent come-ons rewarded me—or was it the military elegance of Dominique's jacket that was rewarded? I played it cool, listened to this or that offer: English, French, Spanish, et cetera.

"Another time," I said and walked on.

Rues des Petites Ecuries, Rue du Château d'Eau, Rue du Désir, Rue du Paradis... If I were a guy, would I seek my thrill on Horse Stable Lane, Water Castle Road, Street of Desire, or Paradise Alley? A few times I had joined a throng of men in front of an Arabian bordello on Boulevard de Clichy, waiting in line by a door with a small window to get a peek into a courtyard where ample women were standing around or lolling on battered chairs. If I were a guy instead of a woman in disguise...which *belle de nuit* would I choose for my own fantasy scene? Every woman, in fact, was in disguise, especially here in the *Kontakthof,* the contact-court of artificialities, of femininity on sale.

When I turned the corner to Boulevard de Strasbourg, shortly before the Gare de l'Est, I caught sight of a couple of women standing on the steps to a nondescript hotel. Both were dressed in mini-kilts and white nylon blouses with ties in the pattern of their kilts. In the dim light of the entrance lamp, they looked like schoolgirls from the fifties, one blond, the other dark. Their shoulder-length hair was held by broad hair bands, the tips curled into outward flips. Their eyes and lips were barely made up. They were chatting; their lack of attention allowed me to approach. Up closer they still looked like girls, girls in uniform. The dark one had set one foot onto the stair, bobbing her foot. She was wearing white socks and ballerina slippers. Her beautiful, smooth thigh and calf muscles bulged and stretched along with her bobbing. The blond one, in white knee socks and flat patent-leather shoes with a strap around her ankles, giggled and whispered something to her companion—then they both looked me over.

Something kept me glued to the spot, but I couldn't have said what it was. My high didn't allow for reasoning. I felt torn between the reality and unreality of their appearance, convinced I had to make a decision. But what decision? They took my hesitation for fascination, as if I couldn't get enough of looking at them, for they laughed, hugged each other, and kissed while observing me from the corner of their eyes. They kissed like little girls in love, and I was stung with lust.

"*Bonsoir, les fillettes*," I said before I could stop myself. "Not yet tucked in like good girls?"

"And you, cutesy?" the blond one said. "Runaway? Underage, I bet."

"Cutting classes," I confessed. Where did I get that from? I went a step closer. The dim light obviously played in my favor.

"Charming. And now you'd like some private lessons, right?" The dark one set her foot bobbing again. Her little kilt bobbed too.

"No way," the blond one said and shoved her elbow in the dark one's ribs. She gave me a sharp look. "He's just trouble..." The rest was said into the other one's ear. I heard the word "milk face."

"Bullshit!" The dark one shoved her in turn. Her gaze wandered over my leather jacket. "What's the story with your pocket money, kiddo? You won't get your private lessons here for nothing. Two hundred francs an hour. Understood?"

"Okay. Sure." I took another step closer while I knew I should say, thank you, another time. "An hour, sure. No problem. I want..." Want? What on earth? I felt high and would have liked to keep staring at the bobbing thigh, the checkered kilt, the white socks, and ballerina slippers. I had to say something, but it took all my concentration to keep my voice low. "I want to watch you, nothing worse—"

"Really, how cute. Nothing worse. We got to lay it on for him so he can get off!" They exchanged an amused look. "We ain't a peepshow, baby boy."

"For that you have to go that way." The dark one pointed her head in the direction of Pigalle.

"No no no, not that, just—" I searched in my foggy head. "I just want a scene, like in a play." I was getting somewhere, but they didn't seem to follow. "Like playing school."

"So young and so perverse already." The blond one clicked her tongue. "He wants to be the schoolmaster! We don't do S/M here, get that?"

"No no, not like that. Just fantasy." I went on looking through my vocabulary, unable to pull away. "I'd like to see you do something together."

"I really can't imagine what that might be!" she mocked, nudging her friend. "You?"

The dark one shrugged. The way she eyed me up told me she found something intriguing about me.

"It's this." I finally got it. "I'm going to film school. I need to stage a scene for class. No sex but sexy, you know? For that, I need two schoolgirls. Here—" I pulled some notes out of my trouser pocket and counted out two hundred Francs. I suddenly was on a roll. I had their attention. "You look just right, the two of you. I study directing, you know. It's easy, no sweat." No sweat? This was a different person, not me. Somebody oddly convincing. "You're going to be my extras for the scene, okay?" If this was reckless, I couldn't care less. "Just a rehearsal, that's all."

"In that case..." They both looked flattered. "Okay then." The blond one turned to walk up to the hotel entrance. "No dirty tricks, baby face," she warned me over her shoulder, "no hidden cameras."

"But when you make your film," the dark one took my arm like a chum and guided me up the stairs, "you'll give us a role, no?"

6

RUE DU DESIRE

THE CAPTIVE

I won't soon forget that room. It smelled of stale cigarette smoke and old
socks, with an attempted cover-up by some air refresher, "lily of the valley"
or something. A lamp on a nightstand threw shallow light onto the bed
and a bedspread in orange-brown circles. There was a cheap wooden closet,
a sink, two chairs. Claustrophobic curtains with the same orange-brown
circles. I slid my franc notes under the foot of the lamp to provide good will.
Then I looked around the room.

"More light?" the dark one asked.

 I shook my head. No details please!

"You are called Claude in my scene," I said to her. "And you are Dominique, okay?" With this I had already come to the end of my plot, but the eager nodding of the two and their expectant looks animated me. I placed myself on a chair in a corner, propped my elbows on my knees and squinted my
eyes. I was suddenly in my element. I was Marcel with his arrogant mouth in
Belle de Jour, when he checks out the female offers chez Madame Anaîs. Too
bad I didn't carry a little silver-embossed walking stick. Or was this rather
Lacenaire, the con man and master thief in *Les Enfants du Paradis*? Of course,
a front tooth in gold would be a welcome addition...

"Why don't you take off your jacket?" The dark one was ready to make
me comfortable, which brought me back to reality.

"No problem," I stopped her. I formed a picture frame with my fingers
in front of my face to gain time, scanning the room. For some reason the

look of my hands didn't matter. I was sure of myself.

"So, Claude. You are Claude." Almost perfect with her dark hair. "You got anything to tie her, a cord or something?"

They exchanged a look.

"No S/M," I reassured them. "Just so Claude looks like she won't run away."

The dark one pulled a pair of handcuffs from her shoulder bag and held them out to me. I shook my head. The closet was straight and simple, the bed had no posts. There was nothing in the room that could serve my scene. I had no choice.

"Claude stretches out on the bed," I said out loud, "her head here, at this end. Right...her hair falls over the edge of the bed. Perfect..." I already felt like Buñuel directing Catherine Deneuve. "So we only need—ah, Dominique, your tie!"

I wound the tie a few times around the crossed ankles of "Claude" and was satisfied with the effect.

"Now to you, Dominique," I said. "You...walk up and down in front of the bed... Yes, very good. Hm..." And then? I was searching for the words. "Could you two be turned on without much action?"

They looked at me as if I'd spoken Chinese.

"Turned on?" the blond one repeated. She unbuttoned her blouse, stuck out her tongue and wiggled it like a snake, her eyes crossed, her eyelids fluttering. We all laughed.

"Hot," I said. "But you are innocent students, remember? I want you to look just like you did outside, thank you." Buñuel at work. "We want to suggest things, you understand?"

They understood zilch. Imperiously, I told "Dominique" to play the director, to get her girlfriend into a position on the bed that was a turn-on. I watched the blond one prowl around the bed with scrutinizing eyes. Exactly as in Liane's photo studio, "Claude's" clothes were rearranged. "Claude" was turned on her side, the little kilt pulled up over her smooth, muscular thigh, and in front, the skirt was pressed slightly between her thighs as if a pleat had got caught there.

"Nice and modest," my blond "Dominique" smirked. She pulled a strand of hair from under the hair band and draped it over "Claude's" cheek. Not satisfied with the effect, she had "Claude" chew on it.

"Look at me," she ordered. "Doesn't she look like you want to eat her up?"

All three of us were enthralled with our film production. "Dominique" played around with "Claude's" hairdo. She pulled off the band and used it to tie up a ponytail. In order to give the ponytail a role, new positions on the bed were tried out. Next she focused on the tie. She stuffed the ends under one undone button of the blouse, then she changed her mind. One end was tugged into the waistband of the kilt so that it formed a dividing line between "Claude's" breasts; the other end was loosely draped onto the bed.

"Fantastic," was all I brought out. I was in a trance, in which I desired nothing more than for time to stand still so that the silent movie in front of my eyes could flicker on. For a while they seemed to have forgotten me in their attempts to direct or, rather, decorate. I imagined being Liane, taking dozens of pictures, all of them much more fascinating than her lamp post scene. They were acting without my interference, accompanied by little sounds—hmm, *oui, non, comme ça*—and their peaceful, concentrated faces looked young in the dim light. They glanced over at me from time to time.

"Go on," I said. "That's what I want to see. Just go on."

It was indeed what I wanted to see, but I was suddenly too high to really want anything. I was glued to the sexy, touching image of the schoolgirl playing a game with her pal, her accomplice. Something in the scene delighted and disturbed me and had me hooked. I felt sucked into a strange paralysis and sadness. I knew that this curious delight couldn't last. Something was wrong. Something was missing.

"Now we've really tried everything." The dark one sat up on the bed and freed her legs. Suddenly both of them seemed bored and impatient. "We can't go on forever with this kid stuff."

The blond one again unbuttoned her blouse to reveal a white lace bra. She gave me a sharp look. "Hey, how about we tie you up a bit now?" She approached me with the tie.

"Ehm, thanks, you were great...but I've got to get going," I tore myself from the chair. "I've got class tomorrow."

I pushed past her and got through the door. I heard them laughing behind me.

"A pervert, that kid, what else?" The voice of the blond one. "Instead of getting off, he bawls!"

In the hallway and outside on the stairs, I felt tears on my face. But why tears, I wondered, when it was simply wonderful? I felt undone, took a taxi home and threw myself on my bed without taking off my clothes.

At some point between night and morning I dreamt—or was it a waking dream?

A pirate with a ponytail and an eye patch made of painted cardboard and rubber band. A captive princess at a ladder, the mast of a ship. No, it's the lamppost in Liane's photo shoot. Someone shouts: "Go!" I am in the studio with Claude who won't look at me. The hooker is coming toward me holding out her handcuffs. I panic. I am suddenly sure that Dominique has staged it all. She's done it for me. But that's absurd. Impossible!

In a sweat, I peeled out of bed, threw my clothes on the bathroom floor and toweled off. I struggled to wake up but my head refused. Nauseated, I threw myself back into the next wave of dreams.

The pirate stuffs a thin Oriental pipe with tobacco from a candy can and puffs heavy smoke clouds, inspecting the captive. "Your story touches me," the pirate says. "You may share my sleeping cove. But I can't grant you freedom, or else you might run away." A record plays a tumultuous piece of orchestral music. The pirate enlaces the captive; they lie on a thick rug. A woman's voice sings with ecstatic fervor. The captive has tears in her eyes.

I was suddenly wide awake. I stared into the first leaden blue of the morning. Tears, I knew. It always ended in tears, no matter how it began.

Was that why I wanted to forget?

Hell! It was no dream. How was this possible? My new classmate, Monique. A girl with a snub nose and a haughty demeanor. "Mo" was like a boy, proud not to belong. She despised girl things. She wore what my mother called "vulgar" jeans and lied the blue out of the sky. I envied her tall tales. She'd sailed halfway around the world, had seen shrunken heads and cannibals with her own eyes, had been spat at by a camel, and fooled by a mirage.

Where did this come from? Mo with her eye patch and pirate pipe—I could smell the sweetish tobacco even now. How many times in my life had a whiff of a certain pipe tobacco floated past me and stopped me in my tracks? Each time I'd been lost in a spell, trying to remember where I had already smelled it. It was like the first notes of a song you can't place or complete. This familiar and yet unreachable candy-smoke scent.

This was real. As real as the thick sheep-wool rug, the first of its kind I had ever seen in a home. Lying down on it felt like lying on the back of a polar bear. And the music—Senta! My musical memory rarely went wrong. *The Flying Dutchman* with Senta's intense, demented desire to sacrifice herself for love of a phantom. A cursed lover whom only eternity could redeem… was I already longing to get away? To sail the seven seas with Mo, leaving everything behind? How could I forget Mo? How could I forget Senta, always hoping with all my heart for Senta's impossible dream to come true?

DOPPELGÄNGER

A phone call tore me from my drug stupor. I looked at my watch. It was Thursday, almost 4 p.m. My editor from Sender Freies Berlin wanted to know if I would cover the literature awards. In my confusion I didn't find anything better to say than "Sorry, I'm already engaged." I had to laugh. Indeed, I was already engaged. My private life had me in its claws—I couldn't care less which male heads would once again be crowned with laurel. I had smoked too much, I was done in from the night. I needed an anchor.

Tanja picked up after eight rings.

"Do you believe in *Doppelgänger*?" I asked.

"Lou? Is something wrong?"

"Remember I was supposed to call when I had news about the redhead?"

"The *asympathetic* haircut? You don't sound exactly thrilled..."

"Could I come by? I'm in shock and have a murderous hangover. But you're at work, aren't you?"

"Yes. No, it's okay. Come right over."

"I've got to pick up my Vespa at the Alliance Française. Had to take a taxi yesterday night. You won't believe what I'm going to tell you."

"Hurry up, but don't do anything stupid!"

The walk to Raspail aired out my head. At the Sélect I downed a double espresso at the bar and felt a bit more like a human being. It was about the same time as the day before when I set out to be Mata Hari in Liane's studio. Now, as I unchained my Vespa, a whole year seemed to have passed.

Arriving in Tanja's neighborhood, I remembered she never had anything edible or drinkable in her studio except bourbon. I made a quick stop at the Algerian market next to her to pick up a bottle of Côte du Rhône, a camembert and a baguette. The owner, a pal of Tanja's, went to the back-room to fetch me a bread—his supply for special customers and his family, he announced with a pleased smile. I instantly tore off one tip of the crusty, glistening bread. Apart from a day-old croissant, I hadn't yet had any food.

I crossed through the ugly, post-war housing block on Rue Jean Moulin and rolled my Vespa down the cobbled lane in the back, a hidden alley lined with trees and ateliers. Tanja had already turned on her lights. A moment later we sat on two chairs, the only furniture apart from a seriously rundown butcher-block and a steel tea-wagon turned into a porcupine of brushes, knives, palettes, and other utensils. The canvases were leaning against the walls, their backs turned. The only visible painting on the easel showed a figure in a garish evening gown with the face and halo of a saint.

"One of your darlings?" I asked, looking at it more closely. "*Phantastique.*"

Tanja was in a phase where she only painted "performances" of this kind. But everything in fact was a performance: the schoolgirls in the shabby hotel, Claude as Saint Sebastian, Dominique as a sailor on leave. We were all the same—me in my street outfit of a boy, Tanja with her wig-like curls framing her austere face. Each one of us was in her own way *phantastique*, was the touching, courageous, at times ridiculous reflection of her erotic obsessions.

"Guess who Claude eloped with?" I told her the story, beginning with the leather jacket and leading to my spy act in Liane's studio. Tanja followed along with enthusiastic shouts—"*Pas possible!*" "What?" "No way!"—and short, throaty laughs.

"So, what's your take on this scene?" I asked nervously.

"A bit of a déjà vu, isn't it? The dress, the red cord... She sure is fond of her own ideas!" Tanja tapped the ashes off her cigarillo. "But Claude could never afford Liane! Why would anyone want a—what's it called—Personal Environment? Seems like a souvenir for a photo album!"

I felt grateful for Tanja's emphasis, the rise and fall of her resonant voice, her sentences ending in exclamation marks.

"Maybe it was a gift," she went on, "from Dominique? She's well off, designer stuff and what not. A little gift tied with a sexy red ribbon!" She laughed.

"Sexy or kitsch?"

"Question of taste, *ma chère*!"

"This is supposed to be hotter than what Claude had with me? All her dreams come true?" I tore off a chunk of baguette for comfort.

"I thought you knew Claude! Every new role is the best she ever played, every new lover the greatest she ever had; don't you get it? It doesn't mean much!" I wanted to object, but she wouldn't let me. "Listen. Let me tell you something. I had a friend back at art school, Michel, the closest friend I ever had. We would have been lovers if he hadn't been gay as a lark! We told each other everything we couldn't tell anyone else. But when he died, at his memorial, six people, men and women, came forward to tell teary stories about how he told them they were his one and only close friend! I could have killed him if he hadn't been dead already! See what I mean? If Claude were to die, some five hundred women would come forward to claim they were her hottest lover because she told them so. I know you don't like to hear this. You should see your face right now!"

I didn't like to see myself in the pack of five hundred. But neither did I wish to reign over that pack and claim her for myself. What did I want, after all?

"Anyway, back to the scene. The primal scene! Your Dominique plays up the *mec*. Does Claude know how you walk through Paris at night?"

"Sure. You think—?"

"What if the scene had something to do with you?"

"No way."

"Ha! A night scene, male dress, ambiguous territory? Consciously or unconsciously, you inspired them! Why not?"

I was baffled, unable to follow. "You know Benjamin Britten's opera *The Turn of the Screw*? The Henry James story with those seduced, haunted kids and their secret ceremonies? Britten put in a line from Yeats that's always puzzled me: 'The ceremony of innocence is drowned.'"

"Yes? No, don't know it. Why?"

"Something reminded me. I can't put my finger on it. It felt like some perverse pact between them. A ceremony of betrayal…"

"Or of separation! You know, people go to greatest lengths when something's in fact over. You get the most lavish gifts when your lover's ready to quit and guilt is mounting."

"I know… isn't it horrible? Claude has every reason to feel guilty." I emptied my glass with a vengeance.

"Wishful thinking, *ma chère*! But this Dominique is after you. Don't huff! And you are German. Lili Marleen! Didn't she already have some fantasy going about you with that opera thing you told me about, in her article?

Hey, maybe she wants *you* at that lamppost. Captivated—her captive!"

"That's what I already was, as a schoolgirl…"

"Meaning?"

"We had this thing going, a game. She was the pirate on a ship and I had to be the captured princess or slave…"

"You—with whom? Not her!"

"Funny, I suddenly see it. I was totally into it. But she was convinced I'd run away. She never believed me. She laughed when I once said I wanted to marry her!"

"Wait a minute! Marry her? What are you talking about?"

"She said, 'Pirates don't marry, that's bourgeois!' And I said, 'Couldn't we just pretend?'" I felt my throat tighten. "But she…no way. She wouldn't talk about it. She'd just put on Senta's ballad or some other heartbreaking music, and never…" I got up from my chair and wandered through the studio, staring at the mute canvas backs.

How confusing it was. How maddening to remember and not re-member. Sometimes I hated her for having such power over me. Sometimes I broke out in tears, which she brushed off my face with a half-amazed, half-pleased look. I yearned to be special to her, so special that it would scare her to think I might run away. And she was scared, I knew she was, even if she never let on. But then we'd lie on her rug again and it was enough to be near her, to lie with my face in the hollow of her neck like on the bottom of the ocean, with Wagner's storms raging overhead. It was enough to feel her warm, beating pulse, and breathe in her skin with its faint smell of milk and cake.

I didn't want to break down in Tanja's studio and have to explain. I couldn't possibly explain this to her.

Tanja was looking at me as if the ship of the Flying Dutchman had sailed into her studio. "Are you telling me you two—? Are you telling me you knew each other?"

I sat down again. "I'm not sure. Can't be sure. It must have been in fifth grade. Maybe..."

She leaned toward me, her North Sea–blue eyes fixed upon mine with force. "The *Doppelgänger!*"

She lit a cigarette for me and I took a long draw. "Yes. Similar face, sim-ilar laughter, similar way of walking...only that Mo was a complete tomboy."

"Mo?"

"Monique. She came from abroad and went off to England with her parents who were never home. Suddenly she was gone. Overnight."

"Monique...Dominique?" Tanja raised her eyebrows.

"Impossible. They aren't alike at all. Mo had a snub nose and soft, dreamy hazelnut eyes, whereas this Dominique has shrill green eyes that stare at you—"

"Hypnotically?"

"—like a glacier!"

Tanja laughed. "Listen, *ma chère*—eyes can be changed as easily as hair and noses! I know this from my girlfriends." Her energetic chin pointed to the easel.

"I had no idea...really?"

"There's nothing that can't be changed. Colored contact lenses—you don't recognize the people!" She leaned back in her chair and waited for it to sink in.

"But even if." I refused to believe it. "This can't be Mo. This high-polish femininity, this exaggeration of style, this designer fashion!"

"Ah, yes, like this fabulous jacket, right?" Tanja leaned over and seized the sleeve of my leather jacket that was hanging on the back of my chair. "You said she was a photo model? I have to say, I like this woman. She's outrageous!" She shook her head. "If she's your Mo, Monique, then *chapeau*! I told you right from the start: watch out, she's dangerous. Remember? Because you were fascinated. You were instantly turned on by her. Don't deny that now!"

I couldn't object. I didn't want Tanja to point her finger at me and say: *Don't tell me you're scared of her!*

"But if it's her," Tanja continued, "why doesn't she simply approach you and say, 'Salut, I am Mo, in case you remember...'? You must have had quite a story, you two, back then." She threw me a look from the corner of her eyes. "*Thérèse et Isabelle*?"

"Never read it," I said with regret. "Is it good?"

"You're asking? It got censored! It's Violette Leduc's own story—girls' passion at a boarding school. You know that Leduc pursued Beauvoir?"

"A mystery to me. I'd never have pursued Beauvoir. I always found her cold and a bit *zopfig*—Miss Schoolmarm."

"You kidding? I would have killed myself for Beauvoir! And for Sartre, too. Anyway, what kind of crimes did you commit, you and this Monique?"

"Mo and I... Nothing special. I only just remembered her again. I can't tell much more."

Tanja started to laugh, then she saw I was serious. "You've repressed it! A moment ago on the phone you said you were in shock. That speaks volumes!" She looked at her watch. "I'm afraid I've got a dinner date. But come to my place and stay over if you like."

"No need, *merci*. I just had to vent a bit."

"And now it's all got to settle. The more I think about it: It's her! Has to be. Take your time—it'll come back to you."

I drove pensively down Rue Jean Moulin toward Blvd Raspail and Montparnasse, unsure what to do with myself. *Take your time!* I hadn't told her the half of it. Nothing about my confused attractions, my feelings for Dominique who was more than ever a mystery. Nothing about getting so close to Claude again. There was no time at all. Too many things had to be figured out all at once. Claude and Dominique! I couldn't get the besotted look in Claude's eyes out of my mind. How could I have been such a fool to believe I was getting close to her again? Close to what? Being part of the pack of five hundred?

All of a sudden, I was so tired I could have fallen off my Vespa. Damn, I didn't put drugs away any more the way I used to in my twenties. Dominique and Claude! If Dominique Araki really was Mo, what was she up to? Why was I clueless? Why was I scared?

HIDE AND SEEK

The next day I spent in a daze, doodling, doing nothing, unwilling to go out and risk running into anybody who might make me nervous. At dinner time Kiki called, worried that she hadn't heard from me "in ages." What on earth had I been up to? Nothing much, I said (the understatement of a lifetime). I promised to fill her in next time we met.

"Tomorrow then," she said, "at the opera!"

Shoot! I had already skipped the literature awards, and now this? Forgetting the opening of *Arabella*! Forgetting to arrange my press tickets; forgetting to check with my German editors whether the production was of interest to them. I was what my mother would call *schlampig*, a slob. Skirting my duties. Neglecting my job. But what did my mother know about the chaotic urgencies of passion?

"Since Pina nothing's been happening, don't you agree?" Kiki complained. She told me about her upcoming Pina film presentation. I only listened with half an ear. Pina had unexpectedly faded from my mind. And so had the lovely music student-*ouvreuse* with another possible rendezvous at the opera. "We are showing excerpts from several pieces. Saturday in a week, at the Institute!"

"What would we do without you, Kiki?"

"We do what we can..." She sounded touched.

"Could I bring someone? Claude for example? Maybe Dominique Araki would also be interested." I suddenly wanted to see the two of them in the same room together, knowing what I knew about them. What kind of a charade would be played out before my eyes?

"Why not? What makes you think of her?"

I didn't explain, and Kiki related some gossip about Dominique and her relationship with men.

"I happen to know she's with women," I said. "At least at present."

"Dominique Araki? Are you sure? I can't imagine…"

"I ran into her at Rue d'Alésia. We had coffee and she told me all about it."

"Women tell you everything, don't they?" She laughed a good-hearted laugh. "In any case, invite her. Invite them both."

What if Dominique really was Mo? I couldn't wrap my mind around Tanja's certitude. It didn't make sense. I didn't recognize her, and she didn't recognize me, so it was irrelevant if there was a foggy backstory. And yet. I couldn't stop trying to conjure the real Mo-face out of the past, trying to explain the familiarity that had struck me when I first met Dominique. But it was useless. No image formed. Dominique's face held off the memory like an unyielding, lacquered mask.

I must have dozed off in the late afternoon. I awoke with a start. I had dreamt I was lying on the bottom of the ocean, happy as a clam, when all of a sudden the water was pressing down on me and I couldn't breathe.

No need for Tanja's analytic aid on this one. The old phantoms of the unconscious push toward the light—her hobby horse. They knock against the coffin cover as if buried alive, until something unforeseen helps them escape: a slip of the tongue, intense pain, a dream, some form of acting out, some "virtuosity."

I found myself thinking of Claude with fresh resentment. Claude at her swooning post, using the same dress that had touched me when I first saw her onstage. This lovely, thin, moist summer dress of the Girl in her play that had stirred my imagination—now turned into a tease for Dominique. Toying with that red cord around her neck as if to mark her eager submission. Did I even know anymore who she was?

The phone rang. As if she knew what I had just been thinking, Claude's voice sent a questioning, caressing "Lou…?" through the ether.

"I can't talk right now," I heard myself say. I hung up.

After a pause, another attempt. Could there be such urgency only two days after her love scenes with Dominique? Should I pick up and tell her straight out what I thought? I counted the rings. Then the click-off. Then quiet.

I propped my elbows on the low cast-iron balustrade of my window and drew in the evening air. Down in the courtyard at the back of my building some men were smoking. The busy clicks of heels on the pavement told me it wasn't late; I must have slept only a moment, just long enough to dream I was drowning. In the ash trees of the yard some bird was still clucking, rehearsing its spring courtship. I listened to the city, the layers of sounds, sirens blaring, cars, Metro trains whooshing and humming nearby, distinct, then echoing from the distance, a wider, fainter chorus. I wanted to rush out again, dive into the night and walk, drift along to bars, cafés that were lit up and pulsing with life.

Okay then, the first schoolgirl love. One remembers or one doesn't. But usually this first craze doesn't reappear half a lifetime later like a mirage, playing a game with one's memories.

If it was Mo, how come she remembered me? Addressing me by my birth name like my schoolteachers. "If it's not a coincidence, then it's really amusing!" Laughing, keeping me guessing. I'd made a fool of myself shouting, "Kismet!" and dancing for her in the street.

Why the whole mystery? And why the gauntlet—"Believe it if you can!"? If Tanja was right, I would have known. A bell would have gone off

saying, "Mo!" But no bell. Just, "Hey, look at that woman! Gorgeous. Fascinating. A Modigliani!" Every time I bore down to the place of memory, my feelings somersaulted sideways like grasshoppers at an approaching step. And yet. There was the jacket, given too easily. The sudden closeness that came out of nowhere. The stab I felt when I saw her in that sailor (or should I say, pirate?) suit.

Was it or wasn't it Mo?

I couldn't stop asking, but did the answer even matter if this was just a game, after all? Making up mysteries for some reason to fool me? How tired I was of all these ambiguities—wanting, not wanting. Desire, in this light, seemed an endless manipulation. A hide-and-seek game that always withheld, never kept its promise, never finally revealed.

Was Dominique like Claude, shifting and changing and never real? Was it another false promise to even think of Mo?

I went to my desk and pulled out the note with Dominique's phone number that she had scribbled down at the café.

I looked at my clock. It wasn't 10 p.m. yet. I dialed her number.

A high male voice answered. The guy with the ponytail, I thought with a stir of curiosity. No, Dominique was not present: might he perhaps convey a message? Accent-free Parisian politesse. He might, I said. I would like to meet Dominique for a coffee. It was important. The day after tomorrow, that was Sunday, at 4 p.m. Unless she let me know otherwise, I would be expecting her at La Coupole.

Perhaps I was dramatizing the whole thing. Why couldn't it be pure coincidence that Dominique had met Claude? Perhaps she had also gone to see Claude's play at the Biennale des Jeunes Artistes. C'est la vie. Seeing me, or rather, observing me at the opera could have been sufficient reason to be "after me," as Tanja put it. There was no need for a long-forgotten childhood story.

Would Dominique accept my invitation? If she wasn't Mo, she might get the wrong sense of my sudden urgency. Would I be disappointed if she ended up having nothing to do with Mo? Maybe I would be relieved. I'd have a story to tell her: how some obscure phantoms from the past made me ask two streetwalkers in their schoolgirl kilts to play out a forgotten tune for me.

SNOW QUEEN

Unable to go to sleep, I pulled *Bonjour Tristesse* out of my bookshelf. Maybe reading again about the sexual confusions of a schoolgirl might trigger my memory. Eluard's poem went through my head, set to music by Poulenc: "*Bonjour tristesse / Amour des corps aimables / ...Tristesse beau visage.*" I thumbed through the book, restless. Finally I called Christiane, for whom the night would have just begun.

She was eager to talk. "How did it work out with Claude?"

"Nothing worked out. The play is over."

"*Ah bon...*" She sounded impressed.

"I found out a few things about her. You won't believe this." My feet propped onto my desk next to the phone, I took comfort in telling the story again, this time beginning with Dominique. I turned off my desk lamp so I could see the city lights and the steady glow of the Eiffel Tower. She let me talk with few interruptions until I came to the last act, Liane's studio, followed by my dream that wasn't a dream about a schoolgirl called Mo.

"You mean...?" She was silent for a beat. "Are you saying this studio scene was playing on a memory?"

"Tanja thinks I repressed it all."

Another silence. "And you—what do you think?"

"I wanted to forget Mo."

"It's not so easy to forget. What else do you remember?"

I wanted to light a cigarette, but my throat and lungs refused.

"Everything she did was strange, out of the ordinary. Her freedom, no mother around to keep an eye on us. I couldn't get enough of her wild stories. And her music, all that Wagner. She was the exact opposite of me—good-girl me!"

"In short, you loved her."

"To no avail! We used to play those kid games. The library ladder of her book case was the mast of her pirate ship. I was the captive and got my hands tied with a bathrobe belt. She never let me touch her!" I laughed.

Christiane didn't laugh. "Perhaps you wanted more from her or were a few steps ahead of her—developmentally, I mean. Sexually."

"I don't know. I know I got tired being a princess on a pirate ship. I wanted to be Senta and her to be my Flying Dutchman!"

"So that you could save her?"

"Save her? From what? Her big, empty apartment?" For a moment I was back at Leni's restaurant, drawn into that strange intimacy I had felt. The loneliness we suddenly shared, at the edge of tears. I pulled myself back. "I wasn't ahead of her. She always decided everything. I'm sure of it. She knew exactly what she wanted, and when I wanted something, it would always be, oh yes, tomorrow. Tomorrow we'll play some other game..."

"So she was incredibly seductive but always kept you at arm's length?"

"I guess." I didn't like the formulation, but why? Because it was true? It sounded too manipulative. Too grown up. Too painful. But I didn't have any better words for it.

"How did it get resolved?"

"It didn't. Her family suddenly left Hamburg, left Germany from one day to the next. I never heard a word from her again."

The room felt stuffy. I leaned across my desk to open the window a crack.

"You mean, one moment she was holding you captive, and the next, you'd lost her?"

I hesitated. "I had a hold on her, too. Come to think of it: I also had stories. I had 'The Snow Queen.' She didn't know the tale. She'd never heard of Hans Christian Andersen. She begged me to loan her my book...and then never gave it back." I paused. "Funny that I should remember that."

"And then?"

"And then? I don't know." I listened to the noises outside. Someone was shouting in the street below. A truck was rumbling by. "Then she was obsessed with the Snow Queen. We had to play Lapland and tundra and whatnot. Oh yes, and listen to Sibelius."

"And she was the Snow Queen?"

"She was the wild robber girl, and I was little Greta. Or was it Gerda? It seems like a hundred years ago..."

"The robber girl with the knife?" She sounded taken aback.

I saw the scene as if a veil had dropped. Mo and I were lying on the rug, listening to some desperately sad music. Mo had pulled her little Swiss folding knife from her pants pocket and whispered into my ear: "Don't be

scared— it's dull."

"She caressed my arms with her old pocket knife," I said, perplexed, "and I—"

"And you?" asked Christiane. The noise of the city had stopped.

It was as if a gathering wave pulled the sand away from under my feet. A yearning to relinquish myself, a sweetness washed over me. Never before had I been in the grip of such overwhelming, violent weakness...

"I can't say. It reminds me... Something I read just yesterday in Françoise Sagan."

"And you?" She waited.

"I think I was beside myself. In tears."

"Yes," Christiane's voice was pensive. "'Loving is considerable work. We don't know if we'll lose our skin to it.' That's Violette Leduc."

"And then she kissed me. I am sure of it. She kissed me for the first time."

The sweet, hot feeling that ran through my entire body. I remembered. A voice inside me said, please please never stop... At that moment, she stopped. She said the devil's glass splinters, the cause of all suffering in "The Snow Queen," had been washed from our eyes. "Now we see the world all new." Her words stood out clearly in my memory.

Now she loves me! I must have been sure of it in that moment. Hadn't her eyes grown moist like mine?

Yes, I did "see the world all new." A face that from a distance was not particularly beautiful—a face with a snub nose, narrow eyes, and a pout mouth—all of a sudden, from close up, was a landscape of light and shadow, misty hazel ponds and eyelash reeds. I discovered what I would never forget: that one can look into eyes, that there is something that rises and falls, something that makes one want to dive after it, catch it, hold onto it. But something in her gaze resisted, turned around, and fastened on me. I must have taken her hand. Our intertwined hands were pressed between my thighs.

NIGHT VISIT

I was back in Françoise Sagan's book when I heard a tap on my door. I froze.
A light, triple tap. A well-known signal.

"*Lou Garoud...*" Claude's voice fluted through the locked door.

I opened. She must have read my eyes.

"I know it's a bit late for Little Red Riding Hood to be out," she said
with her arms stretched down, hands clutched. "Out in the dark, dangerous
forest..." She was watching for my reaction. "But I tried to call you many
times. There's something wrong with your phone, you know? I really wanted
to talk to you, and as I happened to be in the neighborhood, I thought... Can
I come in for a moment? Do you have a moment?"

I stepped to the side and watched her walk in, scanning right and
left, as if looking for any changes in my environment. She went to my
picture shelf with photographs from my dance and theater days and a photo
collage of the writers I admired: Djuna Barnes's profile under her cloche
hat; Isak Dinesen with a lopsided smile at an ornate fireplace; a massive
Gertrude Stein, hands folded on the desk in front of her; a forlorn, dreamy
Virginia Woolf. There were two small lithos Meret had given me, which
Claude had never paid attention to, and a framed snapshot of Meret as a
young beauty at the Café du Dôme, with slicked-back hair like a boy, dark,
brooding, her hand on the shoulder of a blond, feminine friend. Claude
scrutinized the picture as if to read the degree of my infatuation in the
composition of the frame, the pressed white orchid I had added, and the

romantic sketch of a face I had drawn that could have been Meret's face but also Claude's.

"I got worried..." She turned to me. She put her hands on my shoulders. Her almond eyes wandered over my face, questioning. With careful tenderness she kissed my cheeks. "But here you are. You're home."

I steered us to the table, a polished piece of wood on the base of an antique sewing machine from the flea market. In the light of the table lamp I noticed that she was wearing some *raffiné* eyeshadow that enhanced the slant of her eyes. And was that lip gloss? Everything about her was shiny. She was wearing a waist-hugging forties jacket in burgundy with a small collar of white fur that seemed to make her face shimmer.

"Lou, I have a lot to say to you. I have a confession to make. Could we have a glass of wine? I think I need one..."

I brought an open bottle of Beaujolais with two glasses from the kitchen. She was tapping a pack of cigarettes onto the table, fishing one out.

"I know you prefer your tobacco." She waited for me to flick my lighter for her, cupping both hands around my hand with meaning. I filled our glasses.

"This is to you," she lifted hers, "and to the error of my ways." She paused. "You know what I mean, don't you?"

I was busy taking in her shiny presence, the white collar, and her darkly burning eyes.

"Can't you guess?" Maybe she had noticed that until now I hadn't said a word.

"Tell me."

"Where to start? Let's say it was after Pina. You opened whole new doors for me and I was moved...I felt changed, forever." She reached her open palms across the table. "It wasn't only Pina. It was you. You were different, very different. Very giving..." Aha, I thought, her old resentment. It showed in the slightly pained corners of her mouth. "But I never thanked you enough. I wasn't clear yet. You said that night, after Pina, that I didn't treat you well." She sighed. "You were right. I didn't."

"Why?" I rolled myself a cigarette. How many cigarettes had I had this night? This one was one too many.

"I didn't realize I was still angry for something, old stuff really, the way you left me in Nice...well, in the end, I felt stupid about it. Why hang

on to that? Don't you agree? Lou?" She looked at me intensely. "Are you all right? You're looking sort of... Have you been up all night? Doing naughty things?" She smiled, then held up her hand. "No need to confess! I told myself that the past was the past. Why stay distant? What was I doing?"

"You were punishing me."

"Yes, you had withdrawn, and I felt I needed to withdraw too."

I lit up. Was that all it was? Could it be that simple?

"But then I felt I was losing you. Lou, that's the last thing I want! You mean too much to me. Much too much." Her eyes were brimming. "You mean everything."

"Everything?"

"You do!"

"Like that woman of your dreams?"

She looked puzzled. "Oh that! What an innocent I can be! Yes, don't laugh. It's true!" She shrugged with charming helplessness. "I wanted to believe in a dream. Is that so terrible? A childish dream, a *folie*. But even more, I wanted *you* to believe in it. I wanted you to care. To make you jealous." She made a scratchy little laugh. "There, I said it. I confessed!"

"So what happened to the woman of your dreams?"

She waved the back of her hand, chasing a silly idea from her head.

"You mean, *there is no there there*? Or never was?"

"Well, I can't say that. No, as I told you, honestly, it was... what it was."

"How did it end so suddenly?"

"Suddenly? Some things aren't meant to last. Unless, of course..."

A knowing glance.

I was searching in vain for a way to bring up Liane without giving myself away. Maybe the photo shoot really was a parting gift and whatever Claude had with Dominique was over.

"So I've been punished enough?"

"I regret what I did, Lou. That I wasn't more honest with you. I really tried. I let you take me to Pina. Maybe you can forgive me for being such a bitch." Did she read the skepticism in my face? "You had forgiven me that night, I know it, after Pina..."

Dido's lament—"Remember me"—went through my mind. I, too, had been "laid in earth" until she chose to dig me up again.

She cupped her face with both hands, sending a misty look across the table. "It wasn't easy for me, I think I told you. I wasn't myself after Pina. But afterwards I couldn't stop thinking of you. I had sleepless nights. *It is so bright, how can I sleep—I always want to play with you...*" She was reciting from the poem I had left on her doorstep. "The calla lily you gave me is still a dream. Do you know that I often dream of you?" There was her cello voice. "In my dreams we are in a grove of willows by a river. The river is lazy, there is dappled shade, the scent of anise and thyme in the breeze...and we kiss." She looked down, but I thought I knew what was in her eyes. "I feel like floating away on the river, slowly, while we kiss. We kiss forever. Like nobody has ever kissed me...except you."

I flashed back to our hungry kiss after Pina, the ride back through the sleepy streets to Belleville. If you keep talking in this voice, I thought, every cell in my body will awaken again to that first hour when I was burning to touch you and was only allowed to kiss.

"I know you know. How could you not?" She looked up. Her eyes said, *Now I am here, with you...* Her one hand dreamily stroked her fur collar. She is hypnotizing me, I thought. She is willing me to rise up, move over, put my hands on her...

She let the jacket slip off her shoulder and fall behind her. Her dolphin shoulders rose in a matte golden sheen from a tight tank top.

"I miss the red room," she said with a sigh. "Don't you remember our favorite games? Our unbearable erotic attraction?"

Something in her words knocked me awake. Wasn't this what I had said to her not so long ago, when I was pleading? Was she ironic, quoting me like this?

"Lou, I want to concentrate on us again, body and soul."

"Like with that woman who was fulfilling all your dreams? That's what you said about her. Word by word—exactly the same!" Suddenly I couldn't control my indignation. I saw the flicker of shock in her eyes.

"But it was a mistake, Lou. Didn't you hear me? I take it all back. I was wrong to say it then!"

I felt a wave of anger pulling against a slew of other feelings—longing, heartache, pity. How hard she was trying to believe her own words. All those glittering scenes and stories she'd made up on the spur of the moment, always changing, always true in the moment she presented them. I saw the actress at work, performing as she always had—and succeeding because I wanted her to succeed.

"It's too late, Claudine."

"Too late? It's never too late. What do you mean?"

"I can't go back. Pina, yes, we had our chance that night." I still felt the sting of it, the bitterness of giving up. "But things have changed, and there's nothing I can do about it. I've something else in mind." I realized she didn't get it. "Let's say, it's happened to *me* now. Let's say I've met the woman of my dreams."

Her face fell. "Are you saying—?"

"I am. You said it yourself not so long ago: one wants to concentrate." Would I regret this at some point? Something was driving me forward. I felt sorrow and at the same time an unbending resolve. Even if it turned out that there was no dream woman for me, it didn't seem to matter. *Bonjour tristesse, adieu tristesse.*

"I am grateful you came by," I said, "so I could tell you right now, in person." I stopped myself from saying I was sorry. I had to hold back because at any moment I might go over and put my arms around her to comfort her. It pained me to look at her hurt, hungry eyes. I snuffed out my cigarette and got up. "Would you like me to call you a cab?"

She shook her head. "I won't see you again?" She got up in slow motion, picked up her jacket, slowly slipped it on. "Ever?" She raised the collar around her neck as if freezing. The great *tragédienne.*

"Of course you'll see me. No tears, okay?" I watched myself, scared and secretly thrilled by my resolve. Was I playing a part, as she was? "My crystal ball tells me the next *grand amour* is already waiting in the wings." I moved to the door.

"But who is it? Who is she?"

I had to smile. "Your *grand amour*? Or mine?"

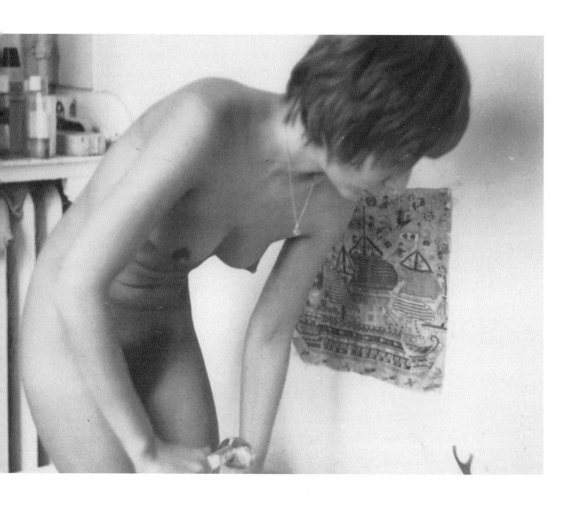

TURKISH BATH

Who was it that said, "In a triangle there is always one person who is betrayed, and often two"?

When I dragged myself out of bed and looked at the mirror, raccoon eyes looked back at me. There was only one remedy, if I wanted to be presentable at La Coupole tomorrow: the Turkish baths. I stuffed towels, shampoo, and body oils into a bag together with some books and papers and was on my way to the *hammam* at the mosque. Halfway there, it occurred to me that the beautiful place with its rose-colored marble pillars, mosaics, and fountains would be the meeting place for *le tout Paris* on a Saturday morning. I would run into any number of women I knew (some of them too well). My private occupations were turning me asocial. What was happening to me? I might end up lonely if I didn't watch out. No Sinners group, no parties, no Katmandou. Not even the opera.

I turned around and drove over to the no-nonsense baths at Rue d'Odessa.

There was nobody in the vestibule. The frequent emptiness of this *établissement* made it a perfect place for escapades on the steamy, slippery tiles. Claude and I had had our share of these in the now-distant past. Coming in from the brightly lit main room, it was impossible to look through the thick fog fast enough to catch what was going on in the sauna. Never mind. I'd promised myself not to think of Claude.

I stripped and went for the showers. When I came out, a towel slung around my belly, I heard voices. A mother was drying her daughter's hair by the locker mirrors, fighting over the girl's hair. The daughter was nine or ten, insisting on her long fringe while her mother wanted the hair out of her face. "You want to look like a sheepdog?" The mother shoved the dryer back into her bag. The girl hung her head and slunk out behind her, her hair still wet. She parted her bangs in a half-hearted way, seeking a compromise when there was none. Just like my mother and me.

In the milky vapor of the eucalyptus steam room I made out a few body shapes prone on the tiled steps that rose up toward the ceiling. Not a motion or sound in any of them. I started on the top step in the thick of heat. When it got too much I carefully stepped around the bodies and went to the lounge room to dip into the shock-cold pool. I scrubbed my skin with a Moroccan loofah and again sweated out my exhaustion.

At my next cold dip, I saw two of the bodies stretched out on a towel by the poolside. One woman was oiling the other one's back, red as a lobster. She was doing it listlessly, keeping an eye on my movements. A couple, I gathered, in their late thirties, both short-haired, getting heavyset. Sharing a single bath bag decorated with beach balls and tennis rackets. Sharing everything, just not much sex anymore? I went back to my top step in the steam room. How I didn't want to be that couple! The idea of a relationship where I didn't have my own towel and bath bag gave me the willies. Did it have to be like that? A cage, with one or both women always peering through the bars, on the lookout for some relief? Or a love-knot where one person controlled the other's hair style and clothes?

The fall from grace into the "marriage coffin"—I knew it firsthand, not just from Frantisek. Uschi! Uschi with her pathological jealousy. Or Käthe! I labored in vain for almost a year to convince her professorial brain of my desire for her Venus de Milo body. Stéphane, with her political activism, was another disaster, followed by Suzette, with her fixation on oral sex. I used to tease her, calling her "*Sucette*," lollipop. She didn't find it funny. Another attempt with Zohra who was so marvelously muscled and so unmusical. How could I be in love with a woman who couldn't stand opera and hated Chopin? Then I finally got it: one woman for sex and spice, another for opera, a third for the intellect, and one more (why not?) for whatever else could be desired.

Was that really all there was?

Once or twice I'd met a couple who seemed fully alive by midlife, engaged but still free enough, still interested in everything the other said or did. Rudi and Lutz, a librarian and a script writer who sometimes collaborated on a screenplay. They were still in love: their gestures and sexy touches gave it away. And there was the old aunt of my one-summer lover Meikje, in Holland, with her lifelong partner. The way the two elders looked at each other bespoke such intelligent appreciation that I treasured every cup of tea I had with them in their little flat on the canal. They were like two plump marzipan cakes, shyly radiating warmth and pleasure.

I had felt something like awe in the presence of these couples. What was their secret? Did they have other lovers? For some reason they seemed to be enough for each other. Why couldn't someone be enough for me?

It was a rhetorical question. A question that wouldn't stop turning up to taunt me. I had been disappointed too many times. I was convinced, deep down, that there wasn't a chance. "Enough" wasn't meant for me. Why did that make me so sad at this moment that my throat got tight? Wasn't it what I had chosen?

I couldn't face the risk of losing out, not again, living in dread of another failure. I also couldn't risk having a sobbing spell here in the sauna. If another meltdown started I might not be able to stop. My chest and belly wanted to heave with a huge wave of self-pity that scared me. I tried to relieve the pressure by forcing my breath absurdly into my toes. I tried squeezing out any feeling through the sweat of my skin. My voice of self-criticism finally came to relieve me. Enough wasn't meant for me because I wanted too much. I wanted everything that was too good to be true: undying passion, never-ending pleasure of looking at a lover and touching her. All-consuming interest in what she was thinking—right now, at any moment. Wanting to be challenged. Surprised. Wanting things in flux, always changing.

Passion, pleasure, challenge, surprise, flux—the words popped up like the bursts of hot condensing water that kept splashing from the ceiling onto my body. All out of reach, like a mirage in a desert. Like my recurring dream, running after someone with that urgency that never stopped haunting me.

I thought of the mysterious body of Dominique who perhaps was Mo— running past me in a tight red skirt, walking ahead of me in stockings with a blue seam. The curve of her buttocks in pants. The way the gray angora sweater was molded around her breasts. What the hell was Dominique Araki doing with Claude the Treacherous, when she was pursuing me? What sense did it make? I knew Claude. I was done with Claude. Then why think of Dominique? I couldn't stand the idea that she was just another game-player. Something about her ran on a deeper current and stirred my imagination. If Dominique really was Mo, there had to be a reason, an explanation for everything.

If Dominique agreed to meet me at La Coupole, I was going to get answers very soon. Suddenly I was restless. I got up and dipped into the icy pool one last time. My body was feeling restored, every cell tingling. One day, I told myself. One more day.

On the way back I kept my impatience under control by humming a Schumann song to the accompaniment of my Vespa: *Im wunderschönen Monat Mai,/ als alle Vögel sangen,/ da hab ich ihr gestanden /mein Sehnen und Verlangen.* (In the beautiful month of May, when all the birds were singing, I dared to speak my heart to her, my yearning and my longing.) The final notes leave the song forever unfinished, in musical suspension, so one has to start all over again—with the beautiful month of May. In short, it's a song you can't get rid of. An ear worm, the celestial kind.

It was a sultry day threatening rain. In Rue de Rennes, a bustle of students, tourists, and early shoppers were milling about. I stopped at a red light and watched the women crossing the street, coming up from the Sorbonne and St. Michel. My eye got snagged by a red flash of hair on the opposite side of the intersection. There was some advantage, after all, to people running around with a lighthouse on their head. Dominique was wearing her belted trench coat and putting on a beret just then. I revved up, almost ran the red light, and hit the brakes at the sidewalk in front of her.

"Dominique!"

She started. When she saw me, she hesitated. I was surprised to see her in sunglasses in this weather. With her dark shades and black beret, she looked like a *vedette*, a star or fashion icon incognito. I caught myself staring.

"Did you get my message?" I shouted past the other pedestrians. She had stopped but seemed undecided on whether to engage with me. Astride on my Vespa, I made an encouraging gesture as if to say: Hello, it's me—remember?

"Got it!" she shouted back. An ambivalent smile. "*Merci.*" She took a step closer, then made her way to the curb. "I'll be there."

That was all? I got the impression she was already going to turn and walk on.

"Is there another secondhand shop around here?" I joked, wanting to stop her for a moment longer. "But hey, I already have what I need!" I extended one arm and presented my leather jacket for her applause, feeling silly.

"Not bad." Now her smile was a little mocking. "Not bad at all." We both seemed at a loss for words. "Well then, see you tomorrow at La Coupole."

"What time is best for you?" I asked, scanning the shops on her side of the street. Then I hit upon the optician.

"4 p.m. is fine," she shrugged.

I turned and whistled through my teeth, one arm raised. "Claude!" I shouted.

Dominique turned around to search the crowd across the street, just as I expected. I saw her face in profile. Below the leg of her sunglasses her eye came into view, distinctly devoid of its shrill green.

7

MO AND LULÚ

TÊTE À TÊTE

At ten minutes to 4 p.m., I was at La Coupole. From the sidewalk I scanned
the bar before walking over to the entrance on the right. In the to and fro
of the swing door, between ladies in fur steering to the *thé dansant* upstairs,
I had an overview of the place. A few people were still sitting at the battle-
field of their *déjeuners*; otherwise it was empty and quiet inside. Should I go
ahead? Walk around? Choose a table?

I caught sight of her seated at one of the square, fresco-painted
columns, far from the windows. She was smoking, eyes closed, head leaning
against the back of the banquette. Dressed in black. Her face was a pale oval
against the henna frame of her hair and the wine-red patina of the leather
seat. Modigliani, I thought again, *The Girl with the Cherry Mouth*.

I had almost arrived at her table when she opened her eyes and took
me into her green gaze.

"*Hallo*, Mo!" I burst out. In German.

"*Hallo*," she said, unstirred. She extinguished her cigarette.

"What on earth did you do to your beautiful eyes?!" I sat down across
from her. I had planned a different opening.

She raised her eyebrows. "How did you finally recognize me?" She
stuck to her French.

"I couldn't be fooled," I said, upset that she so easily admitted being Mo.

"Really? That's why we had to have this sudden meeting?"

"What's this hide-and-seek game we are playing?"

"Tell me how you recognized me."

I stopped her silver-ringed hand from turning a pack of Winstons back and forth on the table. "Your hands couldn't be masked, could they?" This encounter, so late in the game, was too unreal for me to care what I said.

Did she let me hold her hand because she was taken by surprise? It was long enough to feel the fine tremor in her well-groomed fingers.

She looked skeptical. "Unbeatable, your memory."

"Okay. Your laughter. Your voice. Only these eyes of yours..."

"In Japan, as a photo model, I always had to wear blue contacts. Green is more fun than blue." It didn't sound one bit convincing.

"Green like glaciers?" I couldn't resist being provocative.

A shadow flew over her face. "You hadn't yet recognized me at our first coffee date. I know it for sure. And at Leni's? Still not."

"Your *dangerous* jacket had to help me out." I slipped out of the jacket and draped it tenderly over the back of the banquette. It didn't escape me that she was mystified, trying to figure out what I meant. An old factotum of a waiter came shuffling up to us.

"What may I serve the ladies?"

"*Café américain-cognac*," I told him.

"Twice," she said.

With a stiff little bow, he shuffled away.

"For balance," I reminded us.

She raised the corners of her lacquered mouth.

"I don't get it," I returned to my resentment. "The look of your own eyes isn't good enough?"

"I assumed you didn't want to remember me—therefore, it was all the same how I looked."

"What gave you that idea?"

"You never answered me, back then. When I wrote to you. But of course, I could have known."

"You disappeared—and that was that."

"I don't believe it was that simple... for either one of us."

I pulled my cigarette case from my pants pocket. We were on unsafe territory. She offered me one of hers. I declined; I avoided perfumed cigarettes.

"It's all been ages ago." I unceremoniously lit our cigarettes. "Is it even relevant today?"

"I wrote to you often." She sounded troubled.

I wanted to say, Nonsense— you are pulling this out of thin air.

She was looking at the ashtray, tapping off the cigarette she had just lit. "I could never forgive myself for leaving that way." She hesitated. "And not only that."

"Not only?"

"Remember when I came back after the summer break and was wearing skirts for the first time? Everyone was wearing kilts and only I had always refused to step into a skirt?"

I was hit by the image of the two streetwalkers in their kilts and knee socks. It was all I saw, all I wanted to see. Mechanically I shook my head.

She looked at me with disbelief. "And how I had discovered Callas— *Madama Butterfly*—and Japan—and it changed everything?" She waited. Her face was tense; she seemed to have stopped breathing.

Should I feel guilty for coming up short? It seemed I had always known Callas—what did it have to do with Mo and wearing skirts?

"You don't remember that summer when I came back from London? All grown up?" She shook her head in disbelief. "When I was done with our old games?"

Something clicked in my mind. I saw long, thin legs in bobby socks sticking out oddly from under a skirt. It was true. I had hardly recognized her. She was wearing a velvet bow in her hair and acted so superior with her new sophistication and her discovery of Japan that I felt envious, estranged, betrayed even.

"Listen, it wasn't like that at all: it was I who didn't want to play those childish games any longer!" I felt the heat of a resentment I hardly recognized.

"Childish? But we were children, at least until that summer..." Her face had colored. "So you do remember.... But then you must know what it meant to me back then, that I had changed. That I was ready to tell you—" She stopped. Her mouth seemed to be searching for words and not finding any. "I always took it very seriously," she said in a small voice. "This has haunted me ever since. I feared you wouldn't want to go on seeing me."

"But why wouldn't I?"

"You had no idea what it was like. Of course, how could you? I kept secretly opening my father's mail because I was panicked that he might move us again, any day, tell us to pack up and go, when I would have tied myself to you with a chain rather than leave!"

I was shocked by the force of her admission. Her face looked so stricken that I had an impulse to put my arm around her.

"But first it was you," she went on. "You who went away and left me in the cold...not a word from you. What was happening to you, to me? I had no idea. None."

She leaned back, avoiding my eyes as if defeated. What had I done? Left her "in the cold"?

"You mean, after New Year's? When I wasn't back at school in time?"

Where did this come from? It was as if a photo box was tumbling open, spilling its content—faded pictures that rapidly filled with color and pulsed with life. I'd been absent from school after New Years, maybe because my mother had met some old friends on our skiing trip. I hadn't known Mo for long; she couldn't know that my parents often extended school vacations to suit themselves. When Mo saw me back in class, she wouldn't speak to me for days. When she finally came around, she accused me, red-faced. I was not to be trusted; I was tormenting her on purpose. "You don't understand a thing," she had shouted. "You with your mom and dad always married to-gether in the same boring place! What do you know? You think that's love? You know nothing about nothing!"

Even now I found it upsetting to think of the scene.

"When I had to leave Hamburg, not a word from you. You never wrote," Mo said in a toneless voice.

I took a last drag on my cigarette and snuffed it out. "Maybe I wanted to forget you, Mo."

"I knew it. You never forgave me." She closed her eyes for a moment. The shadow of utter defeat on her face brought home to me what I had said. How could I possibly have forgotten her? Was I no better than my parents, my country, everyone who simply refused to look back and remember?

"You were right," she continued. "I didn't deserve any better. I wasn't fair to you. I always promised something and then didn't keep my promise—couldn't keep it."

Yes, I felt it in my bones. It was true.

"I was a coward," she said with the same troubled, defeated air.

"Coward?"

"You know. Always just looking on. It was all I could do."

The opera and her voyeur article flashed before me. Did I really want to hear this? Did I have to?

"Ah, there he is, at long last!" The factotum came skulking toward us with a tray. I was grateful for the interruption. He laboriously placed our drinks on the table.

She raised her glass of cognac with a resigned smile. "To Café Kismet—and the past!"

"And the present..." I knew my way better around the present tense. To my surprise, she downed the whole glass. I poured the rest of mine into my espresso. "But all of this doesn't explain why you had to hide from me now. Your new eye color, hair color, your new first and last name—come on, why make it impossible?"

"What do you mean—impossible?"

"Why this whole disguise?"

I couldn't tell if she was astonished or amused. "This is who I am. If I am hiding myself, it's from the world, not from you in particular. I've needed to put certain things in place to protect myself. The mask of a model, a paper marriage, always leaving one place for another. Refusing to publish what I privately wrote. Playing assistant to men, giving away my ideas. I only show myself when I choose to. *Rarely, but completely.*"

I felt flooded by what she was telling me. Rarely, but completely? She hadn't shown herself to me.

"Do you think you look like the twelve-year-old girl with her long hair and petticoats?" she asked. "But I recognized you."

"Nonsense, I never wore petticoats!"

She laughed with a tenderness that infuriated me. Who did she think she was to know me better than myself? Then it struck me. Of course! Like it or not, at the time of Mo, I still was my mother's *Schatz*, with long hair and probably any number of petticoats.

"I prefer to see myself as a tomboy," I said. "But if this is how you remember me, you couldn't have recognized me now, unless Kiki or whoever told you my family name. It was easy for you."

"You are saying I couldn't see through your disguise? Let me tell you. I saw you at the opera. No, not *Così fan tutte*. It was *Traviata*, almost a year ago. I saw that person, a beautiful boy in a leather jacket, come out of the orchestra, his face washed in tears. I stopped in my tracks. That wasn't a boy, even though she was wearing an aviator scarf. A boy wouldn't cry like that over *Traviata*. It was you. I had no doubt about it. I kept looking for you every time I went to the opera."

I felt as if the ground was sucked from under my feet. I wanted to stop her, stop everything and brood over what she had said.

"Then, sometime later, I heard about you from our American colleague, Mary. The rest you know. You could have recognized me, too, if you hadn't decided to forget me. Don't you think I wanted to put this memory away? Try as I might, it wouldn't let me go."

I struggled for something to say.

"You asked me why I was hiding from you. Why I didn't come up to you at *Così*. I wasn't going to force my memory on you." She had crossed one arm to support the other, holding a fresh cigarette. "But I did everything to get you to figure it out on your own—and it didn't take you long, did it?"

You have no idea what it took, I thought.

"But you still haven't told me," she went on, "how you figured out it was me, after all."

"And Claude? Was she supposed to help me figure it out?" I wasn't going to be swept away.

"That was pure coincidence. *C'est la vie*."

"You want me to believe that?" My elbow knocked her pack of Winston off the table. I retrieved it, flustered.

"Why not? Perhaps you're giving me too much credit?" She blew her smoke past me but kept her eye on me. "Seeing me as a puppet master? And you had nothing to do with any of it? I mean, your story with Claude?"

Touché. My story with Claude. My hang-ups over Claude. Claude the Treacherous, keeping me busy in all the wrong ways.

"Yes, but what did *you* have to do with it? With Claude and me? Why tell her not to see me anymore?"

"Pardon? I? Tell her?" She looked puzzled, then met my doubt with indignation. "Not on my life!"

"May I ask you something? Last week, I invited Claude to see Pina Bausch. Were you waiting for her that night, at her place?" I took a long drag on my cigarette.

"I wasn't in town for Pina Bausch, I'm afraid. Why are you asking?"

"It's not important anymore, but thanks." I slowly exhaled. Claude had played another trick on me. "Still, why Claude? Picking up an affair so close to me, right out of my lap, so to speak?" I wasn't sure where to aim my indignation. "What was she to you? *Ersatz*? A substitute?"

"A lovely adventure. All theater is, isn't it? I quickly got a feel for how Parisian women played together. It was irresistible."

I chewed on my lip, trying to rein in my feelings.

"But what was I for Claude? Could one ever tell if Claude was acting or not? Suddenly playing the *ingénue* in love for the first time?"

So she hadn't fallen for that either? But I couldn't help myself. "Sure, an *ingénue* just like Lilli Marleen!"

She scrutinized me, then something flashed in her eyes. She burst into laughter. "I see. Liane isn't that discreet after all...or did you hear about this parting gift from Claude?"

Bingo, Tanja! A parting gift.

"Claude was no substitute for you, Lou. Never."

She said it with such feeling that I stared.

I was on the point of saying, Sorry, I can't gather my thoughts; all this is more than I can stomach, when she asked to be excused. She slid through the narrow gap between the table and the banquette. Only then did I realize that she was wearing a light, exquisite knit dress. Slung around her hips was the large belt with the triangular buckle that had struck my eye the day she appeared at the Péché Doux, among the Sinners. *Bon Dieu*, how she had laid it on for me! I was in my usual jeans and a simple jeans shirt.

I watched her stride to the bathroom on low-heel boots, her silky hair bouncing, every bit of her smooth, in harmony. The dress ran like a dark jet of water from her shoulders to her calves, gathered in by the leather strap of the belt and fanning out below her hips. I slowly let out my breath. Was she intentionally offering me the occasion to take in her body? She is after me, my mind repeated. All of this is seduction. I am courted by Mo— Mo, who didn't want me to touch her. *Claude was no substitute for you. Never...*

THE HUNTER'S NET

Callas. Callas, I recited. I would have given my life for Callas when I was young. But how young? I remembered courting a girl from my school with the help of Callas; we must have been about fifteen. There, too, tears were part of it. How could it be otherwise when a dark voice, broken from deep inside, sings as if singing were an expression of something incurable. I had never heard such singing before, but I recognized it. A voice vibrating at the edge, a sharply cut edge of an abyss, causing pain as much as ecstasy. My passion for opera had begun with this discovery. I used to believe that all it took was listening to "Un bel di," and my girlfriend would want to cry in my arms. But no, apparently I had only taken what I learned from Mo. What else? What else had she taught me that took us to an unforgivable end?

I didn't notice that Mo had come back to our table. The moment I sensed someone behind me, she had put her arms around me. Her hands gliding over my shoulders, the faint veil of her perfume, the silky hair at my ear instantly drew me into a trance. I stopped dead like an animal caught under a glittering hunter's net. I was hardly aware of her mouth in the hollow of my neck. I registered her kiss, the way it drove into my body, pushing aside everything in its way. It went down like an unmoored elevator crashing to the bottom where it exploded in lust. I couldn't move. I felt an absurd gratitude when she leaned her temple against mine and stayed there, motionless, giving me time to get hold of myself.

She let go of me and slid back into her seat.

"Do you know what you're doing?" I wanted to ask. Before I could get a word out, I saw that she had taken out her contacts and wiped off her lipstick.

There they were, those dreamy hazel eyes. Mo's eyes, narrower than I remembered. Without the lipstick, her face looked young, her mouth unprotected. Only the red of her hair cut into the tender image from the past. What an armature she had acquired with that glossy look of perfection! Without the armor, a naked, vulnerable, young Mo-face offered itself to my eyes. I felt again her daring kiss on my neck. The same elevator crashed through my body. For one long moment I wanted to lose myself in her eyes. I thought feverishly, *Where is the closest hotel*? I saw the excited red spots on her cheeks and felt my own flushed face. As if seeing myself from the outside, I was aware of my incredulous, enamored, greedy look. I noticed the slight tremor that passed over her mouth. Automatically I took the cigarette she was offering me. We smoked in silence, contemplating each other through the cigarette smoke.

I thought, only for Mo would I smoke this horrid, sweetish stuff.

"If it's not a coincidence, it's destiny," she said, quoting one of us, I couldn't remember whom, but the light teasing in her voice broke the spell.

"Destiny is dangerous," I countered as if on automatic pilot.

"The danger is getting what you want."

Did she have to be provocative right at this moment? Suddenly I remembered how she had kissed Claude's neck in Liane's studio. How time had stopped dead when I saw Claude's besotted look.

I took a deep breath and shook off the hunter's net.

"Mo," I said, leaning back, "what do you have in mind? Is this reparation for the past?"

She was visibly taken aback. "If you like…why not?"

"We didn't agree back then—why should we now?"

"A moment ago I got the impression that we agreed. Quite a bit." She played again with her pack of cigarettes.

"But you caught me out. It was a surprise victory."

She burst into laughter, the laughter of Mo that I recognized.

"You really believe the past can be undone?" I asked. "Just like that?"

She took her time before she answered. "I would like to make up for the past." She said it as if it were the most natural thing in the world. She opened her hands. "I want to grant you a wish. I haven't had anything else on my mind all this time."

She must be living on a strange planet, I thought, a fairyland, where she is willing things into being. Here she is trying her magic—willing things on me.

"Not every wish can be fulfilled," I said pointedly.

"Yes, it can, Lou." She leaned forward. "We've always had a passion for each other. We still do, and we have more..."

"More?"

"We are equally strong. Passionate. Obsessive. We have the same thirst for freedom. Shall I continue?"

I didn't want her to continue. We also had Claude in common, hadn't we? I stuck my arm into the path of a waiter and asked him to send our factotum over. We'd been sitting here on the dry for quite a while and I hadn't even noticed.

She leaned in more closely and whispered like a conspirator, "The tiger is afraid to be tamed..."

"You bet," I said fiercely. "I'm not tempted by the repetition."

She calmly said, "If I've been forgotten, it can't be a repetition, can it?"

"I see no way," I said, shaken by her certitude. "No way out of the past."

"Oh Lulú. How can you be so blind?"

Had I misheard her? She had said my name with the accent on the last syllable. Once upon a time, there had been Mo and Lulú. I had completely forgotten. She seemed to read the shock of blindness in my stare, and the dawning recognition. Her half-amazed, half-satisfied gaze was the gaze I knew so well from the past, when I was undone by her. I felt an urgent, panicky need to ask her about those letters she said she'd written. But I didn't want to admit how much I couldn't remember.

"Instead of turning geisha, little Gerda has turned into Don Juan," she went on, leaning her head sideways, inspecting me.

Her provocation gave me room to breathe. "And what about you? Pirate-Mo turned into a photo model, wife, and whatnot."

"True," she conceded. "Maybe I turned into my own opposite in order to be closer to what you were for me in the beginning."

"Closer? All you did was keep me away." The bitterness in my voice surprised me. "As if I scared you to death."

"Well, maybe the strongest attraction creates…the strongest fear?"

Again we silently looked at each other. I saw the shadow in her eyes. She was not urging me on. She was holding off, prepared for anything.

"What do you even know about me?"

"Of course, not much," she allowed with a gracious movement of her hand. "I only know what I know about myself. That it leaves scars when one is separated from one day to the next the way we were. One always tries to find a way back. Yes, Lulú, one does even if one wants to deny it. Or wants to forget."

Her voice had taken on its intensity, and the spots over her cheekbones had flamed up again. I read vulnerability in her eyes mixed with sadness. The image of the schoolgirls on the hotel stairs went through my mind. I felt an old ache of longing, a pull into the past further than I could reach. I had no words for it, only opera words, "*Dahin muß ich zurück, und wär's mein Tod.*" (I have to find my way back to that place, even if I have to die.) Maybe she was right. Maybe she was right with everything she said.

"I am saying this because you recognized me." She folded her hands on the table. "I wanted to tell you the truth. Now you know. We can talk about something else, if you like."

ONE MORE TIME

"I need another coffee," I said.

"Shouldn't we have a bite? I'm dying of hunger. There's a good Vietnamese place around the corner."

Our short walk to Rue Delambre put us into a different gear. At the Vieux Saigon, we didn't touch upon our long-gone history. Mo gave me an overview of her country odyssey with her diplomat father; she told me about Japan, her fascination with men playing women in Noh theater, and a young director, Terayaki (or was it Terayami?) and his experimental version of Artaud's "Theater of Cruelty," based on extreme slow motion and silent screams. I drew parallels with the slow motion work of Robert Wilson and told her how my passion for dance and theater had led me to journalism. I described the exhilarating first moments of dance theater which she had missed—Pina Bausch, Richard Foreman, and of course Wilson's "operatic" forays. We were talking like friends who, after some twenty years, take up the thread as if there had never been an interruption. Such ease—was it just a pretense? Or was it her eyes? Inviting and familiar. More than familiar—I knew again why once upon a time I couldn't get enough of looking into Mo's eyes. I remembered the feeling of wanting to dive into those hazel ponds and touch the warmth that seemed to sleep at the bottom.

Sometimes when I was talking she seemed to only half listen. She had a dreamy expression as if she were listening from below the surface, pursuing something behind our words. But most of the time her eyes were alive

with sparks of amusement, and an observing coolness that wasn't at all unpleasant. It was challenging, knowing. And there was her readiness to burst out in her infectious laughter that seemed to wipe the years off her face.

At moments my mind flashed back to my first "work" rendezvous with Claude, at the Clauserie des Lilas. With her, I had instantly felt the chase was on; at stake was how quickly I would break through the resistance she had put up for the game's sake. With Mo, the question didn't arise.

We chose the same dishes from the menu, competing to see which one of us could turn out the best wraps with our rice galettes. Holding together finger-thin imperial rolls, salad leaves, and finely cut vegetables, the wraps had to be not only aesthetically pleasing, but also solid enough to prevent their contents from falling into the fish sauce after the first bite. Mo won the contest hands down.

She had none of the competitive stubbornness of Claude, whose habit to play out the know-it-all theater-woman against me, the critic, now seemed a bore. Wanting to win the argument because it was a small erotic victory to bring the other to her knees. Mo and I shared the same outsider's perspective. We grinned about our special fondness for *Così fan tutte*. There was a moment when she checked me out before launching into Dorabella's seduction scene, singing a few lines—"Che nuovi diletti! Che dolce penar!" (What new delights! What sweet pain!)—eyes dangerously narrowed. It was the only direct allusion to our recent history. It made me laugh, and her easy singing surprised me the way I had surprised myself when I did my little song and dance routine for her in the street. The Vietnamese madam came a step closer and smiled at us, her eyelids batting graciously, her hands folded inside her sleeves.

"What's your favorite opera?" I asked to steer us away from Così and the opera loge. "What's the biggest turn-on for you?"

She thought for a moment. "The twins, Siegmund and Sieglinde. Falling in love after so many years of being lost to each other. I love the suspense, how Wagner builds and builds their awareness of who they are. This slow awakening. It's the greatest love story, don't you think?"

Another story about memory, it struck me. Another *Marienbad*.

"They are so bold, so irreverent," she went on. "Twin souls who glory in their outlawed love."

Wasn't that what I had felt for the tomboy Mo when I was still a girl? It was what I had always felt about being gay—this bold irreverence and disregard of rules and taboos. *Twin souls who glory in their outlawed love.* How passionately I had been looking for such a love—looking in vain, looking in all the wrong places. I didn't know what to say. The topic was too close to home.

As if guessing my handicap, she said, "Looking at you now, I imagine your favorites are mezzos, boy-girls in love. Cherubino? Zdenka? No, more romantic. More deeply romantic..."

"Me, the cynic?"

She broke out in another laugh.

"Is it that obvious? Okay then."

"How about three women in a triangle—and the one who plays a boy dresses up as a girl? *Rosenkavalier.*"

Only a few days ago, I had imagined myself in a triangle with Mo and Claude. My friends probably had a point, teasing me for confusing life with opera.

"Isn't it odd that these transgressive characters always get the most ecstatic music?" I said to distract her from me. "I mean, Wagner? And a guy like Strauss, who then had to stuff all this buffoonery into his opera?"

"Of course, the forbidden and the erotic. You know how such emotions have to be cooled down, no? Or else one risks getting swept away?" She said it with unmistakable innuendo.

There seemed to be no way around it: wherever we ventured, we would meet an echo of our story. Our opera talk brought us back to Callas. Mo had chanced upon her when Callas was at the end of her career, performing in Japan. She had witnessed the fantastical shipwreck of a voice. And she had got her hands on a pirated video recording of Callas in the second act of *Tosca*, when she still had the full power of her voice.

"It's the only existing opera scene of Callas," she said, eyes brimming with excitement. "A whole act. Staged by Zeffirelli. Callas starved, with matchstick arms, in an empire dress lined with fur. Of course, one can't see the color, the video is just black and white. But I'd bet it's mauve or diva-pink. Her face a mask of pain, like a Noh mask. She sings 'Vissi d'arte' and you tremble for her, her disbelief, her sobs. A woman facing a sadist, facing rape. But when she knifes Scarpia, she shouts '*Muori! Muori!*' with a voice as rough and deep as a man's. A whole life's hatred in her throat. '*Muori! Muori!*' Incredible."

She must have seen the wonder and envy in my face. She smiled. "Don't worry, you'll see it."

Seduction with Callas? Like my ticket for Claude—the proverbial offer one can't refuse? We were eating our dessert, a fresh mango, and I was suddenly gripped by fatigue, a temptation to surrender, no further questions asked. But my mind kept watching as if under siege, as if I had to defend my citadel, my right to choose and refuse.

At the end of the day, when we walked down Blvd Montparnasse to where her car and my Vespa were parked, we returned to our topic. She explained that back in Hamburg, her father had been called off to England, and she had been incapable of taking it in, incapable of saying goodbye to me. She had written from England, hoping her letters would explain, hoping I would understand. It was another moment when I was at a loss. I didn't remember her letters.

She had suddenly stopped, in the middle of the boulevard, at the brightly lit Rotonde where people were having drinks on the terrace. Her eyes seemed to darken with an emotion I had a hard time naming. Was it desire? A plea? A plea for forgiveness? I was drawn into her eyes with unmistakable longing. Everything else was silent. I thought again: why don't we go to the nearest hotel?

She said, "Well then...*à bientôt.*"

"*Très bientôt,*" was all I found to say. My mind raced. A nightcap? We were only minutes away from my flat. We embraced right and left like mere friends. But in slow motion, with hesitation. I hoped she would repeat the kiss on my neck one more time. One more time, something in me said, then all will be clear...

INVITATION

I had a way of letting opportunities slip. She had a way of disappearing. I had
to give it to her: she was keeping her silence. She didn't make a move, didn't
rush forward. The ball was in my court, and all I had done for a day and a half
was dawdle at home by the telephone, trying to work, preparing for a play I
had to cover, still hoping against hope that she would call. How Tanja would
huff at me if she knew I was too nervous to pick up that phone.

The demanding knock on my door could come only from my concierge.

"I'm not dressed," I shouted when I heard her voice. She slid the *pneu*
under my door. D. Araki, I read. In my impatience with the blue envelope and
its four glued seams, I grabbed my kitchen shears.

> *Wo war ich schon einmal?* Lulú, this evening, this very night tonight
> I would like to spend with you. Say yes!
>
> Life so rarely gives lovers (or anyone, if you prefer) a second
> chance. I've never stopped believing that two people can be meant
> for each other. I don't believe you have either. But even if you
> can't believe, perhaps try to imagine?
>
> A place somewhere nearby, on a small island. Rusty stairs winding
> up to a platform, overlooking a river. No furniture, just two chairs, a rug
> and a fireplace. Nearby, a Vietnamese caterer for spring rolls and mangos.
> Would it be a place to begin again? I rented it yesterday. You'll find the
> address on the envelope. Around 6 p.m.?
>
> Mo
>
> P.S. There's that book I've intended to return to you someday.

A wave of heat shot through me. She had done it after all. Done what I had admired her for not doing: not budging, not making a move. She'd done what I so wanted her to do: bridge the silence that had been growing hour after hour.

But this was not what I had expected. Once again she was ahead of me, challenging me to catch up with her. Begin again! A second chance, for "lovers"! I was bowled over. Flattered. Shocked. Tempted. Unsure. First she had thrown me her gauntlet; now it was a rose. A silver rose. *"Wo war ich schon einmal?"* (Where have I once already been and felt such bliss?) Quoting one of my favorite moments in the *Rosenkavalier*—words and music that held such an echo for me. Was it the same for her?

I tigered back and forth between the entry room and my desk, staring holes into the light-blue paper as if to read her thoughts. Where did she find the courage? How the devil could she take such a risk?

I brewed myself a strong cup of coffee and settled into my chair by the window. I had to think. She had made the first move, now the second. I hadn't been up to it, not at La Coupole, not at that moment on the boulevard, not afterwards. Now she was asking directly, not giving me any more time to hedge. "Begin again..."

Why force the issue? Wasn't it obvious that we had already begun? I only had to relive her kiss, her touch, her perfume—and the elevator came crashing down.

Why did it have to be faster or more? There was something troubling about her rashness. But had I taken the initiative and suggested spending the night, I wouldn't call it "forcing the issue." Had I sent the *pneu*, everything would look different. I wouldn't suggest leaping right into "forever after." I would have picked a hotel. A hotel would have lifted the whole affair onto a lighter plane. But she had rented a place, a romantic hideaway.

I jumped out of my chair and picked up my Paris map from my desk. The address was in the fourth *arrondissement*, Quai d'Anjou. The "small island" was Ile St. Louis, the heart of Paris. Was she saying that one could see the Seine from her windows? A place with no furniture to speak of. No history. A place where Claude had never been.

I was torn. Every time I felt my resistance, I had the image of Tanja pointing her finger at me. Mo had hit it right on the head: I had no desire to be tamed. I was not eager to risk it. Those scars she had mentioned, the scars of childhood, might reopen and bleed. Unbearable thought.

But seeing myself as a sexual coward was just as unbearable. Who said I wasn't in control? No matter what Mo had in mind, I ought to have my own mind. I could think of this hideout as another version of a hotel if I liked. I would have no problem deciding if there was a beginning, a middle, or an ending. It was up to me, not just her. Sex was always a leap of faith. Fear of getting tamed? Nobody could tame me unless I let them.

I called the Théâtre de l'Odéon and asked them to postpone my press tickets for the night. Mr. Beckett and Godot would have to wait a little longer.

How should I dress? I went to my back room to cast a critical glance at my wardrobe. My theater jeans with the black silk shirt and my aviator scarf felt outdated. Mo had already seen—and recognized me—in this outfit. I felt the stir again of the moment when she told me how she had spotted me coming out of the opera, a boy who wasn't a boy, in tears.

What would she be wearing this night?

The image of Chiara appeared before my eyes. Chiara—a medical student with blond Monica Vitti strands of hair. At the Maggio Musicale in Florence, some years ago, she shot toward me like an arrow. When I arrived for our tryst, she opened the door naked under the proverbial fur coat, in spite of the Italian heat. I kept my composure. The coat turned out to be a welcome padding on her kitchen floor—*La Notte* in a student kitchen. One never stops learning. Nevertheless, I felt the familiar unease that grips me before an adventure when I dread a faux pas.

Dominique would be wearing something exquisite, for sure. Something exotic. Like the red-golden kimono with its chrysanthemum and waffle patterns that Mo had slipped over me one day.

Out of nowhere, the memory lit up.

The kimono was much too big but Mo liked how it dragged behind me when I promenaded back and forth before her. Or, more to the point: pattered back and forth for her. She had glued and nailed a pair of beach sandals onto two blocks of wood.

The precision of the memory kicked up my heart. In my hurry to light a cigarette, I dropped the match onto my sisal rug. Setting the house on fire with trembling hands? I shook myself. What the hell? I inhaled and counted to ten. It didn't help.

She used to make a whole ritual of dressing me up. Tying the sash with the thick knot in back was its own ceremony; combs and chopsticks had to be stuck into my hair; makeup was a must: a white flour paste stirred up in the kitchen, black eyeliner, a tiny scarlet-red mouth. How did she know all this already? Then we would play tea ceremony on the rug. She would lie propped on her elbow and watch me pour tea. I had to pluck away on her ukulele or sing along with "Un bel di" until my voice cracked.

What on earth did she get out of it? What did I?

I must have reveled in being touched and handled, combed, and made up by Mo. On the other hand, these rituals had to feed my expectations. How was it possible for me to be so patient? Pleasure and pain. Maybe it was Callas. Because we were listening to Callas I held out and didn't move, didn't protest.

I was back in my apartment, in my wicker chair. The piercing calls of town swallows chasing past my window caught my ear and instantly brought back a mood of longing. I felt the pull at my feet, the vertigo of things moving faster and deeper than I could stand. They were tugging at me from a shadowy past beyond my grasp. *We've always had a passion for each other. We still do…*

Never in my life had I found myself in such a roller coaster. Unable to trust her, unable to make up my mind. *Vorrei e non vorrei*. Damn Mozart! I was Zerlina, struggling against Don Giovanni's seduction, the offer she can't refuse.

Try to imagine…

One thing was clear. The offer would never be made again. Once in a lifetime, a voice in my head whispered. An invitation like this only comes once.

N O T H I N G   T O   W E A R

I pulled a shirt from my hanger, fingered it, and inhaled a hint of Indian incense. I hadn't worn it in ages. But back in hippy days, when its style was comparatively understated, it had been my cruising shirt—silver-gray velvet, cut in the shape of a short, slightly waist-hugging jacket. I slipped it on in front of the mirror. The crushed velvet flattered my figure, making me appear more curvy than I was. The two front panels ended in points that reached down to my hip bones. I found the look too girlish. What would it signal to Mo? That I was caving in to her taste?

I tried on my tight black leather vest. Mm-hmm. A certain tight constriction of the body begs to reveal what is hidden underneath. The metal button-studs were as hot as the zipper of Marianne Faithfull's leather body-suit in *The Girl on a Motorcycle*. But my white winter skin against the black spoiled the effect. The vest conveyed something of a "sex knight"—a notion that felt ridiculous in regard to Mo. For discos or parties this little piece of leather had served me often and well, but here it was of no use. I didn't want to appear tough. Neither hunter nor prey.

But which among my few well-chosen clothes would fit in between? Which one would not betray any sexual preference? All the clothes that once seemed perfectly "both-and," as Mo had called it, now looked more or less tendentious. A tad too dykish, and I immediately felt bored. A tad too femmish, and I was overcome by a notion of weakness, a queasy suspicion of wanting to please. Why was that so unbearable?

Something she said came back to me: her studied femininity had been a way to feel closer to me, to my younger self. I didn't remember the exact words. A number of things she said stung me so fast I wasn't able to register them. I kept fighting off their impact, fighting for my composure so she wouldn't see how unsettled I was. I didn't want to give in to her story. But then I had the impulse to put my arm around her. Why? Was it her small voice telling me she'd always taken it very seriously? Because I believed her in that moment? I had felt her loneliness back then, in Hamburg. There it was, her vast, empty apartment devoid of decorations, lights or candles. A cold winter day close to Christmas.

"Don't you have a Christmas tree?" Every German family had a tree long before Christmas, whether they were Catholic, Protestant, or nothing, like mine. "Not even an *Adventskranz*?" Everyone I knew was lighting candles on a pine wreath all through December to prepare—each Sunday another candle until all four were burning. It was the essence of German *Stimmung*, the glow of candle light in winter, the scent of pine needles, the anticipation of high, festive events.

Mo gave a scornful shrug. Her parents were traveling; she was alone with the cook and maid. When my amazement didn't abate, she pointed to an imposing candelabra on a shelf among the books. "That's our tree, can't you see? It's called a menorah. It has nine branches, and it doesn't die afterwards like yours." I must have stared at her. There were little stumps of candles in the branches. But her eyes and the dread of those empty rooms made me urge my mother to invite her. At least for the second day of the three-day celebrations.

It had never occurred to me to bring her home, to be inspected by my mother and probably laughed at for her boyish ways by my sister. They had seen her at our school concert in the fall where she played Debussy and I sang two Mozart songs. For the occasion, she had appeared in a much-too-adult dark blue dress, her pigtail in a French clasp. I had felt intimidated by her unexpected elegance. I couldn't stop staring. It wasn't all that different now, when I saw her in her dark blue outfit at Kiki's podium. But the memory didn't come to me then. The Christmas invitation hadn't gone over too well.

That year, our tree was decorated the way it used to be in my childhood days in Berlin, with tinsel, angels, tiny painted toys, and sweets—sugar-coated

Kringels and miniature marzipan fruits. Mo, hands folded at her back, walked around and inspected the tree like a strange zoo animal. She suddenly had a laughing fit, pointing to a pink marzipan pig hanging from the tip of a branch. She carried on until I tore off the pig, bit off its head, and offered her the butt to eat. That stopped it. But my mother was displeased. She had a rule of not eating from the tree until the set date of ritual "plundering," on January 6. Now that I thought about it, my mother was probably miffed by other things as well. Maybe she happened upon the butt of the pig that Mo had shoved under the tree. Mo didn't touch the special Christmas cakes and cookies my mother had baked for weeks, not even her famous *Lebkuchen*. She must have produced her tall stories, her shrunken heads, or snake-catching, to entertain my family. "I don't think this is an appropriate friend for you," my mother said afterwards in her voice of hurt superiority. "She wears expensive clothes, but she's a liar."

What a trickster, my memory!

I grabbed the blue message from my table and went over every word again. She was going to give me back a book—"that book"? Was she speaking of Hans Christian Andersen's fairy tales? She'd taken off with my book. It was illustrated with nineteenth-century engravings of girls with long curls sitting at the feet of an old crone storyteller. I loved the drawings, especially in "The Snow Queen," showing Kay and little Gerda in their rooftop hideaway, the spot where the two roofs of their houses met, with a potted rosebush as shelter.

So this old book went to London, traveled to Japan, and all the way here, to Paris? As if she knew that one day, against all odds, she'd give it back to me? Like little Gerda, tracking to the end of the world to find her lost playmate Kay, who had forgotten her, frozen in his heart...

I bent over the cast-iron balustrade of my window and let the cool air brush over my arms and shoulders. Everything with Mo was unfathomable. *Equally strong and equally obsessive...* Was she right? Was Mo right and I was blind?

I looked out at the roofs with their chimney pots, the mist-gray high-rises of La Défense in the distance, past the Eiffel Tower. What did it mean to be meant for one another?

I saw myself writing in a new notebook, or perhaps working on a review. I felt Mo's presence, bending down to look at what I was doing, one arm around my shoulder, nodding, laughing... We'd been at the theater together, no, at the opera. We were inspired, had seen the same thing, seen with the same eyes. I saw a desk, two desks, one above, on the platform overlooking the Seine, the other at the lower level, looking right into the branches of a plane tree on the quay. Impatient footsteps cluttering up and down the metal staircase. I heard our voices. Mo's melodious voice, her mischievous laughter. Arguments, heated debates. She was writing on Japanese aesthetics or on a film we'd seen with different eyes, like *Last Year in Marienbad*. Or maybe we were both writing stories, looking at a paragraph that had just been finished, commenting, editing each other, getting another idea. Always another idea. Talking and writing in bed all day, barricaded, *Les Enfants Terribles*. Bowls of fruit and chocolate next to the bed. Reading out loud. Reading in front of the fireplace. Books everywhere, bookshelves from floor to ceiling. A record collection on another shelf...

I got it. Being meant for each other meant furnishing her place! Why not go ahead and add a balcony and an umbrella? Or a small roof terrace with potted trees and roses. Hadn't someone told me about a garden of English roses that were entirely from the nineteenth century? We would have such a garden somewhere, in the south of France, and of course it would mean buying the ruin of a "Mas," an old farmhouse, rebuilding it, and planting roses named Emily, George, Edith, Virginia, Vita! I could have sworn that I caught the scent of George Sand's dark red rose after a long summer day. It floated through my nose and palate as insistently as the whiffs of sweet-scented tobacco that used to mesmerize me.

Back at my closet I pulled two T-shirts, one black, one white, from the shelf and tried them on. Black cotton was lame, lacking juice. In white, I looked like a Sunday child ready for a round of gymnastics. Out of the question—and to imagine Mo in something shimmering, exotic... She had grabbed a big advantage, being able to await me at her place, in a déshabillé or whatever, whereas I had to arrive in my leather jacket, in the unknown.

I had to laugh at myself: I had nothing to wear.

But I didn't laugh for long. The possibility of feeling vulnerable, unsure of myself, made me weak-kneed, gave me an apprehension of falling again into the same old pattern: tied up, her captive. Unthinkable—and yet. *The strongest attraction creates the strongest fear…*

It was the old trap of my youth—hesitation, ambivalence. An incapacity to make up my mind. Had I really not made any progress? I was acting like the countess in *Capriccio*, debating whether she is in love, and if so, with whom, and in that case, what should she do about it? As if I, too, had to find the ending of an opera I had commissioned—but, "Is there an ending that isn't trivial?" What an irony. Here I was pacing from one room to the next, staring out the window, staring at my closet, looking at the phone for an answer. I couldn't call Christiane for advice; I couldn't discuss this with Tanja. I had to figure it out myself, and I only had a few hours.

Could it possibly end up being trivial? Trivial could only mean bad sex. Bad sex meant dishonest sex. Lying, pretending, cheating oneself. Out of the question. I had felt her touch. Trivial meant unconscious errors of judgment, lack of subtlety. We were both writers. She had asked me the question in the restaurant, while we were waiting for our dessert. What do you write? With a lightness in her voice that was offering me an easy way out. Like a buoy bobbing on the surface, but I sensed the deeper anchoring. I couldn't take it lightly; I had to answer.

What really interested me in writing, I said, was capturing time passing, life passing. Like in a haiku: watching a leaf falling through space and quite forgetting oneself, while another self knows that in this moment, one is changed.

She listened with quiet attention, her hand under her chin, one silver-ringed finger pressed over her mouth. And you? I asked.

She gave me a probing, pondering look. She was writing broken stories, she said. Then she used my metaphor. When a leaf falls, she said, something shifts, slips imperceptibly out of balance, is lost, and one does strange things on impulse that change one's life.

I sat down again by my window, rolled another cigarette, and inhaled nervously. What had she said at La Coupole about her intentions?

"I want to grant you a wish…"

The way she said it made it sound like a contract, the same way she shook hands with me over my offer of a coffee. If I believed her, she literally wanted to hand me this power—the power of asking for anything. It meant she was utterly confident in her capacity to meet me, wherever I came from, wherever I wanted to go. My heart skipped a beat. If destiny was dangerous, she wasn't the least intimidated.

What if we were a match in bed the way we were outside of it? What would it be like? I searched my memories, my favorite fantasies, but no image came to settle. It was as if part of me refused to tie me to an expectation of anything I already knew.

I tried out the idea of traveling with her to Tokyo, London, New York—every place where she had been. An opera in Vienna: *Rosenkavalier*, of course, with Elisabeth Schwarzkopf and Sena Jurinac. We would sit in the fourth row on the left aisle, away from the brass but close enough to see every gesture and glance of the two women in bed. I would get press tickets for any performance we desired. *La Traviata* at La Scala, the same box where the old goat Onassis used to sit, brooding over what the devil Callas was doing, crying her eyes out over her young beau onstage. We would go to Wuppertal to see the latest performance by Pina; to Bayreuth to hear the *Flying Dutchman* again, and the *Ring*... I was surprised that Germany was on this fantasy map. Yes, perhaps we would even go, one day, to revisit the places of our school days, in Hamburg.

Try to imagine...

If only I could believe in her this time.

POSTCARD

The metal suitcase I pulled from the back of my closet was covered with stickers and torn address labels. I rummaged through packs of old papers, letters, photographs, diaries, until I had dug out my "Poesiealbum." The once bright red booklet had yellowed, but the pages were unfaded. My first diary. Thirteen years old.

"Dear diary! No shining grades this year, but my new girlfriend Gisela says many great minds were zeros at school…"

I turned the pages. Bad grades were not the usual fare in my Good Girl journey through school. The diary was filled with sketches, movie tickets glued to the pages (*Roman Holiday* and *Gone with the Wind*), and a handwriting that betrayed chaos under its applied orderliness. Not a word about Mo. No package of unopened letters. Was it one of her stories that couldn't be proved but also not rejected out of hand? Nothing stood out from the papers strewn across my rug, the mass of words holding my past, hiding keys to my memory.

Arriving at the last page of a diary, I used to gather my loose notes and souvenirs into a craft envelope and slip it between the last page and the cover. But carrying my suitcase around, from Hamburg to Munich to Paris to Berlin and back, had made a jumble of my attempt at order. I thumbed through some envelopes at random and drew out a bunch of letters and pictures. Family snapshots— the safe smile of the Good Girl in the bosom of her family, the brooding look of the Good Girl in retreat, a few years later. A crumpled newspaper cutout of Man Ray's famous photograph of Gertrude

Stein wearing makeup. A "Cubist" poem by Frantisek. Drafts of love letters to my French teacher.

I lifted a Japanese postcard from the pile. Two smiling geishas, hand-colored in pastel tones. On the back side, an English stamp with Queen Elizabeth. The date on the stamp unreadable. No sender's address. In the scrawled handwriting of a schoolgirl, next to the address: "Believe it if you can!"

I was dumbfounded. Had this been a common phrase, a joke between us? Dominique's gauntlet, when she appeared a few weeks ago, hadn't been a gauntlet at all? Just a way to get my attention and drop me a message from the past?

What else had I missed or misunderstood?

I recognized Mo's face in one of the geishas. She had stuck her head through a cardboard figure for a postcard photograph. There was her snub nose, an impish look in her eyes. She looked ready to trick her way into becoming a geisha—and I'd better believe it! With Mo anything seemed possible. She had ended up in Japan, as a photo model with a new (Modigliani) nose, and got married to a Japanese man. I couldn't wrap my mind around her. But I only had to think of her uncontrolled laughter and her sailor manners in Liane's studio to recognize Mo, the tomboy who wanted to kill a fly with a whip. I thought of Tanja's analysis of the asymmetrical haircut: "She can do it both ways." I recalled how she had first blinded me like Diana, the Huntress. If I added her brazen ways of being after me, there was only one conclusion to draw: Mo had quite an *éducation sexuelle*. It was not for nothing that Claude had been over the moon. Even if she had laid it on as thick as a brick to make me jealous, the fact remained. Mo had picked up in no time "how Parisian women were playing." She had jumped in and chosen one of the best players. *A lovely adventure, all theater...*

I turned the postcard over again, intrigued by the handwriting. The way the long uprights of her letters mingled with the long tails of the letters on the previous line of my address touched a familiar chord. It must have been shortly after her disappearance. A hotel envelope from London, an elegant sheet of paper with a letterhead, Hotel King Edward or something. The whole page filled with "I love you I love you I love you..." The *l* of *love* enlacing the *y* of *you* all over the page, like a love tangle that could never get sorted out.

And that was all she'd come up with? The fine hotel stationery, the fact

that she was trekking around the world again while I was still attached to my mother's apron-strings, in sixth grade, and in Germany of all places! I hadn't wanted that letter. Mo couldn't be trusted. What hadn't she promised—and never kept!

The last day with her stood before my eyes, clear as glass.

We had gone to her place after school as usual, because nobody was home. Mo had the velvet band in her ponytail. I saw her on her piano stool, her too long, thin legs sticking out from the crisp pleats of her kilt. On the piano, the kimono was already spread out. She was going to pull it toward her when I said, out of the blue, that I was done.

"Done?"

"With these kid games. This infantile stuff."

She scrutinized me with squinted eyes as if taking an X-ray. I had to look away. She laughed. She jumped up and pulled a book from under her piano scores. "Of course we're done with that, don't you know? I have a new idea...."

She wound the velvet band around her head so that her hair fell to her shoulders behind her ears. She reached out her hand. "Come. Listen and be amazed."

We stretched out on the polar bear rug as usual. There was no record on the turntable this time. Just a tense silence. Mo opened an antiquated book with the title *Geisha*. She read me something—but here my memory left me. What was it? There was a word that intrigued me because it was unknown to me. Intimacy? Initiative? It was something ominous, exciting, something sensuous. Initiation! That's what it was. Rites of initiation...rites of an old geisha tradition. I remembered.

When the time was ripe, the story went, the young apprentice was given over to an experienced older friend by the madam of the geisha house. For seven days, he would visit her once a day, each day break a fresh egg, dip his finger into the egg white, and make her familiar with his finger. The old-fashioned, flowery language of this initiation was a strange sort of poetry and the vagueness of it all conveyed to me an urgent sense of redemption.

"Would you like to play initiation?" Mo asked. I pondered the question. She had again said, "play." I wanted to ask who would play what? Maybe it didn't matter.

"When? Now?"

She nodded with a serious face. "It's a ritual, you understand? One can't jump into a ritual just like that. We have to learn more about it, both of us. Let's go on reading. Tomorrow…" She kissed me lightly but with meaning. Then she played *Madama Butterfly* with Callas and let me look into her eyes for a long time.

The next day, Mo didn't show up in class. She was sick, and before we could continue with her "new idea," she had left Germany.

The pain and dismay of childhood love welled up in me all over again. How many more things had I forced myself to forget?

Callas, I reminded myself, I hadn't allowed her to take Callas away from me. Perhaps because this voice seemed to know everything I had to disown and yet could never disown. At the restaurant, Mo had made a little remark, "You still love Callas, I see…" I hadn't let her take Callas away from me. I could see now that it might have felt like a victory. But no matter how successfully I cut the string that connected this music to Mo, every time I listened to Callas my heart broke a little. With every performance of *Madama Butterfly* I was undone, without a clue that the story of the childlike Cio Cio San and her abandonment had anything to do with me.

What else had I lost because I had to lose Mo?

Everything I had embodied for her? The good little German girl's compliance and pliability? Velvet and silk, innocence and abandon, milk-and-cake trust, the patience of worship, of adoration?

Not lost, I corrected myself—put into doubt, under suspicion within myself. If I wanted to be sarcastic, I could say I had started out as Butterfly and ended up as Pinkerton. Life as a sailor, the "Yankee vagabond," with a woman in every port. The less you are reachable, the less you get hurt. I had vanquished the pain by trying to imitate Mo's elusiveness, her capacity to hold back and not be swept away. I had copied her independence, her tomboy determination not to please but to do as she pleased. Yes, even without sarcasm I could say I took on the desirable role, her role, and kept everything else carefully at bay.

I felt the tight pit in my stomach when I tried to turn around and see the past with her eyes. What had I done to her by burning her letters, her love declarations? What had I done to her with my stone silence? Turning sides, I saw Mo, the girl with the vast imagination and the sexual shyness, overwhelmed by my desire, my longing to give myself up to her. She had said it herself, her cheeks burning: it was all too much for her.

She hadn't made up the letters, hadn't made up anything. "I love you I love you I love you...." Everything made sense; everything was still a mystery.

I heard the longing in Mo's invitation. "Say yes!" I saw her silver-ringed hands, her way of holding the cigarette between thumb and middle finger. I recalled the scent of her perfume, the tips of her hair at my cheek. The elevator started down. I saw her hazel eyes when she sat down again at La Coupole, her naked, insecure gaze, the tremor on her lips. I saw the way she had looked at me on the Boulevard, pleading with me to forgive her. She had put herself on the line just as much as I would have to.

And that kiss...

I grabbed my washed-out light blue jeans from the closet and pulled them over a pair of black Tangas. Another moment and my dove-blue gilet came off the hanger. Its back was black satin with a little belt and buckle. The front was knitted in fine silk. As there was no lining and the stitches were slightly transparent, I usually wore it over a shirt or T-Shirt. This time I wore nothing underneath. Instead of appearing winter-pale, my skin shone cream-like through the bluish stitches. The gilet had a single hook closure in front and was cut loose enough to appear closed when I stood still. When I moved, it fell open, and the silver buckle of my jeans belt came into view together with a strip of skin. I probed my appearance from every angle. My image could be seen—according to taste or preference—as somewhere in between, neither boy nor girl. Both-and. I clicked a small gold hoop into my left ear, with a quick gesture, messed up my hair, brushed a hint of per-fume-powder on my neck, slipped on the leather jacket, and snatched my silver cigarette case from the table.

My mirror reflection said, *Vas-y, ma belle*, let it be love: you don't risk anything but your skin.

ILE ST. LOUIS

Stone steps, worn down through centuries. The smell reminded me of the
dry, pleasant sandstone air in Meret Oppenheim's ground-floor atelier.
Another stonemason building, not far, almost right across the river, in fact.
The door at the landing had a note attached: "Come in and make yourself
at home. I'll be right there, M." I pushed the door open. An arm of light
stretched from a high window across the floor to my feet. A crossbeam
supported a mezzanine platform, and smaller beams rising like spokes of
a wheel made for a balustrade. A metal staircase spiraled up with battered
grace. The rest of the room lay in semidarkness. A few logs were burning in
a sandstone fireplace. Two rocking chairs nearby. A standing lamp threw a
small pool of light over a coffee table.

I wondered if Mo had gone out for Vietnamese food. I was grateful
to be alone.

Accidentally or on purpose, she had given me time. I slipped out of
my jacket. A standing rack at the door held her trench coat and black beret.
Now with my leather jacket joining in, two people seemed to be living
here. A couple?

In this mere sketch of a living place her presence felt as light as her
touch. A glass bottle with a branch of lilac on the mantelpiece was the only
decoration. The rocking chairs had an air of a different time; curving their
colonial rattan on a threadbare oriental rug, they seemed to come out of a
story by Marguerite Duras.

I was drawn to the book lying on the coffee table. My lost Hans Christian Andersen book of fairy tales! It had shed its paper cover, but the thick leather binding in dark red was still holding together, the imprinted title legible. I slid down on the rug under the lamp, leaning on my elbow, the book against my knees. I didn't have to consult the table of contents. The book fell open by itself. "The Snow Queen." The picture of the two children, Hans and little Gerda, showed them nestled into their hiding place where the roofs of their houses met, between small, boxed rosebushes. I imagined the scent of lilac was sifting down from the branch on the mantel. There was the first page, the devil laughing into his mirror, laughing so hard that the mirror fell and cracked, sending its tiniest splinters into the eyes of people, showing them ugliness, making them cold and cynical.

Now we see the world all new...

It was so still, I barely heard the hum of cars from the quay.

I put the book down and strolled around, restless, tempted to climb

up the stairs to see the sleeping platform and the view she had mentioned in her *pneu*. On another round I came upon a tall menorah in the shaded area below the mezzanine. I knelt to look at it more closely. There was no doubt, I had seen it before. Yes, it was the same nine-branched "tree" that wouldn't die when Christmas was over.

Mo was late. Should I doubt that she would come? I fought back a wave of nausea. Was it possible that this invitation was another disappearance act? That she would leave me alone here with my memories? Or come waltzing in arm in arm with Claude?

What the devil. I was here because I accepted the dare. Accepted it with all the consequences imaginable. Not that I could imagine any one of them. My imagination had raised its white flag. But wasn't that the point? That something was promised and neither one of us could know what it was? And hadn't she set it up like that, the door open for escape? I could still change my mind, this very moment, while I was still free. Was I still free?

The tiger is afraid to be tamed...

A faint clicking sound right next to me made me turn. I hadn't noticed the beaded curtain in the shaded back corner, leading perhaps to a kitchen and bathroom. There she was. I saw Mo's dark silhouette behind the strings of ivory beads, one hand ready to part the curtain. The tightness in my chest, my throat made it impossible to move as if from fear—her fear? My own? Time slipped away. How long had she been there? How long had we been in the same room together?

"Mo," I said, reaching for her hand.

She slowly stepped out and remained still, the curtain clicking back and forth into place behind her. In the pale oval of her face her eyes were filled with darkness. Her red hair cut across her cheek like a blade. She was wearing the waterfall dress with the belt. It struck me that she hadn't moved from the moment we had separated two days ago. She had been there then, she had risked it, and she was still there, holding on to a small, very small possibility. It seemed we were both holding our breath.

Thoughts rushed through my mind, words I couldn't say. She must have come back noiselessly while I was absorbed in the book. Perhaps she hadn't noticed me on the floor between the chairs and the table.

"You have come," she said, her voice catching. "You have come. Lulú."

I saw the sob in her eyes before I heard it. I pulled her toward me and enclosed her in my arms, feeling the same sob in me. I don't know how long we stood there, leaning against each other's shoulders.

She detached herself, slipped back through the clicking curtain, and returned with two sheets of paper towel. We blew our noses and laughed. She tucked the towel into her belt like a tattered butterfly. I tucked mine into my jeans belt. We laughed and cried at the same time. The brief moments when we were able to look at each other were too vulnerable to bear; I fled back into the embrace and we stood there, leaning our temples against each other with no other motion than our breathing. My eyes closed, I felt the silk of her skin, her hair with the dusky perfume nested in it. Felt the surprising delicacy of her shoulders and shoulder blades and the reassuring fullness of her breasts against mine. My heart beat hard—perhaps it was her heart as well. She had not raised her arms to meet my embrace, as if it would be too much, as if it was enough to bring our faces together so our cheeks would touch. I felt the warmth of her face with deep relief, like a wave slowly coming home and rolling out onto a beach. Coming home.

Where have I once already been…

I caught a tear coming down her cheek and crushed it between my lips, tasting its faint salt. The pounding of my pulse resumed. Our lips had met. The sweet flesh I had known from our shy kisses so long ago—the girl with the cherry mouth. The touch went through my body with such an ache of desire that my knees wanted to cave in. She must have felt it. She bent her face away so she could look at me. I let her see me—my nakedness, pain, longing to go under in her tear-washed eyes.

"First, come, let me show you…" She kissed me lightly and with meaning, the way she had the last time before she disappeared.

She led me to the table by the fireplace, knelt down, and waited for me to kneel next to her. Noticing the book on the floor, she gave me the briefest smile of recognition. She opened the coffee table, a traveler's metal trunk with a keyhole and stamped letters on the side. Inside, in the pool of light from the lamp, the waffle-chrysanthemum pattern of a kimono shone up with a matte glitter. Next to its intricate folds, a lacquered box looked like a bento box, but instead of food, the little rectangles and squares held pencils, a powder brush, a small hair brush, combs, and pots of white makeup and rouge. I looked at her, troubled, scared.

She shook her head. "Later—never."

I pressed her hand to my heart, hiding my face from the storm racing through me. Butterfly, Callas, geisha, being made up and handled, waiting, always waiting for her to release and redeem me. "Un bel di" rushed through my mind with its tenderness cutting to the core. "*Que dira? Que dira?*" (What will he say? What will he say?) "He will call Butterfly from the distance and I, remaining silent, will stay hidden, a little to tease him, a little so as not to die…"

It dawned on me that while I had fantasized about our future in this place near the Seine, she had been waiting and preparing—the same magician she had always been—to take us right back into the past. To the place where everything had vanished, where we had felt betrayed. I might never have remembered it without her. The place where I had lost, forgotten, the innocence of love. She was restoring us to the moment, the exact moment when we hadn't been able to go any further.

I felt her arm around my shoulder, the tickle of hair, her mouth in the hollow of my neck. A spatter of excitement rushed down my skin, aching in my body.

Now, I knew. Now we can go on. She pulled me close against her, gathered me in with her body, her breathing. Kiss me, I thought. Kiss me again.

She did.

————

THE END

CULTURAL GLOSSARY

PARIS BY NIGHT / 1

THE WOMAN IN RED   14

COSÌ VAN TUTTE Opera by Mozart about the seduction of two sisters by each other's fiancé.

RAMEAU, LULLY, GLUCK, HANDEL Major Baroque composers.

BOHEMIAN The free-wheeling lifestyle of artists under the roofs of Paris, as celebrated in Puccini's opera La Bohème.

GUSTAV MAHLER'S VIENNA Austrian-Jewish composer and conductor in Vienna, at the turn of the century.

LUDWIG WITTGENSTEIN Austrian-Jewish language philosopher ("Whereof one cannot speak, thereof one must be silent.")

KAFKA'S PRAGUE The German-speaking, Jewish writer, Frank Kafka, lived in Prague in the first half of the twentieth century; he became world-famous after his death. Scholars now suggest he was gay.

GERTRUDE STEIN'S PARIS The Jewish-American writer revolutionized language in Paris, her chosen exile, where she moved in 1903. Together with her lover, Alice B. Toklas, she held a famous salon at 27 rue de Fleurus, near Montparnasse.

JEAN-PAUL SARTRE French writer and philosopher of existentialism and nihilism, lifelong partner of Simone de Beauvoir.

JEAN GENET French gay writer whose work romanticizes violent criminals.

MARQUIS DE SADE Eighteenth-century French writer of scandalous sadomasochist books.

FIORDILIGI AND DORABELLA The two tempted sisters in Mozart's opera Così fan tutte.

CARMEN Opera by French composer Bizet about a sexually intrepid gypsy woman.

RUDOLF NUREYEV Bisexual Russian dancer who defected from the Soviet Union in 1961 and reached world fame in the West.

SWAN LAKE Tchaikovsky's Russian ballet classic about young women turned into swans.

GISELLE Russian ballet about a betrayed young girl who turns into a "Wili," or ghost.

OUVREUSE Usher.

MEZZO The lower register of a soprano voice in opera.

CHERUBINO Trouser role in Mozart's opera The Marriage of Figaro, a woman singing the role of a boy.

OCTAVIAN Male lead, a sixteen-year-old boy, sung by a woman in Richard Strauss's opera Der Rosenkavalier.

APOLLO Greek god of music, son of Zeus.

CATHERINE DENEUVE IN BELLE DE JOUR: French actress in her breakout film by Luis Buñuel.

GUGLIELMO One of the two irresistible tempters in Mozart's opera *Così fan tutte*.

THE GOOD GIRL   26

MOZARTIADE From Schubertiade—term for the intimate time spent at the house (or in the presence) of the composer Schubert.

ARABELLA Romantic opera by Richard Strauss.

MOLIERE'S L'ECOLE DES FEMMES Play about women's education.

LE MONDE Major liberal daily paper.

"VISSI D'ARTE" ("I LIVED FOR ART") Dramatic aria in Puccini's opera *Tosca*—a diva's lament about injustice as she is facing rape by a tyrant.

LE LOUVRE Major art museum in Paris.

NIGHT WANDERER   32

DIEGO VELÁZQUEZ Leading painter of the Spanish Golden Age (seventeenth century), possibly of Jewish lineage.

BATEAU MOUCHE Tourist boat for sightseeing on the Seine.

CARLOS CASTENADA American writer who experimented with hallucinogenic drugs in Mexico.

WAGNER'S VALKYRIES Warrior-goddesses in Richard Wagner's operatic cycle *The Ring* (*Der Ring des Nibelungen*).

SHAKESPEARE & CO English-language bookstore in the Quartier Latin, close to the Seine.

LA COUPOLE, MIDNIGHT   39

LA COUPOLE, LE DÔME, LE SELECT, LA ROTONDE famous artist cafés of Montparnasse.

LES ENFANTS DU PARADIS Marcel Carné's 1946 classic movie, *Children of Paradise*.

MIREILLE French chansonneuse and pop singer Mireille Mathieu.

PYGMALION Play by George Bernard Shaw, inspired by a Greek tale about a sculptor falling in love with the statue he created. (*My Fair Lady* was based on this play.)

KIKI DE MONTPARNASSE Artists' model, actress, nightclub singer, and painter in the 1920s.

MERET OPPENHEIM German-Jewish bisexual artist who began her career in Paris among the Surrealists.

MAN RAY American-Jewish artist known for his photographs of artists and beautiful women in Paris.

MAX ERNST, GIACOMETTI (Jewish) Modernist artists in Paris.

SURREALISM Avant-garde movement (starting around 1920) of writers and painters working with the unconscious.

EDOUARD MANET French painter, precursor of Impressionism.

LE DEJEUNER SUR L'HERBE Scandalous painting by Manet, showing a naked woman at an artists' picnic.

OUT OF THE BLUE   52

LIBÉRATION Left-wing newspaper.

CLAUDE / 2

AMOUR FOU   60

MONIQUE WITTIG Award-winning lesbian writer and feminist activist.

CHRISTIANE ROCHEFORT Award-winning and bestselling feminist writer.

VIRGINIA WOOLF Avant-garde English writer and feminist (*A Room of One's Own*) who had a love affair with writer Vita Sackville-West.

SIMONE DE BEAUVOIR Bisexual writer, intellectual, feminist. Life companion of Jean-Paul Sartre.

THEATER OF CRUELTY Theater theory by early twentieth-century avant-garde playwright Antonin Artaud.

MAO SUIT Buttoned-up, blue Chinese workers pantsuit.

BRECHTIAN Derived from the German play-wright and theater director Berthold Brecht.

ROBERT WILSON (Gay), PETER BROOK (Gay, Jewish), RICHARD FOREMAN Exponents of the new theater movement of the seventies.

CROCE DELICIA   74
(Torment and Delight)

THE LADY AND THE UNICORN Series of Flemish tapestries circa 1500.

LA TRAVIATA Opera by Puccini about a courtesan.

KLIMT Viennese fin-de-siècle (turn-of-the-century) artist.

OBSESSION   81

LA SYLPHIDE Classical romantic ballet about woman-spirits.

BELGIAN BALLET AVANT-GARDE French choreographer Maurice Béjart and his "Ballet du 20ème Siècle," based in Brussels.

DISTRACTION   89

BEAUX-ARTS School of Fine Arts in Paris.

COLETTE Bisexual author of *Gigi*, nominated for a Nobel Prize in 1948.

COCO CHANEL Fashion designer.

"VAGINA AND ITS DISCONTENTS" Word play on Freud's *Civilization and Its Discontents*.

JAMES JOYCE Irish avant-garde author of *Ulysses*.

HOTEL VIOLET   105

"PARLEZ-MOI D'AMOUR" (Speak to Me about Love) song by Edith Piaf.

ART NOUVEAU Art movement of the turn of the century, using sumptuous, curvy forms derived from nature.

BELLE EPOQUE Period of European history before World War I, a Golden Age for the arts.

DAWN   110

27 RUE DE FLEURUS Address of the salon of Gertrude Stein, started in 1905, displaying the best collection of modern art in any museum at the time.

PARIS FRANCE Gertrude Stein's 1939 book portraying the French.

SWEET SIN / 3

PLAISIRS D'AMOUR   118

DON GIOVANNI Hero of Mozart's opera, notorious womanizer.

LEPORELLO Don Giovanni's servant who keeps a many-folded list of his master's conquests.

DIANA Roman goddess of the moon and the hunt.

MODIGLIANI Italian-Jewish painter of women with long, narrow eyes.

ROMAN DE GARE Cheap novel, literally "train-station novel."

MARIMEKKO Finnish design house known for its bold, colorful prints.

TOP OR BOTTOM   123

S'ENCANAILLER (From *canaille*, "beast") Mixing with lower-class people, adopting their behavior, slumming.

ZERLINA Peasant bride in Mozart's opera *Don Giovanni*, who is almost seduced by the irresistible rogue.

L'ART POUR L'ART (Art for art's sake) Bohemian creed that art doesn't have to serve any ulterior purpose.

SAPPHO SHOW   127

SAPPHO Greek lesbian poet on the isle of Lesbos, circa 600 B.C.

LA BOHÈME Puccini's iconic opera about young, penniless artists in Paris.

APHRODITE Greek goddess of love.

THE PLEIADES Star constellation.

THE TENTH MUSE Greek philosopher Plato added the poet Sappho to the Nine Muses of Greek mythology.

PALAIS ROYAL 138

OVID Influential Roman poet from the beginning of the first millennium.

COUP DE FOUDRE Literally "flash of lightning", metaphor for falling head-over-heels in love.

CAFÉ DU COIN Neighborhood café.

STRATÉGIE D'AMOUR 149

TANZTHEATER WUPPERTAL Pina Bausch's experimental dance theater company, founded in 1973 in the German town Wuppertal.

MARCEL PROUST (Jewish) Gay author of *A la recherche du temps perdu*, (*Remembrance of Things Past*), a novel of long, elaborate sentences and memories triggered by the taste of a madeleine (that very French cookie).

TOM JONES Novel by eighteenth-century author Henry Fielding, about the rowdy adventures of a charming hero.

FELIX KRULL Protagonist of the novel *Confessions of Felix Krull, Confidence Man*, by bisexual German author Thomas Mann.

THE CHESHIRE CAT The grinning cat in *Alice's Adventures in Wonderland*.

LA SOMNAMBULA Opera by Bellini about a sleepwalking young woman.

MONSTER 158

TAMARA DE LEMPICKA Bisexual Polish-Jewish painter of portraits in Art Deco style.

THE STRANGER / 4

TEMPLE SEX 166

INGMAR BERGMAN Prominent Swedish film director.

HERODOTUS Greek historian, fifth century B.C.

HENRI MATISSE French painter, rival of Picasso.

PARTHENOGENESIS Literally, asexual reproduction, "virgin creation".

THE SILENCE 174

LOLITA Novel by Vladimir Nabokov about the sexual abuse of a young girl.

DÉJÀ VU 190

JACQUES LACAN Half-Jewish psychoanalyst and intellectual who influenced post-structuralism.

LAST YEAR IN MARIENBAD 204

ALAIN RESNAIS Major French filmmaker, known for *Hiroshima mon amour*.

DELPHINE Actress Delphine Seyrig.

NOUVELLE VAGUE Term ("New Wave") for the films by a group of young French filmmakers in the late fifties and sixties.

THE LEATHER JACKET / 5

PINA BAUSCH 227

DIDO'S LAMENT "When I am laid in earth," Aria from the baroque opera *Dido and Aeneas* by Henry Purcell, regarded as one of the most beautiful arias in all of music.

SAMUEL BECKETT Irish avant-garde writer (*Waiting for Godot*).

MAGGIO MUSICALE IN FLORENCE Yearly May festival of classical music.

LA NOTTE Film by Michelangelo about alienation.

NOTHING TO WEAR 327

STIMMUNG German term for mood, atmosphere.

LES ENFANTS TERRIBLES Novel by gay writer Jean Cocteau about siblings who spend their days in bed.

EMILY, GEORGE, EDITH, VIRGINIA, VITA Writers Emily Dickinson (presumed gay), George Elliott, Edith Wharton, Virginia Woolf (bisexual), Vita Sackville-West (bisexual).

CAPRICCIO Opera by Richard Strauss about what comes first and is more important in opera: words or music?

ELIZABETH SCHWARZKOPF AND SENA JURINAC The two lovers (soprano and mezzo) in a celebrated DVD of the opera *Der Rosenkavalier* (Richard Strauss).

ONASSIS Greek tycoon who married diva Maria Callas.

BAYREUTH Famous opera house in the Bavarian town Bayreuth, designed by composer Richard Wagner for his own operas.

THE RING *Der Ring des Nibelungen*, Wagner's sixteen-hour "Ring Cycle" of four operas.

POSTCARD 336

CIO CIO SAN Geisha, tragic heroine of Puccini's opera *Madama Butterfly*.

PINKERTON Name of the naval officer in *Madama Butterfly*, who marries her and then leaves her after a few months

VAS-Y, MA BELLE "Go ahead, honey."

MARGUERITE DURAS French author (*The Lover*), screenwriter (*Hiroshima mon amour*), and filmmaker, whose work is often set in exotic places such as French Indochina (Vietnam), where she grew up.

LIST OF PHOTOGRAPHY

Most of the vintage snapshots were taken by me at the time of this memoir; a few, by lovers and friends. Press photographs and portraits were given to me with permission by the artists and writers depicted: Meret Oppenheim, Christiane Rochefort, and Monique Wittig.

In addition, permission has been granted by the following photographers: Catherine Conway Honig (page 57), Nichole Robertson (page 189), and Catherine Deudon (pages 129 and 328).

Every woman depicted in these pages belonged to my intimate Paris circle of women loving women. To protect their privacy, most of them are not named.

ACKNOWLEDGMENTS

Regarding the poetic license I took with certain players in this memoir, French readers or expatriates who were present at the scene might detect elements of a "memoir à clef," with "keys" given to unlock the disguises of certain people and events in an otherwise accurate account of an era and a time of my youth.

With pleasure and gratitude, I would like to acknowledge my first readers. As always, Kim Chernin, writer par excellence, who also knew how to become Willy to my Colette when my courage flagged. Some of my writer friends were repeatedly supportive, critical readers over the years: above all, my friend and mentor Marilyn Yalom, and my friends Gail Reitano, Cornelia Durrant, and Lise Weil, who proved that there is nothing more productive and exciting than manuscript exchanges. Other inspiring readers were Lea Ann Roddan, Catherine Conway Honig, Alix Dobkin, Laura Stokes, Amy Schliftman, Jim van Buskirk, Niki Burzig, Daniela Wenzel, Christa Littman, Margie Adams, Jeanne Stark-Jochmans, Sonja Hopf, and my late friend, Helmut Frielinghaus,

For their artistic and emotional support I warmly thank Maj Skadegaard, Amy Rennert, Louise Kollenbaum, Joan Gelfand, and my German publishers, Elisabeth Raabe and Regine Vitali.

For his unconventional daring and integrity as a publisher (and also admired writer) I am grateful to Brooks Roddan and IF SF Publishing, in tandem with the much loved design team of Tom Ingalls and junior designer Megan Lotter. I also thank my brilliant VAs (Virtual Assistants), Daniella Granados and, at present, writer Andrew MacDonald. In short, it takes a village to write and publish a memoir!

Last but not least, I am tenderly in debt to my late father, Edgar Neumann, whose photo album from 1935 supplied several classical Paris sites to this book. He also took the youth photo of me, age 14.

COLOPHON

TYPOGRAPHY

ITC Berkeley Oldstyle, Frederic W. Goudy
revival by Tony Stan 1983
Chaparral, Carol Twombly
Grotesque MT, Monotype

PAPER

70lb Matte White, 526 PPI

PRINTING & BINDING

McNaughton & Gunn, Saline, Michigan

DESIGN

Ingalls Design, San Francisco
Tom Ingalls and Megan Lotter